6

William N Jacks

MORE THAN A WISH

MORE THAN A WISH

SERMONS AT SHADYSIDE PRESBYTERIAN CHURCH
PITTSBURGH, PENNSYLVANIA

by

William N. Jackson

Lighthouse Point Press
Pittsburgh, Pennsylvania

More Than a Wish
Sermons at Shadyside Presbyterian Church
by William N. Jackson

Published by:

Lighthouse Point Press
100 First Avenue, Suite 525
Pittsburgh, PA 15222

Copyright © 2004 by William N. Jackson
Printed in the United States of America
Library of Congress Control Number: 2003113332

Publisher's Cataloging in Publication Data
Jackson, William N.
More Than a Wish: Sermons at Shadyside Presbyterian Church
        p.   cm.

1.   Religious
2.   Inspirational
ISBN 0-9637966-0-7: $21.95 Hardcover

This book is printed on acid-free stock.
First Printing, February 2004

DEDICATION

This book of sermons is dedicated to:

The Rev. Dr. Richard K. Kennedy
and
The Rev. Dr. John Magill,

my first and most important mentors.

"(I) always give thanks to God for (both) of you and mention you in (my) prayers, constantly remembering before our God and Father your work of faith and labor of love and steadfastness of hope in our Lord Jesus Christ."

— adapted from I Thessalonians 1:2

INTRODUCTION

It was my honor to listen to Dr. William Jackson preach while he filled the pulpit of the Shadyside Presbyterian Church in Pittsburgh. I had just joined the faculty of a nearby seminary, after serving as a preacher myself for over twenty years, and wasn't certain I could survive sitting in the pews. However, after I heard one of Bill's sermons, I knew I had found not only a stellar preacher but also a pastor. Now, after a year of hearing him preach, I realize how parched my soul had become to find both of these things. In every sermon, he gently leads his congregation back to the well and invites us to taste again of the living water, Jesus Christ.

Preaching is clearly a pastoral function for Bill, and that will soon become clear to the reader of this volume of sermons. His sermons are not didactic, in the sense of teaching the congregation things they ought to know by now. Nor does he strive to provide silver-tongued orations that draw attention only to his abundant eloquence. Rather, his sermons carry on a sacred conversation between the worshipers and the Savior they desperately want to believe is involved. Thus, each sermon speaks from both below and above. He isn't afraid to lift up the old dreams that lie discarded beneath our many coping devices, the hurts we thought we had buried long ago, or even the questions about God that we dare not admit having. Then, in the same sermon, he always responds to our frail words of lament and anxiety with the words of life from on high.

I stood in the Narthex after worship and heard members, while walking through the line, take his hand and say, "You wrote that sermon just for me." He didn't, of course. He would also be the first to avoid any credit for the work of the Holy Spirit. But, over many years of loving his congregations, he has learned how to preach into the human soul – the secret, tender place of life where we are most ourselves, and where we yearn for the God for whom we were created.

In these sermons, you will get a sense of his gift for climbing down into your own soul with the good news that God also yearns for you. As Bill would be careful to add, through Jesus Christ all that yearning can now turn into joyful reunion.

M. Craig Barnes, Ph.D.
Meneilly Professor of Ministry
Pittsburgh Theological Seminary

FOREWORD

From the heart and mind of one of America's most thoughtful and respected preachers comes this book of sermons. The Rev. Dr. William N. Jackson, now serving Shadyside Presbyterian Church, Pittsburgh, Pennsylvania, has ministered to thousands throughout his career. Of particular note was his time as Director of the Department of Religion and pastor to the historic Chautauqua Institution, where he served from 1984 to 1989.

Bill Jackson, during his tenure, was a bridge builder. He built bridges of trust and understanding to America's African American Community. During his time at Chautauqua, notable African American preachers offered their gifts to the Institution, including the late Bishop John Walker, Episcopal Bishop of Washington, D.C.; the Rev. Dr. James Forbes, currently at the Riverside Church, New York City; and the Rev. Dr. William Watley, now at St. James African Methodist Episcopal Church, Newark, New Jersey.

Dr. Jackson's sermons bridge the theological gap between conservative and liberal Christians. His deep personal faith informs his preaching, and his commitment to a just society gives his sermons prophetic power.

Dr. Jackson's time at the Chautauqua Institution was highlighted by a growing relationship between Chautauqua's Jewish and Christian community. His vision of a world where the faith of all people is honored and respected laid the groundwork for today's Chautauqua that has responded to a religiously plural America with the building of the Abrahamic Community.

This book of sermons will serve as a rich resource for students preparing for ministry and as inspiration for all seeking guidance in their daily lives.

Joan Brown Campbell, Director
Department of Religion
Chautauqua Institution

TABLE OF CONTENTS

TOPICAL SERMONS

SPIRITUAL DIRECTION AND GROWTH SERMONS

A SERIES INTRODUCING THE CHURCH'S SELF-STUDY PROCESS

COMMITMENT AND DEDICATION SERMONS

PREFACE

I am indebted to the Session and Staff of Shadyside Presbyterian Church and the Milton G. Hulme Charitable Foundation for their encouragement in putting together this book of sermons. However, I must admit that, as I began my work on this project, I found it to be a daunting challenge. For while my sermons have been carefully and prayerfully prepared, they were delivered without notes and much of what was said was accentuated by gestures, facial expressions, tone of voice, volume (high and low), and appropriate pauses. Preparing these sermons for reading required the extra discipline and effort of attempting to recapture the original meaning and intent of the messages.

The sermons were chosen by random selection with thought for seasons of the Church Year, as well as the particular themes, series, or significant events of the time. Because of that broad choice of sermons, the reader will find some duplication of favorite texts, as well as a few partial repetitions of illustrations or quotes. One advantage of this for the reader will be to discover the conspicuous direction and passion for the message I hope to bring.

There was much prayer in the preparation of this book. I want to share two that have become most helpful and inspiring to me. The first is an anonymous prayer from the Middle Ages, and one which I frequently pray before a sermon:

Come Holy Spirit, come;
Come as the fire and burn;
Come as the wind and cleanse;
Come as the light and reveal.
Convict, convert, and consecrate
Until I am wholly Thine.

The second prayer comes from the Gospel according to Mark and reflects my ongoing desire to continue to grow, learn new lessons, and become more trusting and faithful: "I believe; help Thou my unbelief." (Mark 9:24b)

Perhaps these prayers will also be of help to you as you read these sermons and continue in your own personal Christian walk.

I do want to express my personal thanks to my Associate Pastor, the Reverend Calvin Coolidge Wilson, for promoting this project and offering regular and frequent encouragement. Also, to Sylvia Feldman, not only for her outstanding skill in transcribing the original texts, but for her incredible – and much appreciated – patience in typing several drafts of each sermon. She also gave much helpful advice and many wise suggestions, and a generous and gracious amount of loving constructive criticism and encouragement. I thank Tiffany Bodem for her thorough work in the initial editing process. Most of all, I thank my wife, Vail, for her love and affirmation. Because of her intimate knowledge of me and my preaching, she was of invaluable help in transcending the gap from the spoken to the written word, and thereby helped to clarify and highlight exactly what I wanted to say.

Finally, I want to thank the faithful and patient people in the pews who have prayed for me and with me, listened with discernment, encouraged me to maintain a faithful discipline and commitment to my calling, and responded with genuine love and devoted service in the name of Jesus Christ.

As I close, allow me to borrow from Johann Sebastian Bach, who on all of his works put the letters S. D. G., representing the Latin phrase, *Soli Deo Gloria*, "To God alone be the glory!"

William N. Jackson

More Than a Wish

Psalm 103:1-12
Ephesians 3:14-21
II Corinthians 13:13

"It was the best of times, it was the worst of times; it was the age of wisdom, it was the age of foolishness; it was the epoch of belief, the epoch of incredulity; it was the season of light, it was the season of darkness; it was the spring of hope, it was the winter of despair; we had everything before us, we had nothing before us." Perhaps most of you here recognize those words as the opening words of Dickens' *A Tale of Two Cities*, written over a hundred years ago. Yet, they still seem very appropriate because they describe for us the way that you and I live everyday. "The best of days, the worst of days; the spring of light, the winter of despair; everything before us, nothing before us."

Now, I know when I am having a good day – that is rather easy for me to recognize. But someone gave me a list not long ago to help me know when I am having a bad day. You're having a bad day when you call the crisis center and they put you on hold. You're having a bad day when you have a blind date and it turns out to be your old boyfriend – that's a bad day. You're having a bad day when the bird singing outside your window is a buzzard – that's a bad day!

13

There was a professor giving a demonstration to a class. He was going to dissect a frog, so he walked to the front of the class, reached in the pocket of his smock, took out a piece of wax paper and opened it up. There before him was an egg salad sandwich. At which time he said, "I thought I ate my lunch." That's a bad day!

There was a diver who went all the way to the bottom of the ocean and, just as his feet hit the floor of the ocean, over his intercom came these words, "Come up quickly, the ship is sinking." That is a bad day! Well, when we have good days and bad days, how does the world usually respond?

The typical greeting we hear most often today is, have a good day, have a good week, have a good vacation, or have a good time. That is the world's wish for us. However, the Apostle Paul understood the reality that we all have good days and bad days. He knew the Corinthians had good days and bad days. He knew them very well; he knew exactly that with which they were struggling in those days. He knew the times when they were hurting; he knew the times when they were rejoicing – he knew their good days and bad days. But, what he gave them was more than a wish. At the very end of those two letters, he gives them the words that you and I know as the Apostolic Benediction. "The grace of the Lord, Jesus Christ, the love of God, the Father, and the fellowship and power of the Holy Spirit be with you all." Most of us have heard those words so often that we are sure that we understand them. But let me comment on each one of the phrases of that text in the hope that they may be a blessing for you and for me, today, and cause us to examine what God has to say to us in these special words.

"The grace of the Lord, Jesus Christ, be with you." Most of us think we know what grace is. In fact, I heard a television preacher say just a couple of days ago, "Grace is God's undeserved love that we do not merit in any way." He was absolutely right! Unmerited love – we don't deserve it, and we cannot earn it. We understand that definition, but I think we understand it better when we see it lived out in the world in which we live.

Once, during the time I was serving my second church, I was traveling with a funeral director all the way across the state of Ohio for an interment. He didn't know me very well and I didn't know him, so we talked to get better acquainted. He told me about his life, how irresponsible and promiscuous it was, how irreverent it was, and how carelessly he had lived his life. The more he talked, the more I believed him. Then he said that about six or seven years after high school and college, he had done so many embarrassing things that his whole family asked him to leave. He was gone for a number of years. Later on, he wrote and asked to come home, but no one wanted him back, no one, that is, except his father. That sounds familiar, doesn't it, like a story we have heard in the New Testament? He said pensively, "My father loved me when no one else would." I wanted to copy that down, thinking that perhaps I could use it for a sermon. All of a sudden, with a tear coming down his cheek, looking straight ahead, he said something even more profound, "He not only loved me when no one else would, he loved me when no one else could." That is the powerful gift of grace. God, in Jesus Christ, loved us not only when no one else would, but also when no one else could. No one else could go to the cross and love us as God did in Jesus Christ. Paul prays in our text today from Ephesians, "That the fullness of Christ may dwell in you through faith, that you, being rooted and grounded in love, may have the power to comprehend with all the saints what is the breadth and length and height and depth to know the love of Christ, which surpasses all knowledge."

There is another phrase that perhaps you have heard or used, "God helps those who help themselves." I don't want to shock you, but that is not in Scripture. Benjamin Franklin wrote that. It is true that God blesses good stewardship. He blesses the good work that we do in His name. God blesses all those who do faithful work. The bottom line of Scripture, though, is that God not only blesses those who help themselves, God blesses those who *cannot* help themselves. That includes you, and that includes me. The grace of the Lord, Jesus Christ, be with you, not that you just receive it, but also that you give it. When we receive this grace, we are to pass that grace on to others around us; in our families, in our church, in our relationships, in our community, and in our workplaces. We have the opportunity to forgive people who are truly sorry. John says in his first letter, "If we confess our sins, God is faithful and just to forgive us our sins and cleanse us from all unrighteousness." So then, if we are to forgive others as God in Christ has forgiven us, then people who are truly sorry for the way they have wronged us should receive that same forgiving grace.

A number of years ago, I was in Florida watching a newscast. There were two newscasters there, a man and a woman. At the end of the newscast, a picture of the Pope was shown. He had his back to the camera and his hands outstretched to Mehmet Ali Agca, the man who once tried to assassinate him. The male newscaster said, "How can he do that? That's the man who tried to kill him." The woman said, "Perhaps he knows something about grace that we haven't learned yet." The grace of the Lord is the love that Paul describes as "the love of God which surpasses all knowledge."

"The grace of the Lord, Jesus Christ, be with you all." The forgiving grace of the Lord, Jesus Christ, be with you and through you and in you – and that is more than a wish.

The second phrase is, "The love of God be with you." Now it sounds as if we are repeating ourselves. Grace is love, and here we speak again about the love of God. However, this is a different kind of love. This is a parental kind of love; an affirming, encouraging kind of love. That is the kind of love that God, the Father, gives to us as Paul describes it, "The love of God, the Father, be with you." Paul uses a very specific word for fatherhood in that passage. Here, it does not mean just paternity, which simply means fathering a child physically. The word Paul uses for fatherhood here describes an encouragement, an affirmation, an instruction, a companionship, and a presence that is generous and unconditional. We might translate it today as "Daddy."

A number of years ago at Chautauqua, New York, Robert Schuller told the story of walking out in a field with his young daughter. He played the game that many of us have played. He picked a flower, and he took it apart petal by petal repeating, "She loves me, she loves me not, she loves me, she loves me not," being very careful to end on the positive, "She loves me." When he finished, his daughter, who was maybe four or five, picked a flower, and she said, "He loves me, he loves me, he loves me, he loves me." I expect that Robert Schuller had disciplined his daughter and had said no to her at times, but still she knew, in spite of all that, his love was constant. That is what Paul is talking about; the love of God, who loves us and loves us and loves us and loves us. That is what Paul says in this passage from Ephesians, "That you may know the fullness of God," even at times when we don't see it.

There was a man walking down a street. He came across a young boy with a spool of string and saw the line going up, around a tree, and behind a building. He said, "What are you doing?" The little boy said, "I'm flying a kite." The man said, "I don't see a kite; how do you know it is there?" The little boy pulled on the string and said, "I can feel the tug." There are times when I really don't see God present in *my* life. There are times when the suffering is deep and the loneliness is very intense. And there are times that I really don't see what God is doing or what God is all about, but I can feel the tug. "The love of God be with you."

Well, how do we respond to that? We respond in the best way humanly possible, to give our love back to God – we do that. My parents taught me a game when I was little. We were able to walk together down the street and we could say "I love you" to each other

17

without actually saying a word out loud. We would just hold hands and squeeze three times, which meant, "I love you." The answer back was two squeezes. "How much?" Then the first person would hold on for a long time to let the other person know just how much they were loved. I taught the same game to my children, as well. One day while driving down the road with my twelve-year-old daughter, I reached over and took her hand, squeezed it three times, "I love you." She answered, "How much?" I held on for a long time. I watched the odometer to make sure she knew that I really loved her and then, after awhile, I let go. Down the road she took my hand and squeezed three times, "I love you" and I answered back, "How much?" She took my hand and squeezed it, and she held it a lot longer than I had held hers. Then she used both hands on my hand, and then she clenched her teeth together and breathed rapidly, as children will often do. Finally, she let go and said, "I can't hold on long enough or tight enough." By that time, I would have given her the car! What I knew was that she gave me as much of her love as she could in her childlike way, with her childlike faith. That is what God asks of us. He doesn't ask us to be God, he asks us to be ourselves. He asks us to be as complete as we are able; to show our praise for God, our love for God, in the best way we can – holding on as long as we can. It is impossible just to wish for that kind of love.

The grace of the Lord, Jesus Christ, be with you. The love of God, the Father, be with you. Finally, "The fellowship of the Holy Spirit be with you." Now Paul didn't just add that third phrase so preachers would have a nice three-point sermon. He had a very important reason for saying, "The fellowship of the Holy Spirit be with you." For Paul, this was not theory; this was not academic projection. This was something he had experienced. When Paul said, "the fellowship of the Holy Spirit be with you," he wanted the Corinthians, and now those of us who read that same passage, to know the power of the Holy Spirit to change lives. When Paul said "the fellowship of the Holy Spirit be with you," he was thinking of his own life. All you need to do is to move to Galatians and see what he says about the fruits of the flesh and the fruits of the Spirit. The fruits of the flesh, the things we do when we are out of the Spirit, are very sobering: *They are immorality, impurity, idolatry, sorcery, enmity, strife, jealousy, anger, selfishness, drunkenness, and the party spirit.* Paul knew all that. Either on his own or from that which he had observed, Paul knew what it was to live apart from the Spirit, in the fruits of the flesh. But after the Damascus road, after he met Jesus Christ in that life-transforming experience, after he lived with the Holy Spirit, after he lived those years in serving Christ, he said, *"The fruits of the Spirit are love, joy, peace, patience, kindness, goodness, faithfulness, humility, and self-control."* That was a significant change. That was what Paul was talking about when he said, "The fellowship of the Holy Spirit be with you" – that life-changing power! In Ephesians, in our passage today, he says, "For this reason, I bow the knee before the Father, before whom the whole family in heaven and earth is named, that according to the riches of His glory He may grant you to be strengthened with might *through His Spirit* in your inner being," that you might be totally changed.

Back in the Philippines in 1942, Douglas MacArthur fled the islands because the Japanese were taking over. But he made a promise. He said, "I shall return." Not many people believed him, military people or anybody else. It just seemed impossible that he would ever be able to return; but later, he did. All of us who are old enough remember that picture of him coming off the landing craft with his very distinctive hat, his sunglasses, and his corncob pipe, wading in water up to his knees. He had come back! To this day in the Philippine Islands, when the military groups call the roll, they call everybody's name and each one answers for himself. At the end of the roll call, the commander calls out one more name, "General Douglas MacArthur," and the whole group answers, "Present in spirit." Jesus said, "I shall return." It is the only promise He made in Scripture that has not yet been kept, and I fully believe that it will happen. Until He comes again, He can call your name and mine, and we should respond, "Here am I, send me; here am I, I will follow." Give your name as one of His servants, as a brother or sister in Christ. After all of our names are called, we could call one more name, "Jesus Christ," and we can all answer, "Present in spirit."

"The fellowship of the Holy Spirit be with you. The love of God, the Father, be with you. The grace of the Lord, Jesus Christ, be with you."

When shall we incorporate all of this into our lives? Shall we do it this afternoon after we get home and have a good dinner and, perhaps, a nap? Maybe we could think about these things all this next week, perhaps next summer, perhaps when we have a vacation and we have more time, after we have established our career or family, or maybe when we've retired, then we might have time to think about these things. However, there is an urgency, an imperative, in the Christian Gospel. Each one must claim these precious promises for the first time, or renew or reclaim them from time to time throughout our lives. Either way, it is an urgency that all of us should consider, every moment of our lives.

When our son was about four, he was a very anxious little boy. He liked to do things quickly. One time, there was something he and I were going to do and he kept pestering me, "Daddy, when are we going to do it?" I said, "Jim, it is not going to happen any sooner just because you keep asking; it is going to happen tomorrow; please don't ask me one more time." He honored that. The next morning, at five o'clock (do you know how you wake up and someone is looking at you?), I awoke with one eye open, and there he stood, fully dressed. He waited until my second eye was open, and then he said, "Daddy, tomorrow is now!" Tomorrow is now everyday for us as Christians. Paul knew it when he talked to the Corinthians once again. He said,

"I have helped you on the day of salvation, I have kept you on the day of need." Then he said, quoting from Isaiah in II Corinthians 6:2, "I have listened to you and helped you on the day of salvation. Behold, now is the acceptable time; behold, now is the day of salvation."

"Best of days, worst of days, spring of hope, winter of despair, season of light, season of darkness, we have everything before us, we have nothing before us," and the world says to all of that, "Have a good day, have a good time." But I say to you as a friend and brother in Christ, as one who gratefully shares with you this relationship that God has given to us, something that I think is much more powerful than anything the world has to offer. Once again, today, I say: the forgiving, redeeming grace of the Lord, Jesus Christ, be with you, each one of you; the affirming, encouraging love of God, the Father, be with you, all of you; and the life changing power of the Holy Spirit be with you. And that, my dear friends, is much more than a wish!

Choosing When Our Christmas Begins

Luke 1:26-38

She could have said "No!" There was no reason why she could not have said "No." The angel had come and announced, "Blessed one, God is with you and gracious to you. You are in His favor." Mary was deeply troubled by those words. Who wouldn't be? Even more astounding was what the angel said next. "God has a purpose for you; you will be the mother of a son named Jesus." She was dumbfounded and deeply disturbed by this announcement, and we are, too. We can think of many legitimate reasons why Mary could have said "No." This had come to her suddenly, without warning, like a bolt right out of the blue. She was far too young; perhaps, 12, or 14, maybe 16 at the most. It was not the right time; it was not the right place; it was not the right partner; it was not the right family; it was not the right plan for her future. This proposition seemed to her too abrupt; too much, too soon.

She could have said "No." She knew then what everybody knows even now, that it is more politically correct and socially acceptable to have babies *in* marriage and not out of wedlock. She could have said "No." Had she gone to others in her family and community, I

23

firmly believe that they would have given her the same advice. Out of their own experience, out of their own wisdom, they would have told her to "just say 'No.' " Any reasonable adult who had Mary's best interest at heart would have advised this way. They were, after all, older and wiser, and this kind of situation should be avoided at all costs. Consequently, for them, her only acceptable response should be "just say 'No.' " And, realizing that she was immature and impressionable, they did not want her to think that perhaps she was just living up to her name in Hebrew, which literally meant "bitterness and rebellion." That would probably have strengthened their resolve to advise her to "just say 'No.' "

Mary could have said "No"; the people around her could have said "No," but in the end, that was not what happened. After the angel made the announcement that she was to have a child, Mary asked questions for clarification. "How can this be? How can this happen to me? I am a young person. I am a virgin. I have not yet conceived." Naturally, she had many misgivings, apprehensions, and fears, not only for herself but about what others would think once her pregnancy was discovered. The answer to her questions came directly from the angel once again. "God has chosen you; God is with you; it is God's will for you. You will conceive by the Holy Spirit, and the child will be called the Son of God." And then this assuring promise, "For with God, nothing is impossible."

That is the point at which Mary gave her answer; perhaps one of the strongest, most powerful, personal testimonies in all of Scripture. "I am a servant of the Lord; may it happen to me as You have said." Mary had said, "Yes!" I am not sure many of us would have, but Mary said "Yes."

Martin Luther said there were three miracles in the Christmas message. One miracle was that Jesus was born of a virgin. The second miracle was that God in Jesus Christ became human. And the third miracle was that Mary said "Yes," she would accept this call from

24

God. She responded positively to what God had promised through the voice of the angel. This is the point at which the Christmas story becomes good news – the Gospel. This is the point at which the Christmas story comes alive. Not because Christmas is a day of celebration, not because of any ceremony, or ritual, or tradition, but because somebody, Mary, said "Yes" to the invitation of God to be a servant; to follow God's call.

There are several stirring paintings and statues of this annunciation scene. Raphael has a moving scene of the angel standing near Mary as she sits off to one side. Michelangelo created both a painting and a statue. In Westminster Abbey, there is a captivating picture in a stained glass window done by Sir Edmund Burns Jones. All of these pictures, all of these portrayals, express the same message. All of them show a young, demure, innocent Mary, looking away from the angel, pondering what has been said to her. Her expression indicates that she is perplexed and overwhelmed by this encounter. Then the angel, in all these scenes, stands a few feet away, not threatening, not intimidating, but rather, with arms outstretched in welcome, in love, and in grace, waiting patiently and longingly for Mary to make her decision and give her answer.

These thought-provoking artistic scenes mark the point at which this Gospel, this story, touches us. As it was with Mary, so it is with us. God is waiting for our response, your response and mine, to what will be done with the invitation offered to us in the Christ Child. Will we receive the Christ Child when He is offered to us? God did not force Mary. He did not threaten her or manipulate her. Neither will He do this to any one of us. However, the answer that Mary gave was crucial, and our answer is crucial, as well. The answer for Mary had critical implications, and our answer will be equally critical. She could have said no, but she didn't. When she said, "Yes, I am the Lord's servant, let it happen to me as you have said," it was the beginning of the Gospel, and it is at that same point that Christmas begins for us.

We need to see that Mary was not simply thinking with her head, but she was also feeling with her heart. It is an easy temptation to look only at the facts that surround us, those things we can see or touch. That objective approach is very valuable because it is through precise thinking that we are able to build bridges and skyscrapers, go to the moon, and balance our family budget. But, if we are honest with ourselves, we know that in our lives there is also a need to go beyond, from the objective to the subjective. We need to grasp the inner message this story is revealing to us. It is very subjective, very visceral, internal, and very personal. Here we see Mary dealing with subjective feelings – feelings that are down deep within her heart. We have often heard that the longest line in the world is from the head to the heart. It is frequently difficult to get what we are thinking to be in touch with what we feel. However, I happen to think there is a longer line. It is from the heart to the head. What we feel emotionally and spiritually deep down inside ourselves has a great deal of difficulty informing what we think we know. Blaise Pascal, a seventeenth century French philosopher, theologian, and scientist said, "The heart has reasons the mind knows not of." And then later, this same insightful scholar said, "The confidence that we have through our hearts and through our faith gives us more knowledge and more understanding than our thinking could ever provide."

A frequent phrase we often use is, "Seeing is believing." I have learned that if I can see an object, I can believe it is there. If I see you, I believe you are there. But I also happen to believe, because of my faith, and because of my experience, that the opposite is true, "Believing is seeing." For instance, I believe in Jesus Christ and, therefore, because of that belief, I am able to see the power of His cross and the meaning of grace, redemption, and reconciliation. I believe in Christ, so, therefore, I know what the cross means. I believe in Jesus Christ and, therefore, it is possible to comprehend the power of the resurrection, life abundant, here and eternal beyond. We believe certain things, and, therefore, we can know it, something we can find no other way. For instance, when a child snuggles up on our lap, puts his or her arms around our neck and hugs us tightly, we have a tender, warm understanding of what love is. That did not come from the head. It came from the heart. Suppose we have lost a loved one and, as we stand at the grave, someone comes and embraces us. In that touch, in that embrace, even when no words have been spoken, there is matchless understanding of the eternal presence of God and the power of Christ's eternal victory. Just from the touch, and the embrace, from feeling together the love and hope deep within, our minds are transformed into a victorious moment, a moment which can move us even beyond our tears. We are not always sure where that originates, nor do we understand how it comes. But from our experience, this one thing we do know; it is real, and it is authentic.

Mary could have said "No," but she didn't. And, in so doing, she said "Yes" to Jesus Christ; she said "Yes, I believe; Yes, I trust" and when she did, she discovered something deep within her that can only come by way of faith. Don't misunderstand me. I am not rejecting logical analysis, objective thought, and rational thinking – not at all. I am a Presbyterian, steeped in reformed theology. Therefore, I believe in the disciplines of study and learning. However, I also believe that, with Mary, we need to think about the matters of the heart. We must not ignore that which uses all of our senses, and especially, what we feel. I believe that it is important for us to have an encounter that comes from within, a precious encounter, experienced by knowing Jesus Christ personally, an encounter which leads us to that moment when you and I can say for ourselves individually, "I believe, I am the Lord's servant, may it happen to me, as God has said." And my prayer, today, is threefold: that you and I can open our hearts so we can be touched by God down deep inside of us; that you and I can encounter Jesus personally; and, that right now will be the moment when we will respond to His touch.

Too often we attend church – especially at Christmas time – because of habit and tradition. But what should really motivate us to come? We could have said "No" today. We could have stayed home, drinking a second cup of coffee, and watching the news on television, all of those incessant spin shows. We could have read the paper, or snoozed by the fire. We could have said "no" to a spouse, parent, child, or friend who had invited us to come with them, saying, "I just don't want to go today." To us, our excuses could have been just as valid and as convincing as the ones Mary could have given. However, we are here. Why? Perhaps we came because we work here. That is why I'm here. (The Commandment says, "Remember the Sabbath Day, to keep it holy," and for many that means no work on Sunday. But not for me! Some may think it is the only day I work, and that I only work twenty-five minutes of that day.) However, many others of us do come because we work here; we sing in the choir, we usher, we have teaching responsibilities, or we have responsibility to care for the building. Or, perhaps, we come because it is a special time of the year. We love to come to sing the familiar carols, hear the Scriptures, and pray the traditional prayers. We come because that is what we have always done in Advent and at Christmas.

But just perhaps there is a strong possibility that we have come here today because this is *exactly* the right place and the right time for us – this may just be our moment. And somehow, in this moment, while we are surrounded by the Scriptures, the anthems, the carols, the messages, and the company of God's people, the Spirit may move within us and, in this moment, may touch us. Perhaps some of us will experience that touch for the first time. Perhaps, for many, it will just be a renewal and reconsecration of that feeling down deep inside of us. Whichever it is, that moment is precious and personal. We should always be seeking for and open to that moment, so that when we come to worship, it is not just to sit, sing, and then to go home. It can be a moment when we hear the claims of the Gospel and are confronted by the invitation of God in Jesus Christ to become His servant, and to answer "Yes," to say, "I believe."

That is happening here. When our answer is spontaneous and voluntary, then the Christian living that we see and want, that peace that we desire, that forgiveness that we receive and give, happens naturally, from the heart. As an example, we don't have to tell our muscles how to form a smile if we see a friend whom we love. The smile just happens from within. We don't have to know the etymology of the word love, the history, the philosophy or semantics of the word, to be able to say sincerely and genuinely, "I love you." Those things can happen automatically, or naturally, when there is an encounter from the heart which has been warmed by Christ.

Madeleine L'Engle, in her short writing called, *The Weather of the Heart*, said this, "In this sensational, superficial, secular theological season, it is important for us to remind ourselves of that genuine, refreshing, revitalizing love of Jesus Christ that flows from the heart of God to our heart, and through our heart to others." That is what I'm proclaiming. We can intellectualize about many things, but what I'm sharing is deeper than that. Jesus meets you and me personally, and He instills His love in our hearts. That is the encounter I want you to experience today! When we accept the gift He offers, we are immediately on the edge of a great adventure, on the way to something, or someone very special – the Lord and Savior, Jesus Christ. We are crossing the threshold into being held by the strength and touch of the Cross and Resurrection of Jesus Christ. There, however, is one significant difference between Mary and us. When Mary heard the angel, she could have said "No," but she didn't. She said "Yes," even though all she had was a promise. She had no idea how great an adventure was before her, or that her son would some day speak to thousands of people, feeding and healing them, bringing sight to the blind, and wholeness to the lepers. She also had no idea that He would be spit upon, and crucified, and derided. She couldn't even imagine all that. All she had was a promise, and on that promise alone, she said, "Yes, I believe."

Fred Craddock, theologian and inspiring homiletician, says, "You and I have the opportunity of being on this side of the Cross." Mary didn't – we do. We have the luxury of looking back to see what has already been accomplished and what has been fulfilled in the 2000 years since the time of Jesus Christ. We have learned much through Scripture. Jesus came and taught, healed and died upon the Cross. We know that; it is a historical fact. The atonement for our sins has been fulfilled. Jesus Christ was dead and rose again, and we know that victory has been fulfilled. So, when the angel says to us, "God is with you; you are in God's favor, and God wants to use you!" we have no excuse because we already have been on this side of the Cross, where we have seen all that has been fulfilled. Nothing has been held back, we are not separated from anything that God has promised for us and accomplished in Christ. That is the message of Christmas.

A great carol we sing so often is entitled, "Good Christian Friends, Rejoice." That particular carol has a vital and complete message. At its core are the claims of the Gospel, the promise of Good News in Jesus Christ that comes into our hearts. "Good Christian friends rejoice with heart, soul and voice. Now you need not fear the grave. Jesus Christ was born to save . . . He has opened Heaven's doors and we are blessed evermore . . . Christ was born for this. Christ was born for this." Through that promise, which has been accomplished and is available to us through Christ, in that moment when God touches our hearts, we begin to realize that there is no effort God will not make to pursue us, even to the cross. There is no distance to which God will not go to reach us, even all the way to our hearts. There is no depth to which God will not stoop to lift us, all of which He has done in Jesus Christ and which we receive through our faith in the Living Christ.

When will your Christmas begin? Will it begin when your decorations are finished inside and out? When your cards are all finished and mailed? Will it be when you have done all your shopping and wrapped all your presents? Will it be when you come to all the services and all the programs which are available? Or, when you exchange gifts on Christmas morning and have a dinner together with family and friends? Is that when your Christmas begins? Well, that is all very important. But that is all tradition pointing us to the real reason we do all of this celebrating. Ultimately, Christmas begins when each one encounters what God has done in Jesus Christ. It begins when the incarnation – when God sent His only Son in human flesh to save the world – becomes a reality. When we acknowledge that reality and respond, "Yes, I believe. I am Your servant; let your will happen in me and through me," then that is when we discover that Christmas has finally begun, and in the mercy and grace of the Lord, and the power and presence of the Holy Spirit, it will never end.

JUST WHAT WE NEEDED!

Psalm 89:1-7, 15-18 (Good News Bible)
I Corinthians 1:4-9

I suspect that several times in the last few days you have said, or perhaps you have heard it said, "That's just what I needed." It is, after all, a very gracious thing to say. It is very courteous; and also politically correct to show our genuine gratitude. We want the people who have given us the gifts to feel good about what they have given to us. And very often, because of their sensitivity and their thoughtfulness, it is a true statement. What they gave us is just what we needed. But there are times we say it to convince ourselves that the loud socks, garish tie, oversized sweater or unexplainable gadget is essential and indispensable to our lives; it's "just what we needed."

It is valid to examine every gift we receive to see if we just want it, or whether it is something we really need. Author James Michener told a wonderful story about his childhood in Doylestown, Pennsylvania. He cut grass all summer long for a widow lady. She made him this promise: "I can't pay you now, but at Christmas time I will give you a very special surprise – a very special gift – something you need." So all summer long, as he cut the grass, he tried to imagine what that special present might be. When fall came, he had finally decided what he was sure she would give to him. He felt that the perfect reward, her special gift, something he felt he needed, would have to be a pair of ice skates.

So on Christmas Eve, he went to her house, and she brought out the package. When he saw it, he was shocked and more than a little disappointed because it was obviously too small, too flat, too thin, and too light to be ice-skates. As he opened it, she said, "This is something that I know you can really use, and it will be something that will bless you your entire life." When he opened it, he was totally surprised because it was ten pieces of carbon paper. Now you might try to give your children ten pieces of carbon paper. But I suspect if you do, it will not be warmly received.

Even though he was bitterly disappointed, he took the gift home and began to use it. Putting a sheet of carbon paper between two sheets of paper, he began to write. He wrote some words, then other words, and even more words. He said that exercise began his fascination with words. It opened a whole new world for him. Later he said, while evaluating the impact of this experience, "The average gift satisfies just the temporary – the things we think we want, as the ice skates would have done. But the great gift illumines all of life before us." This simple gift of ten pieces of carbon paper was not an average gift; it was an extraordinary gift that illumined all Michener's life. It blessed his life, and all of us who have read his works have been blessed, as well.

Jesus is not the average temporary gift. Paul says, "We look not for things that are seen, but for things that are unseen. Because things that are seen are temporary; the things that are unseen are eternal." (II Corinthians 4:18) This unseen gift in Jesus Christ is an extraordinary gift that illumines all of our lives. Paul says it this way in II Corinthians 9:51, "Thanks be to God for His inexpressible gift." The Greek word for inexpressible is translated several ways in the various versions of Scripture. In the Revised Standard Version and Jerusalem Bible, it says, "an inexpressible gift." In the King James

34

Version, it says, "unspeakable gift." In the Living Bible and the New English Bible, it says, "a gift too wonderful for words." In the Phillips Paraphrase and the New International Version, it says, "the indescribable gift." In the Good News Bible, it says, "the priceless gift." Bible scholar Walter Wuest calls it, "the gift which is irresistible." William Barclay says, "It is the gift that can never totally be told."

Whatever word we use, we are announcing that this gift God has given us is "just what we needed." If we look at the Christmas gift of God in Jesus Christ, we realize it is *exactly* what we need. It is important for us to see why that is true. First of all, this gift in Jesus Christ is forgiveness – forgiveness for our sin – God's generous grace given to us; the love of God which we cannot earn and we do not deserve, which God gives so graciously to us; offering us the opportunity to repent of our sin, grow in grace, and to find new life in Him.

Back in the eighteenth century, there was a young man who was very vulgar and crude. He was undisciplined and intolerable to people around him, not only in his own home but also in the wider world. When he left home, late in his twenties, he heard an evangelist speaking about Jesus Christ. It changed his life, and he wrote a poem, which described his conversion. It says, "*In evil, long I have lived my life, un-awed by shame or fear. 'Til this new message claimed my life and stopped my vile career.*" He said that message was just what he needed. You perhaps do not recognize that first verse of poetry. The one you recognize is the second verse; "*Amazing grace, how sweet the sound that saved a wretch like me. I once was lost but now I'm found; was blind but now I see.*" John Newton wrote that, claiming it was exactly what he needed: the message of God's forgiveness in Jesus Christ. It is an amazing gift! As Paul says in Romans 5:8, "While we were still sinners, Christ died for us." We need that gift – that cleansing gift, that amazing gift of grace and generous love in Jesus Christ to save us from our sin.

Forgiveness is a powerful gift and we need it. We also need to be able to share it. "Forgive one another as God in Christ has forgiven you." (Colossians 3:13) We pray in The Lord's Prayer: "Forgive us our debts, as we forgive our debtors." To be able to forgive is part of the gift that we need. God gives us the blessing of being forgiven and the opportunity, yes, reponsibility to forgive others. One day while Leonardo Da Vinci was painting, he found that his brush strokes were failing to produce on canvas the images of color and light he saw in his mind's eye. Nothing seemed in focus for him. This frustrated him because he was unable to concentrate on what he was creating. He kept remembering that a few days earlier he had been insulted and publicly attacked by a person who had later asked for forgiveness. He was sure that the man was truly sorry for what he had done, but Da Vinci would have none of that. He was more interested in retribution and revenge. He realized that he was so preoccupied with his feeling of vengeance and reprisal that he was not able to focus on his work. So he went out, found the man and forgave him. Being willing and able to give that forgiveness liberated him from the desire for revenge that had restrained him. Forgiveness enabled him to go from feeling restricted to being refreshed, reawakening his ability and his desire to paint. Being able to forgive was *just what he needed*, and it is just what we need as well.

Also this gift in Jesus Christ is just what we need because it teaches us a lesson of humility. It teaches us to recognize God as our source of strength. In our humanity, there are times when we are awfully cocky and arrogant. Sometimes, I think we are too proud to be shepherds and too self-satisfied to be wise men. Consequently, we are not able to recognize one of our greatest needs as human beings – to be humble enough to see our needs, which God *alone* can fulfill.

I once sat at a dinner table with the late Vince Lombardi's wife at the Hall of Fame in Canton, Ohio. She told me this story. "One day we were sitting at a restaurant and, way across on the other side, a little boy kept looking and smiling and nodding back and forth, and my husband said to himself, 'He knows who I am.' The little boy got up and walked across the restaurant. My husband, assuming he knew what the boy wanted, picked up a pencil and wrote his name on the placemat to give him an autograph. The little boy arrived and Vince said, 'Here is my autograph.' The little boy said, 'Oh, I don't want that; I was going to ask if I could borrow your ketchup.' " Mrs. Lombardi turned to me and said, "That day, Vince Lombardi learned a great lesson in humility."

C. S. Lewis talks about a similar lesson in his life. Before he became Christian, this great scholar and intellect thought that if he worked long enough, and thought deeply enough, and studied as much as he possibly could, he could solve every problem, break down every barrier, and find every solution to the problems in life. Needless to say, he found that didn't work. The more he tried, the more restless and unfulfilled he became. Then he was confronted by the person and the power of Jesus Christ in the cross and resurrection. He read these words in Romans: "By the grace given to you in Jesus Christ, I beg all of you, not to think of yourselves more highly than you ought to think, but with sober judgment, consider the grace that God has given to you in Jesus Christ, each according to your need." (Romans 12:3) Beyond that, he looked at the text today in the first chapter of I Corinthians (1:21-24): "For since, in the wisdom of God, the world did not know God through wisdom; it pleased God through the foolish message that we preach to save those who believe. For the Jews seek signs and the Greeks seek wisdom, but we preach Christ crucified, a stumbling block to Jews and foolishness to Gentiles, but to those who are being saved, those who are called, Christ, the power of God and the wisdom of God."

In an article, just before he died, C. S. Lewis wrote this: "I discovered this new wisdom in the cross and resurrection of Jesus Christ did not take away my mind; it did not take away the need to study or my respect for scholarship. The Gospel simply sifted down through my arrogance, self-importance, pseudo sophistication, and self-satisfaction, and it confronted me, melting down my self-righteousness and over-confidence, and astounding me with a marvelous gift of wisdom, which at one-in-the-same-time was profound and also plain and simple." It may have been the foundation for his widely read and influential book *Mere Christianity*. Therein can be found a plain, simple testimony of faith – a blessing to him, an inspiration to countless others.

We discover that humility, which is ours in Christ. He gave Himself. He humbled Himself so that we might understand what it means to be humble before God. *"That was just what we needed."* It is through the humility of Christ that God gives us strength. Thus the humility enables us to understand God's gift of unconditional love – unconditional love that loves us, not for what we are or have done, but for what we can become, when God dwells within us. That is the wonderful gift that we have in Christ. Christ refuses to see us as we are and continues to see us as the new creatures we are promised that we can become.

Twenty-four years ago on inauguration day, Jimmy Carter was making his way back to the White House through a crowd of reporters. Beside him was his mother, Miss Lillian, and behind him was his brother, Billy, who had a wayward reputation, to put it mildly. As they went through the crowd, one of the reporters called out and said to Mrs. Carter, "Miss Lillian, aren't you proud of your son today?" And she responded, "Which one?" Unconditional love! God refuses to see us as we are, but always in the potential of what we can become.

Unconditional love is not just something we need to receive; it is also the unrestricted love in Christ we need to share. Do you remember O. Henry's touching short story about a young couple's first Christmas together? They wanted to give personal gifts to each other. The husband took his precious pocket watch and sold it so that he could

38

buy beautiful jeweled combs for his wife's gorgeous hair. Unaware of what he had done, she sold her hair so that she could buy a very handsome leather watch fob for his pocket watch. O. Henry said, "Neither one of those gifts was useful anymore" – a watch fob with no watch; the combs for the hair that now was too short. He said, "Their gifts were no longer useful, nor did they now have any meaning, but the couple did discover what it meant to give sacrificially, with unconditional love, to be blest to be able to give as Christ has given to us."

"Thanks be to God for this inexpressible gift," and it is *just what we need* – the unconditional gift of love, which is available to us in Christ Jesus.

We need the gift of forgiveness; to be forgiven and to be able to forgive; to have the humility to know that God is our strength; to have this sense of unconditional love, which we can share and give. But also we have the gift of life. *And it is just what we need!*

Ben Weir is a Presbyterian pastor who was held as a hostage in Lebanon. He was imprisoned in a basement room, with no windows, and only one bare light bulb hanging on a single wire from the ceiling. He had a cot, but he was fastened to the floor by a long, bulky chain. Food came in small quantities, sometimes once, sometimes twice a day. Somehow, he kept track of the days so that he knew when it was Sunday. During the week, he would hide a small piece of bread. On Sunday, when he was alone he would take the piece of bread and a small sip of water, repeat the words of the consecration of those very common elements and there, all alone, celebrate the Sacrament of the Lord's Supper. In addition to the word of consecration, he would also quietly recite these words from Scripture: "Do not be afraid, I am the first and the last, and the living one," (Revelation 1:17) and "Because I live, you, too, shall live." (John 14:19c) He said, "With those powerful words, and with a small piece of dry bread and sip of water, I was reminded each time of the gift of abundant and eternal life in Jesus Christ. And in those circumstances, which seemed so hopeless, I found a small ray of hope and it was *just what I needed*. I was able to cope!"

As Victor Frankl learned in a concentration camp during World War II, if a person has something to live for, he or she usually has the ability to cope. When one has that gift, one then finds a reason for hope. This is the great gift of Easter – the gift of the resurrected life in Christ, which is the basis for our hope. This gift puts us in touch with strength and courage for living, which is not possible any other way. We all need this; in fact, *it is exactly what we need*.

This is a free gift. We cannot purchase it! This free gift, which God has given, is only available to us by grace in Jesus Christ. In Acts (8:14-24), there is a story of John and Peter, who were ministering in Samaria. A man named Simon, a magician, observed them carefully. He heard what they were preaching and watched them healing the sick. He said, "I want to buy the power you have." (paraphrase) They replied, "Your silver and gold perish with you because you think you can buy this gift. What you need is a new heart." If our heart is humble and open to Jesus Christ, this gift that is available is given to us, "without money or without price," only through the generous, gracious gift of Christ. No matter how hard we try, we cannot buy it.

Finally, this gift is one which we need to use. If this gift is ours in Jesus Christ, forgiveness, humility, unconditional love, and abundant and eternal life, then it becomes something to live for and to put into practice.

When I was a boy, my mother was accustomed to cooking with double boilers. This was before the days of microwaves. She had two well-worn old double boilers that she used all of the time. She had used them so long that the bottoms were uneven and wobbly. The sides were badly dented and the lids didn't fit very well. Their handles were loose. I decided to get her a new one for Christmas. I saved my money for a long time and then went out and bought a brand new double boiler, one of those fancy ones with a copper bottom. I was so excited! On Christmas morning, she opened my gift, admired it, said she appreciated the sacrifice I had made to buy it, and thanked me. Then she went to the kitchen, dusted off a place on the shelf and put the new double boiler there. And then, she went right back to work and cooked the Christmas dinner that day with the old double boilers!

Think about that in light of our spiritual lives. God has given us this brand new gift in Jesus Christ, one we know we need. And yet, we come again at Christmas time, dust off the shelf called tradition, put that gift in a place called ceremony, admire it, and then we go on living our lives with our wobbly, old, dented, loose-handled ways. A line from an anthem says, "Let not our slothful hearts refuse the guidance of Thy light to us." I would like to change one word in that phrase: "Let not our slothful hearts refuse the guidance of *Thy gift* to us."

Paul knew what this gift was. In I Corinthians 1:4-7 he says, "I thank God always for the gift of grace that you have in Jesus Christ and for the fact that the testimony is being sustained and strengthened among you, that you are not lacking in any spiritual gift, so you will have all that you need." He wanted us to know and receive this gift in Christ Jesus, which is so complete, inexpressible, indescribable, irresistible, too wonderful for words, and unspeakable. The gift in Christ is all of that, and more, and it is *"just what we needed."*

A New Rugged Cross

(An old familiar tune with a new perspective.)

1. Just ahead in my life stands a new rugged cross
   On which Jesus has written my name;
   I accept that new cross as the dearest and best
   A disciple of Jesus can claim.
   > *Refrain: I will cherish this new rugged cross*
   > *As a loving response in Christ's name;*
   > *I will carry my new rugged cross*
   > *And the glory of Jesus proclaim.*

2. From the old rugged cross once endured by my Lord,
   I have learned of God's message of love –
   How Christ died for my sin, and by faith brought me in
   To his grace and his glory above.
   > *Refrain*

3. As I look at the world and discover the pain,
   And the sadness, and sorrow, and loss;
   I say "No" to myself, and remember God's Word,
   And respond with my new rugged cross.
   > *Refrain*

4. Still ahead in my life stands that new rugged cross,
   And Jesus says, "Take this and live!"
   So I take that new cross, as the only response
   One who follows the master should give.
   > *Refrain*

(William Jackson wrote these words and adapted them to the original tune "The Old Rugged Cross," written by George Bennard.)

FROM THE LAST MINUTE TO ETERNITY

Psalm 130
Luke 23:39-43 and 11:9-13

One thief in particular was especially terrified by what was happening. He was frightened. How could this be happening to him? He never thought that in those days when he was stealing from the market place, or robbing the rich caravans, or burglarizing the wealthy homes that it would come to this for himself and for his friend. Now here he was, carrying his cross up to Golgotha, the place of crucifixion. And something else was terrifying him; this was not the first time he had ever seen a crucifixion; he had been here before. It was common practice for crowds to come and watch – to be curious. But this crowd seemed especially malicious. It was louder, larger, angrier, and more vicious – all of this apparently directed toward the man in the middle, named Jesus. He remembered in the courtyard, when the people were given a choice of what to do with this Jesus, they were in a frenzy; and in their rage, they began to cry out with a deafening roar, "Crucify him." So not only did they pronounce the sentence, now they had also followed along to Golgotha, still shouting, still screaming, still laughing, still jeering – celebrating their victory, making absolutely certain that this man named Jesus would die as painfully and grotesquely as possible.

And now, at the height of all of the chaos and fear, he heard from this man in the middle words that were extraordinary. As the nails were piercing his hands, he called out, "Father, forgive them for they know not what they do." Not hate nor violence, instead this man in the middle was expressing his love, so different from any other victim he had observed on a cross. That word was just the spark, just the thing to raise in his mind, arouse in him the possibility that this one who was so different, so courageous, so controlled, and so confident – seemingly bigger than life – might have something more to say also to him.

So, just as the crosses were raised erect and jolted into the ground, when it was most excruciating, the thief turned to the one in the middle. He took a chance and said, "Jesus, remember me when you come into Your Kingdom"; a very candid and sincere request. He could have gone elsewhere with his request. The thief could have turned to the crowd and said, "In the name of all decency, stop this inhumanity!" And to the leaders of the synagogue, he could have said, "In the name of God, stop this!" Or to the women, "Let me appeal to your compassion and to your pity." But the paradox here is, that the thief does not turn to the apparent victors, he turns to the victim. Instead of turning to those who apparently were the more powerful, he turned to one who seemed to be the most vulnerable. And characteristically, Christ does here what He always did and still does. He turned directly to the one in imminent danger and responded to the one crying for help. The first word He spoke had been a prayer for His crucifiers, but this was a word to someone who had made a personal request. Jesus focused His eyes, centered His attention, on that request and on that man and said, "Today you will be with me in paradise."

This was characteristic of the style of Jesus. From the very beginning of His ministry, Luke and Matthew both record His promise: "Ask and you shall receive, seek and you shall find, knock and it shall be opened unto you." (Matthew 7:7) He also said early in His ministry, "Those who hunger and thirst after righteousness will be satisfied." In the Gospel of John, He said, "Him that cometh unto me, I will not turn away, I will not cast out." Jesus made it very plain all through His ministry, what was becoming clear in this experience on the cross; if someone came with a genuine request for God's presence. He would respond, there would be an answer; there would be a response. The old Gospel hymn says, *If with all your heart you truly seek me, you shall surely find me.*

But this word of comfort, consolation, and confidence to the thief is not just to him, it is also to each one of us. Because each one of us from time to time must bear a cross, not as difficult or as cruel or as torturous as the one that the thief was on, but, nonetheless, just as emotionally and spiritually negative, hopeless, and unbearable. If our request to Jesus, even today, is genuine and sincere and authentic, Jesus will reply in the same gracious, generous, compassionate way.

If this is true, and it is, what can we learn from the thief, from this one last word that Jesus speaks? First of all, I suggest to you that this thief got more than he deserved. The law of the day said that, having been captured and convicted of a crime, he should, therefore, be crucified. He was getting what the law prescribed. He was getting what he deserved, but he got more than he deserved. He said it himself, "We are getting what we deserve, but this one has done nothing wrong." That is when Jesus turned to him and said, "Today you will be with me in paradise." Crucifixion was what he deserved; Jesus gave him an eternal promise; more than he deserved.

The Apostle Paul helps us as we struggle with that same thing in our lives, seeing that God gives to each one of us more than we deserve. Paul says to us, "The wages of sin is death, but the free gift of God is eternal life." (Romans 6:23) Do you remember what Paul said about his own struggle, his own difficulty? He said, "The good I want to do, I can't do, and the evil I don't want to do, I keep on doing." (Romans 7:19) Then he said this, "Wretched man that I am! Who is there to rescue me out of this body, doomed to death? Thanks be to God through Jesus Christ." (Romans 7:24) Does Paul's struggle with good and evil sound painfully familiar to you? It does to me. It does, because we are struggling with the same kind of contrast. While we deserve sin's sentence of death, we have also been offered the free gift of eternal life in God. Peter said, "He Himself bore our sins in His body on the tree, that we might die to sin and live to righteousness. By His wounds you have been healed" – the free gift of God. (I Peter 2:24, RSV)

Let me clarify what is meant by the free gift. Dietrich Bonhoeffer says that this is not cheap grace. It's not a forgiveness that is handed out randomly or indiscriminately; there is a cost to pay. But we can't possibly pay the price. There is nothing we can give that can buy that forgiveness and salvation. However, it is free to us because of the price that Christ paid on the cross for us. What we hear in this word from Jesus is that there is no cost too high; there is no love too costly that God is not willing to pay, even to the extent of giving His own Son for us – taking our place on the cross. We can't afford it, we can't buy it, and we're not entitled to it. God gave us a gift in the cross of Jesus Christ that we do not deserve, but He willingly and lovingly gave.

A young pastor recently said to Billy Graham, "You must be impressed with the staggering number of people, over the fifty years plus that you have been an Evangelist, who have come forward and given their hearts to Christ." Billy Graham in typical style said, "I am grateful, most of all, that God has given me the opportunity to share the message that what He has provided for me and for all who are slaves to sin, is the answer of life and love and hope, which no one of us deserves." He was humbled by that gift.

When Jesus says today, "You shall be with me in paradise," He says to the thief, and to you and me, this is a gift that is more than you deserve. It is also something that is more than we expect. When the crucifixion was over, the crowd went home. They all thought it was successful, all three of the men were dead, especially this rabble-rouser, Jesus; they thought it was finished – it was over.

Fred Craddock says we must remember that we have the advantage of seeing from two thousand years, this side of the cross. When we look back, we see something the crowd did not see. They thought everything was finished, for those two thieves, and for Jesus. But there was something more, more than the crowd expected, more than they thought would or could happen. Jesus said that for the thief this was not the end, it was just the beginning; "Today you will be with me . . . ," not maybe, or could be, or just for this moment, "Today you will be with me. . . ." When we hear these words from Jesus, this thief, and you and I, get much more than we expect – the beginning of life – the victory of life.

When Dietrich Bonhoeffer was executed for his participation in an attempt to assassinate Hitler, he gave these last words to his friends before he went to the gallows, "This is the end, for me the beginning of life." One of his friends said, "The Third Reich, the Nazis, convicted him, that was the law. But God had converted him, and so he had a victory which neither the Nazis nor anyone else ever expected." When Jesus said, "Today you shall be with me in paradise," he gave us a victory which no one expected. Paul says it this way in Corinthians, "O death, where is your victory? O grave, where is the power you had hoped to win? But thanks be to God, who gives us the victory through our Lord Jesus Christ." (I Corinthians 15:55, 57) More than you and I could possibly expect is this eternal gift; eternal victory.

This victory changes our outlook, our perspective, and our attitude. The late Bishop Fulton Sheen, in the early days of television, used to give marvelous straightforward theological messages. Once, when speaking about these two thieves, he said that the difference between them was, one wanted only to be taken down, and that was temporary.

The other thief wanted to be taken up, and that was eternal. When we desire to be "taken up with Jesus," something victorious happens.

When we hear Jesus say, "I am the resurrection and the life. Those who believe in me, even though they die, yet shall they live; and whosoever liveth and believeth in me will never die," (John 11:25) that is a victory we do not expect. When we are hurting, when we are suffering, when we are facing death, when we are facing guilt or shame or fear or disappointment and discouragement, Jesus is there beside us. And if we say sincerely, "Jesus, remember me," there is an answer, there is a presence, there is a healing, there is a power, there is a possibility which most of us don't expect.

When Jesus said, "Today you will be with me . . . ," the thief and you and I get more than we deserve, more than we expect, but also, more than we have asked for. Think of that! All this man said was, "Remember me." That was all he said. Jesus didn't say, "I will *remember* you; I *won't forget* you." He said, "Today you *will be with me in paradise*" – with Jesus in His victory over the cross and death, and in companionship with Christ in eternity. It was the last word of this thief on the cross, but it took him from the last minute to eternity, to an everlasting companionship.

That is a victorious gift, and more than we could ask for, something we should think about more often. In our home, we often have discussions around the table. One night, we were talking about the persons we would like to talk to in heaven, when we get there. My wife, Vail, said, "I'd like to talk to the Apostle Paul, because I have some questions about what he has to say about women." I said, "I'd like to talk to David, because I would like to talk to this man who wrote these meaningful Psalms and these wonderful hymns, and was so brave and courageous." Then Vail turned to our daughter, Anne, and said, "Anne, with whom would you like to visit?" Anne simply said, "I just want to hang around Jesus." This promise, "Today you will be with me in paradise," is more than we have asked for!

That's what the psalmist was saying in that psalm we read today: "Out of the depths, I cried to you, Lord. Lord, listen to my cry for help, listen to my plea. If you would mark iniquities, who could stand? No one! But with you, there is that surprising promise, more than we could ask for – a steadfast love and a plenteous power of redemption." (paraphrased) That's much more than we could ask for. Remember also what the Apostle Paul said in the Ephesian letter in the third chapter: "And now, unto him, who is able to do more than we could ask for or think. . . ." (Ephesians 3:19-21) What a wonderful phrase; what a wonderful benediction, "able to do more than we could ask or think." We are given more than we could possibly ask for. That is the meaning of grace – God's full, liberating gift.

But what we have received is not just referring to the future. It is also an urgent truth that we need to consider for the here and now. This last word of Jesus to the penitent thief becomes a first word for us when we realize there is an urgency here. There is always an imperative in the Christian faith. Are we ready to approach Jesus with our request for His presence in our lives? Is there openness in our lives to find what Jesus is saying in answering our requests and petitions? We are not just bystanders here; we are participants with the thief. We do not have the same kind of crosses, or the same accusations or charges he faced, but we often deal with the same fears and the same anxieties. That is the point at which Jesus comes and responds to us in the same way He did with the thief, who was facing the questions of life and death.

This past week, Maria Shriver did a documentary program on NBC, where she traced the tragic deaths of children by firearms, and confronted the violence which had been experienced by children in one short week. It was a distressing and very disturbing program to watch. In the end of that same time period, that one short week, it was reported that thirty-seven young people had been killed. That was disturbing enough, but then she said that if you take the entire

51

number of people from the teenage and childhood years who are killed by guns throughout any given year, the average is not thirty-seven per week, but seventy-three.

After the most recent shooting in a San Diego public school, on a local television talk show, there were lots of people offering their considered professional opinions and drawing certain conclusions. One psychologist said, "Children don't seem to understand how fragile life is, just how tenuous life is." That is true, not just for children, but for us. Our life is just as tenuous; it is just as fragile, as it was for the thief. We may not be on the cross beside Jesus, we may not be dying, we may not be terminal; but this is the moment, *our* moment to make the decision to come to Christ. It is imperative! Paul said to the Corinthians, "Now is the day of salvation, now is the acceptable time." (II Corinthians 6:2) It is important for us, if we are to hear this word of Jesus, this last word of Jesus to the thief and to us, perhaps for the first time, we need to say, "Jesus, remember me." When our request is genuine and sincere, I promise you that Jesus will answer with more than we deserve, more than we expect, and more than we ask for.

About fifteen years ago, I heard Wayne Watson, a young Christian performer and songwriter, singing a song in which he described in a dramatic way the scene from this morning's text. He sang about the pathos, the suffering, the anger, the struggling, and the pain. The refrain, which was also the song's title, captured my attention. It simply said, "The man in the middle kept giving His love away." When you and I look at the life in which we find ourselves, the personal struggles which are ours, fears that we have, the questions that we have, that scene may be very familiar for us in one form or another. We need to remember, whatever our place in life, whatever our minute or moment in life, that the man in the middle still keeps giving His love away, to you, and to me, and to everyone who says,

"Remember me." And by the grace and mercy of God, we will receive at that point more than we deserve, more than we expect, and more than we ask for, all summed up in the words of Jesus, "Today you will be with me in paradise." Amen.

THE DEEP DESIRE

John 19:28-29
Mark 9:38-41

We are indebted to all four Gospel writers: Matthew, Mark, Luke, and John, who from time to time painted for us vivid, sharp, and penetrating pictures of the humanity of Christ. They didn't have to do this. Yet, at just the right time, when the divinity of Christ seemed to be unapproachable, the holiness of Christ seemed to be untouchable, and the perfection of Christ unparalleled, these writers speak up and remind us, DO NOT FORGET that Jesus was also human; He was the Word Made Flesh. At just the right time, these four evangelists made known to us the fact that Jesus, to whom we pray, knew our feelings; He knew our temptations. He knew our discouragement; He knew what it meant to be hungry, and to be exhausted. He had dealt with squabbling disciples who wanted special favors. He also understood when He heard us pray in anger; He welcomed children; He smiled when we confessed our weariness; He was touched when we were overwhelmed and empathized when we had too much to do with too little time.

All of those things express to us the humanity of Christ. I am indebted, as all of us are, that in this scene from our text today, there are the words "I thirst," which Jesus spoke from the cross. Here His humanity is visibly portrayed in the midst of His divinity. Last summer, during my fourth visit to the Oberammergau Passion Play, this scene had a very profound effect on me. There in the portrayal of the crucifixion was clear evidence of the humanity and the divinity of Christ. This word, "I thirst," is different from the other six that Jesus spoke. The other six seemed to be in character. They were what we expected: "Today you shall be with me in paradise; Forgive them for their sins; Mother, behold your son, son your mother; My God, my God, why hast Thou forsaken me?" Right at the time when we become comfortable with those nice religious "-*ation*" words, like sanctification, purification, justification, and propitiation, the writers remind us of incarnation: His humanity.

This one we call "Savior" did not wear a bulletproof vest or wear rubber gloves; He did not wear an impenetrable suit of armor. No, this one who pioneered and perfected our salvation lived right in the middle of the same kind of daily life that you and I live. While we might call Him, as the writers did, "King of Kings," "Lord of Lords," "Prince of Peace," "Morning Star," we need to remember that at the same time, while He was all of that, He also was the one who restored and renewed us by his personal suffering as the Word made Flesh. Don't forget, Jesus Christ was not only divine, He was also human. The two candles on the communion table are there for a purpose. They represent the divinity and the humanity of Christ in picturesque form. That is why those two candles burn there week after week. Jesus Christ in His humanity knew what it meant to be thirsty, and He also knew the pain of what it meant to be crucified.

One of the reasons this was so important in the latter part of the first century, when John was writing his Gospel account, was because a theological and philosophical heresy called gnosticism was prevalent. It taught that everything of spirit is good; all matter is evil. The conclusion was that God who was good was spirit, and, therefore,

God could not take on human form because human form was matter, and that was evil. As a result, they felt that Jesus could not have had a real body. The gnostics said that Jesus, as the disciples knew Him, was just a phantom, an illusion. They said that when He walked there were no footprints, and on the cross there was no pain, and there was no suffering. In all honesty, it was an attempt by the gnostics to honor God on their own terms, but in so doing they also were taking away His full nature which was, in fact, both divine and human.

Having said all that – that the humanity of Jesus is expressed in His thirst on the cross, I also want to say I am firmly convinced that as Jesus hung on the cross that day, there was not only human thirst, there was a divine thirst, as well. From the cross, as He looked upon those who were standing there – His family, His friends, and His tormentors – His soul was arid, his spirit was dry. The deep cry within Him was not simply for something to satisfy His physical need, but it was also a cry for living water, for the souls standing around the cross and, thereby, for all humanity. That cry, "I thirst," was for all of us, for our salvation and for our redemption.

As we look at the people around the cross, we see a composite of the same kind of people you and I are, with the same needs we have today. Jesus looked down and He saw only one disciple, knowing that the others had fled, and so His word, "I thirst," was for their renewal – for reclaiming and restoring the lives of those who ran away. Just as many of us flee from time to time, He thirsts for us to come back, to be reclaimed, and restored. He looked down and saw the women in their love, loyalty, and courage, and He offered them a word of reassurance, for their self-esteem, for their worth, just as we all need, from time to time, the reassurance of God's love for us. Jesus still longs for that love for us. He looked and saw the two people, one on each side of Him, and He thirsted for their rebirth – one accepted, one did not, but the thirst for their souls was equally the same. As Jesus looked at the other people around the cross, His

57

tormentors and persecutors, He also thirsted for their redemption, their reconciliation, and their return to the love of God.

It is important to understand that as Jesus said, "I thirst," He was thirsting for your soul and mine, for the souls and salvation of the whole world. In the Nicene Creed we hear a phrase, "For us and for our salvation. . . ." He did all this: He was born, He suffered, He died, He rose again "For us and for our salvation." In the classic passage in Philippians 2:6-9, Paul writes, "He did not count equality with God a thing to be grasped, but emptied Himself, becoming a servant, being born in human form. And being found in human form, He humbled Himself and became obedient even to the death on the cross. Therefore, God has highly exalted Him." This was a divine thirst as well as a human thirst.

How do we respond and react to all of this? How do we look at this and begin to understand what our response should be to what Jesus says about His thirst for Himself and for us? Karl Barth said at one time, "Every time we hear the last words, 'from the cross,' we need to consider what our words should be back to the cross." I think the first response that day was no accident; it was very instinctive, spontaneous, humane, and compassionate. One of the soldiers took a sponge of that sour wine, which you and I would probably call vinegar, and put it on a long reed called a hyssop, placing it on his lips. Hyssop was thought to have some type of medicinal use. Most soldiers carried with them a little vial of this sour wine, or vinegar, to use in case they were wounded in battle. Consequently, it was very natural for it to be there at the crucifixion site. Nevertheless, it was a humane response, a compassionate response, and an immediate response.

We can still respond today. We can still be just as proactive. We can still be just as instinctive, compassionate, and caring. That love for us, as we respond to Christ, can continue to expand in our lives. Back in 1948, a little solitary nun left what was the security of a school in Calcutta and stepped out into the disease-ridden streets of

58

that city. You know exactly about whom I am speaking; she is known as Mother Teresa. She stepped out and initiated a tremendous ministry, and fifty-three years later, even after her death, the ministry continues to grow. It began with the missionary Sisters of Charity; later, a men's group was started. There are 400 orders in the world today that follow Christ in her name. Over 8,000 lay volunteers and over a million people work in this ministry. What began in a very unpretentious way, with one little nun walking out into those streets, has become a universal movement.

What is the clue we get from that reality? What is the motivation for what they have done? What is the inspiration for what they do? The clue, found on every wall of every chapel of the missionary Sisters of Charity, is this one simple phrase, " I thirst." At the center of their ministry and mission is this deep conviction, this deep desire to respond to the thirst of Christ as you and I also encounter it in the world where we live; the desire to minister physically and spiritually, not only with those who are suffering and hurting, but those who are discouraged, defeated, and depressed. One man said to Mother Teresa, shortly before she died, "I would never touch the lips of a leper, even if you gave me a thousand pounds." Her response was, "Neither would I, but I would willingly do so for the love of God."

We are asked to think about what it means for us to respond. The thirst of Christ for the souls of others around us is our ministry, our mission; it is what this word is saying to us today. That is the challenge and our mandate! Leslie Weatherhead, a great British preacher, once told about a devotional time in his family. After they had studied the crucifixion story together, he asked them, "What person do you see in this story that you envy most?" He said, "Let me begin. I envy the angel who came to Jesus in the Garden of Gethsemane, when He was full of anxiety, anguish, and anticipating the cross." One of his children said, "I would envy the soldier who touched His lips with the wine." We don't need to keep envying that soldier. We can still do what he did because Jesus told us, "Inasmuch as you do it to the least of these, my brothers and sisters, you do it also to me."

Our ministry may not be as dramatic, outgoing, or universal as Mother Teresa's great orders of the Church, but it can be just as effective. When you and I are comforting those who are sick and dying, we are touching the lips of Jesus. When we are consoling those who are bereaved, we are touching the lips of Jesus. When you and I are opposing all the injustices and inequities we find in the world around us, when we are protecting and defending those who are abused in every way, we are touching the lips of Jesus. When we work at whatever level to relieve those who are hungry and homeless in this world – the suffering in Malawi, the suffering in Sudan, the downtrodden on the streets of Pittsburgh, whatever we do in that regard, we are touching the lips of Jesus.

Once again, we have gone through another week of a shooting in a public school, and we hear the theories as to why this is happening. I would suggest to you that when you and I reach out to those who are loners, who are isolated, rejected, picked upon and teased, we are touching the lips of Jesus. When we offer redemption and hope to those who are burdened by guilt and shame for what they have done, when we offer forgiveness to those who are contrite, even those who may have offended us, we are touching the lips of Jesus. When we assist those who have been defeated to start over again, we are touching the lips of Jesus. When we affirm our family, our spouse, our children, our parents, our colleagues, our friends, even those with whom we disagree from time to time, in that very moment, we are literally satisfying Christ's thirst through us, and touching the lips of Jesus.

There is a song that I learned at camp several years ago, which I still love very much. Its chorus asks, "Have you seen Jesus, my Lord? He's here in plain view." One of the verses says, "Have you ever stood in the family with the Lord Christ in your midst, see the face of Christ on another? Then I'd say you've seen Jesus, my Lord. He is here in plain view."

Henri Nouwen, the great Catholic theologian said, "We, as we touch the lips of Jesus in the needs of people around us, offer them something upon which they can take hold."

George Allen, a psychiatrist, worked in Europe after World War II and his job was to work with the orphans who were roaming around, homeless, scrounging and begging for food. He, and those with whom he worked, provided a temporary camp for them, where there was a bed, food, warmth, and care. The thing that bothered the workers most was that it was very difficult for these children to fall asleep. Then one night, by accident, they discovered if they gave the children a piece of bread when they prayed with them at night, and let the children hold the bread in their hands as they were dozing off, they fell asleep immediately. The children felt that they would still have something when they awoke. There would still be something to eat, and someone there to love them. That was true in the camps in Europe. It is also true when you and I offer to the world around us the bread of life in Jesus Christ. If they accept it, they will always have something to hold onto, and a love which holds onto them.

Our reaching out to others can be very costly. There was another nun, Jacquiline D'Becker, who went to India about two years before Mother Teresa. She was delayed in fulfilling her dream to go by the Second World War. She also had been injured in a diving accident and, consequently, her body had limited movement and she experienced a great deal of pain. She was ill; nevertheless, when the opportunity was offered, she went. After a couple of years, she heard of Mother Teresa, and joined her in her ministry. How excited she was about their work. However, the pain and disease made it necessary for her to return home. The doctors refused to allow her to go back to

India. She wrote to Mother Teresa, expressing her devastation and dismay, because the work in India had been her dream. To remain at home was a bitter pill.

In 1952, Mother Teresa wrote her a letter. Let me share a few of the things the letter said: "I know how you have longed all your life and dreamed to be a missionary. I would invite you to bond yourself with us spiritually. As we work with the people in the slums, I invite you to pray for us, and with us, and for these people whom you love deeply." Then Mother Teresa added, "We need souls just like you, for in that prayer you are touching us and the people with whom we work. Whether you are touching us personally, or whether you are touching in prayer, when you have that thirst for souls, whom Christ loves, the thirst grows daily and expands." Think of how our love and our life would expand if, in our work and in our prayers, we would be thirsting for the souls of people who need to hear the good news. The good news for Jacquiline D'Becker was that she did keep praying and her body became strong enough that she began to do a similar ministry at home. Although she walked around with a full body brace, and with disease that was riddling her body, she was able to minister to people who were suffering. She said her life grew, as did her thirst for those in need.

There is a prayer by a Japanese Christian, which I love, because I think it speaks personally to me, and I hope it will to you. Listen to these very meaningful words: *"Lord, when I am hungry, give me someone in need of food. When I am thirsty, send me someone who is in need of a drink. When I am cold, send me someone to warm. When I am grieved, offer me someone to console. When I am found in poverty, lead me to someone who is in deeper need. When I feel as though I have no time, give me someone to whom I can give help even for a little while. When I am humiliated, let me have someone I can praise. When I am disheartened, send me someone to cheer. When I need the understanding of people around me, give me someone who needs my understanding. When I want to be looked after, send me someone to care for. When I think only of myself, draw my thoughts and concerns to another. And when my cross grows heavy, let me share the cross of another."*

The answer to that prayer, in your life and mine, will help us to know how the deep desire of Christ is finally and completely fulfilled, in and through our lives. Amen.

OUR JOURNEY TO JERUSALEM:
IN MAJESTIC SIMPLICITY

Luke 9:51 and 19:28
1 Peter 2:21
Hebrews 12:1, 2

Several years ago, I stood outside the old wall of Jerusalem, on the east side of the city, trying to imagine in my mind's eye that humble procession making its way down the road from Bethany and Bethphage to the base of the Mount of Olives and across the Kidron Valley to the Golden Gate. I thought about how that scene has changed over the centuries. It was hardly like the eye-popping parades that we see now. There were no floats, no marching bands, and no horseback riders or clowns. There was just this humble person on a donkey, surrounded by some children and a few people who were his followers, working their way down through the crowd that had gathered for the Passover Feast, on the way to Jerusalem. It was what we still call *The Triumphal Entry*, in spite of the fact that it was a very small and a very modest procession. St. Augustine said that this was the most majestic procession the world has ever known. Then he added, "It was also the most prosaic, singular, simple, straightforward portrayal of the Gospel that the world has ever seen; the best testimony of the Gospel that the world has ever heard."

Without contradiction, this was a messianic act. Jesus came fully intending to be announced as a king – not the king the people were looking for, albeit a king, nonetheless. It was an invitation to the people then, and to us now, an invitation to see in the living presence, Christ making this brave entry into Jerusalem, the unalloyed, unadulterated, unembellished, simple, straightforward message of God; the Word made Flesh, the Incarnation, majestic, but also straightforward and simple. We would call it an oxymoron, describing two extremes in one phrase, in "*majestic simplicity.*" What a powerful promise. One hymn we often sing on Palm Sunday picks up that thought in the second stanza, "Ride on! Ride on in majesty! In lowly pomp, ride on to die" – in majestic simplicity. And we must not miss that!

The Apostle Paul, in Corinthians, tells the Corinthian people that they will hear other messages, other stories, and other proclamations and philosophies, and then he says, "Do not be led astray from the simplicity of the Gospel in Jesus Christ." (II Corinthians 11:3b) In other words, we should not be led astray from, or miss, the majestic simplicity of the Gospel in Jesus Christ. There are some qualities in that majestic simplicity that I want to discuss with you today.

It was, first of all, an obvious display of the unparalleled courage of Jesus Christ. I love each Palm Sunday when the children march in, waving their palms, and singing the traditional anthems and hymns. But we must not forget that the actual event was a harsh and tragic experience. It was a difficult reality. Sometimes we gloss it over; we mask it with our traditional celebrations. The fact is that this was a glorious act of brave defiance. The people present in Jerusalem for the Passover, the large crowds, were very unfriendly; in fact, they were hostile because there was a price on Jesus' head! We cannot exaggerate the courage of Jesus who came on that day, into that crowd, even while the people were shouting, "Hosanna."

While we view this, we also need to remember that when Jesus entered this city, He was also inviting us, as Peter said, to enter with Him. "For this," Peter said, "you have been called, because Christ also suffered for you, leaving you an example that you should follow in His steps." (I Peter 2:21) He's giving us the courage to go with Him, as well. Jesus coming into Jerusalem does not simply display courage, He also dispersed it; "You shall receive power when the Holy Spirit is come upon you." (Acts 1:8) And Paul said, "I can do all things through Jesus Christ who strengthens me." (Philippians 4:13) There is that seed of courage within us.

The classic trilogy *Lord of the Rings* by J. R. R. Tolkien has been discovered anew by many, thanks to the enormous popularity of the current film. Both the book and film are very powerful, not because they avoid nudity, profane language, or graphic sex, things to which our society has become so accustomed. They are powerful because they embody the profound message of the Christian faith. Early in the classic work, the hobbit Frodo Baggins, accompanied by three friends, reluctantly begins a journey to return a ring of immense significance to the fires of Mount Doom, in order to rid the world of its domination. As they travel, the small company falls under the control of the Barrow-wights, demonic spirits who entrap people to use in sacrifice. Frodo is gripped with fear. Hope seems lost! However, at this moment, he suddenly feels strength within. It is described this way in the book: "There is a seed of courage hidden within each of us, just waiting for the final, desperate danger to make it grow."

There is a seed of courage within Jesus, and He says it can also be within us. Let us be very frank. We are also confronting a difficult world; a very unfriendly world, a hostile world who rejects our standards and values as Christians; a world that tells us that we are irrelevant, immaterial, that we don't really matter – we are just a sideshow in the culture of our day. Again, we must remember that Jesus not only displayed courage, He also dispersed it. We need that courage. Paul wrote to Timothy and said, "For God did not give you

a spirit of timidity but a spirit of courage and love and self-control."
(II Timothy 1:7) An African-American spiritual says, "Precious Lord,
take my hand, lead me on, let me stand" – with Jesus Christ on the
journey to Jerusalem, possessing through Him unparalleled courage.

The Triumphal Entry was also a display of uncompromising
integrity. Integrity means "all in one piece"; every impulse of our
heart, every thought of our mind, every word of our mouth, every
action of our hand is an expression of this wholeness – one being,
like the seamless robe of Jesus. Jesus came in integrity, one
unblemished revelation from God. He was not trying to escape, He
was not excusing Himself, He was not hiding anything; He came just
as He was, with all the honesty, all the truth, all the integrity that He
had to offer. It was prominently displayed for everybody to see!

Jesus does not just display that integrity, He also demands it. He
said, "Blessed are the pure in heart, for they shall see God." The
word for "pure" in Greek has several meanings; it means unmixed,
uncomplicated, unalloyed, uncompromised. In light of this, the
Beatitude could also be said this way: "Blessed are those who are
unmixed or uncompromised in their motives, who are striving to see
God – a clear display of integrity." A great Scottish preacher, George
MacDonald, was asked, "What is the first duty for us as Christians?"
He answered, "It is for us to live with consistency, with the integrity
we have in Jesus Christ, and to appear to the world around us what
we claim we are."

"Blessed are the pure in heart (the ones with unmixed motives
who live with integrity) for they shall see God."

"Precious Lord, take our hands, lead us on, let us stand," with
that righteous, honest, truthful, uncompromising integrity.

At that triumphal entry, there was a display of humility. This is
completely in character for Jesus. He came as a vulnerable servant;
He came laying His life on the line; He was humble before the Lord.
He said, "I did not come to be served, but to serve." He washed the

feet of Peter and the other Disciples – a sign of His service, humility, and vulnerability. The Apostle Paul writes it this way in Philippians, "He did not count equality with God a thing to be exploited. . . ." (Philippians 2:6) In other words, He did not count equality with God the thing to hold onto, but let it go, humbled Himself, emptied Himself, and became obedient, even to death on the cross.

Humility is perhaps one of the most misunderstood words in the New Testament. Humility does not mean to think less of ourselves. Humility enables us to see more of what we are, and what we can be, through our weakness, because we are willing to see less of ourselves. Jesus said, "Blessed are the poor in spirit (the humble), for theirs is the Kingdom of Heaven. Blessed are the meek (the gentle), for they shall inherit the earth." It is important to realize that, to us as God's people, Jesus is displaying this humility in His life and asking us to also walk that same way. Wouldn't it be wonderful if we would let the humility of Christ shine in us? Just a single light! We do not need to think that we need to shine like stars, but we must radiate whatever light of faith we have at our disposal. Remember Jesus' parable about the woman, who had one small candle, looking for her lost coin? The children's song says, "This little light of mine, I'm going to let it shine."

Sometimes it is just one single light that allows us, in our humility, to give worth and dignity to others. Could it be that, if we are willing to be humble people and walk in the way of Christ, we might be able to avoid unhealthy, inordinate competition? I'm not against competition. I think competition in its best sense is very worthwhile and very valuable. But unhealthy competition is not. For instance, wouldn't it be better if all of us would be able to say to someone, "You have done very well. You are a good person," without thinking that we have to make odious comparisons and ask ourselves, "Are they as good as we are," or "Are we as good as they are?" How liberating to say someone is a good person without thinking that it threatens us. Wouldn't it be more edifying and enriching for us to be able to rejoice with someone? Wouldn't it be elevating for us to rejoice with someone and allow them to rejoice with us, doing it all in humility. John Henry Jowett, the Scottish preacher, said, "A Christian is like ripening corn; the riper the corn becomes, the more lowly and bent is its head." Paul says to the Romans, "We who are strong need to be concerned for those who are weak." (Romans 15:1)

"Precious Lord, take our hands, lead us on, let us stand with unashamed, unapologetic humility."

When Jesus came, it was a display of matchless sanctity, sacredness, and spirituality – a spiritual life. A spiritual life is that life which allows us to do what we know God wants us to do. It seems rather simple, and the way to do this is look at the life of Jesus. Jesus set His mind, His face, to go to Jerusalem. He knew what God wanted Him to do. He was obedient. To be in matchless sanctity is to be totally obedient, to do that which God calls us to do. Jesus describes that for us. In Matthew 16, He calls us to be servants, to take up our cross and follow after Him. Paul says it this way, "Do nothing from selfishness or conceit, but in humility count others better than yourselves." (Philippians 2:3) God calls us to sacred spiritual living – to use the basic things that God tells us to use.

Someone once asked Willie Mays how he was so successful in baseball. He said, "It's very simple; what they throw, I hit, what they hit, I catch." That is just basic, fundamental stuff, the primary requisites of one of the most popular games in the world. Coaches in almost every sport say we just need to learn the basics. If we can obediently cling to the basics – which are there before us in the matchless, spiritual, sacred sanctity of life in Christ – if we can do that, perhaps the fundamentals of our faith will be very apparent to us, and the results of our effort would be inexhaustible – like the fundamentals and results of a great athlete.

Malcolm Muggeridge in his book, *Something Beautiful for God,* describes the person who was responsible for his conversion: Mother Teresa. He said this: "Mother Teresa went from task to task with enormous serenity, while the rest of us, with far fewer demands, live in quiet desperation. She did what she did, not because she was clever, but because she was good. She knew what God wanted her to do and, through the love of Jesus Christ, she did it. She knew what she had to do. She did it beautifully and faithfully." And then he quoted from the title of his book, when he said, "She did something beautiful for God."

"Precious Lord take our hands, lead us on, let us stand . . ." in the matchless sanctity, sacred, spirituality of Jesus Christ, which was so evident as he marched into that city in majestic simplicity.

C. S. Lewis has an illuminating book that perhaps most of us have read. The title is intriguing, *Mere Christianity* – simple, plain, straightforward, unadulterated Christianity; not complex, not complicated. In that book, he says this, "God is not asking us through His message of Jesus Christ to improve, to get better. He is asking us to be transformed." If we look at what God has shown us in Jesus Christ, and if we accept this call to courage, to integrity, to humility, and to sacred living, then we will be on the journey to Jerusalem with Jesus, and well beyond, and with Him, we will be going in *majestic simplicity.* Jesus invites us to take His hand, and join with Him in that triumphal march.

"Precious Lord take my hand. . . ."

(At the end of the sermon a soloist sang the African-American spiritual, "Precious Lord, Take My Hand.")

DEAD MAN – LIVING!

Luke 24:13-32
Matthew 28:1-7
Romans 8:5, 9-11

A few nights ago, a television commentator gave a very detailed description of the procedure for Timothy McVeigh's execution. I was instantly reminded of a riveting execution scene from a movie I had seen a few years ago. It was a penetrating story and one of the most compelling scenes I had ever seen in a movie: a convicted murderer led away in chains, surrounded by guards, with a spiritual advisor walking with him – Sister Helen Prejean, a Roman Catholic nun, who was attending him in those last moments.

As I watched the faces of the people in the procession, and also observed those in the glass booth, who were there to witness the execution, I began to conjure up a whole medley of possible emotions. The emotions were all-encompassing – anger, anxiety, disbelief, fear, frustration, panic, exhaustion, revenge – all standing against the shattered background of dreams, which would never make it to life; dreams of love, forgiveness, hope, and potential. As I watched, I began to realize the sharp contrast between the dreams that had been so lofty and the dreams that were now so totally shattered.

Then came that significant moment in the movie when the very short, stocky little man in the front of the procession began to cry out his macabre, chilling announcement, "Dead man walking!" It is often a tradition in prison when someone is going to the execution chamber that someone calls that out, "Dead man walking!" How poignant that was then for me, and still is even today, as I examine deep convictions and feelings found in the friends of Jesus on the first Easter Day.

There is a razor-sharp comparison here. The same medley of emotions and feelings felt in that movie scene, were felt by the two men on the road as they made their way home from Jerusalem to Emmaus, on the evening of the first day of the week. It was a difficult time, because they had just seen an execution. Their friend, their rabbi, their teacher, the one whom they had agreed to follow, whom they thought was the Savior, the Messiah, had died a horrible and humiliating death on a cross. As far as they knew, Jesus was still dead, and as they made their way along on that sad, homeward journey, they were despondent and disconsolate.

However, that is where the comparison between the movie and the story of Emmaus ends. Now it changes completely – there is a definite contrast. On the journey to Emmaus, Jesus appears alongside these two men, walking and talking with them about their doubts and their fears, and what had been prophesied in all of Scripture concerning Himself. Beginning with Abraham, and later Moses, through the poetic books to the prophets, Jesus explains to them all of the pertinent implications of what had just happened, without either man recognizing who He was. When they reached their home, they invited this stranger in to stay the night and to eat a meal with them. Here Luke reports that something very special occurred: "When He was at the table with them, He broke bread, their eyes were opened, and they recognized Him. Then He vanished from their sight. They said, 'Did not our hearts burn within us as He talked to us on the road and opened to us the Scriptures?' " (Luke 24:30-32)

74

Immediately, they returned to Jerusalem to make known the news that they had seen and heard, which had been verified for them by His teaching and His appearance. We can only imagine the change in their step from a shuffling, stumbling gait to a triumphant victorious march of joy and exhilaration. We can also imagine the change in their message: "Jesus Christ is risen, as the women had said! Now we believe it! And now we say to all of you, this man whom we thought was dead is now living!" Jesus Christ was risen, and their entire lives were changed and transformed. Just as you and I can be changed and transformed as we find the Risen Christ in our hearts today, on our road, on our way. Because our shuffling, stumbling feet from Maundy Thursday and Good Friday, our hesitating steps, are changed on this day to the marching steps of triumph and victory and hope and life. So we come today, discovering that the announcement is still new and vital – Jesus Christ is Risen! He is risen indeed!

Paul says to us, "Since Jesus Christ has been raised to new life, we are walking in newness of life." (Romans 6:4) What is it to walk in the newness of life as the Easter people, as God's people of the Resurrection?

First, let me suggest to you that we are walking in the unconditional love of Jesus Christ. If we are walking in the newness of life in Christ, we are walking in His love. While Francis Bernadone, whom we all know as St. Francis of Assisi, was studying the Gospel of John, he came upon this passage, "As a Father has loved me, so have I loved you; continue in my love. If you keep my Commandments, you will abide in my love, just as I have kept my Father's Commandments and abide in His love. Love one another as I have loved you." (John 15:9-10,12) That last phrase captured his attention, and he asked himself, "How has Christ loved us?" From the Scripture, St. Francis remembered that Jesus welcomed the lonely and the outcast. He touched the untouchable. He healed the afflicted.

He fed the hungry. He embraced and affirmed the children – children of all ages. He was sensitive and caring, being fair and equitable to those around Him and showing them respect and dignity. St. Francis remembered this mandate given by Jesus: "As the Father has loved me, so have I loved you." St. Francis also recalled that we are empowered by Jesus Christ to love others in His presence through the Holy Spirit. As Paul said in Romans 8:10, "If Christ dwells in you, though the body is dead because of sin, the Spirit is alive because of righteousness." We are empowered to live by a new righteousness.

Fred Buechner, a contemporary pastor and preacher, has said that when we discover and receive the outlandish, incomparable love of God in the cross and resurrection of Christ, we then discover that ordinary people like you and I are able to do extraordinary, impossible things. The poet Robert Frost wrote, "The Risen Christ, the love of Christ, which is seen in the cross and resurrection, has affected the way I love others; my spouse, my children, my friends, my colleagues, even those with whom I have disagreement." Someone asked him, "How does that affect you? How is that accomplished?" He simply answered, "When the love of Christ holds us, we believe it into fulfillment; we believe it into reality." Then he said, "It's much better to bear a cross, than to bear a grudge."

We walk in a victorious life by the unconditional and unfailing love of Jesus Christ. Secondly, we also walk in the newness of life, which integrates in us an invincible hope and assurance that totally relies on Jesus Christ. That is important for us to remember because not one of us always has an easy time in life; we face difficult times, hard decisions, periods of grief, and disappointment. Back in 1954, Billy Graham went to meet Winston Churchill at 10 Downing Street. The prime minister did not stand when the evangelist arrived. He remained slumped in his chair, hunched over. As Billy Graham came in, Churchill greeted him with this question. "Young man, in this troubled world, is there any hope?" Billy Graham answered, "Yes, there is hope in the Risen Christ." Then this famous evangelist reminded the prime minister that Jesus also said, "In this world, you will have tribulation (trial, suffering), but be of good cheer, I have overcome the world." Hope!

The Risen Christ can overcome our hopelessness, but too often we still seek our own solutions. For instance, we feel hopeless when we begin to lose our youthful image and energy – we don't move as quickly or as easily as we once did, so we desperately attempt to hold on to youth. We use cosmetics, or we buy the latest frames for our bifocals and trifocals, and some of us get false teeth. We have transplants of kidneys, hearts, or livers. Sometimes, we even get hair transplants. We have knees and hips replaced. We take pills of all sizes and shapes, and vitamins with every letter of the alphabet. We use all kinds of notions, lotions, and potions to regain our youthful image and appearance. It often occurs to me that there are many of us walking around with a lot more than we had when we started. Of course, I am being facetious. However, it is true that these examples point out to us that when we give in to the hopelessness in our lives, we usually find that we have been overexposed to the world and underexposed to the Gospel. We keep looking and hoping for the miracle that will change our appearance and capacity. But the hope of Jesus Christ does not depend on our face or our physique, as important as that may seem to be to us in our daily living. The hope of Jesus Christ is found in the heart, in the depth of our soul. Hope grows in the hearts that know the victory of Christ.

Henry Francis Lyte wrote the inspiring hymn, "Abide With Me," while he was lying on his deathbed. He left the poem for his family to read after he died. At the bottom of that poem, there were no words of scripture, but just these textual notations: "I Peter 1:3, II Corinthians 4:16-18, Romans 6:4." His family looked up those verses. In Peter, it says, "Praise be to the God and Father of our Lord, Jesus Christ, who in His mercy has given us living hope by the Resurrection of Jesus

Christ from the dead." In II Corinthians, it says, "So we do not lose heart. Even though our outer nature is wasting away, our inner nature is being renewed every day. For this slight temporary affliction is just preparing us for an eternal weight of glory beyond all comparison; for we look not to the things that are seen but to things that are unseen; for the things that are seen are temporary (transient), but the things that are unseen are eternal." That is hope! Then in Romans, "Just as Jesus Christ was raised to new life for the glory of God, so we also may be given newness of life." All of that refers to the hope which is eternal – the newness of life in Jesus Christ.

Thirdly, there is a newness of life which we find in the great verities of life, in the truth, honesty, and justice of life. Several years ago, when I was working at Lake Chautauqua as the Director of the Department of Religion, I had the unique opportunity to attend a luncheon with Sandra Day O'Connor, her husband, and three other people. We had an enjoyable and stimulating conversation. Near the end of our time together, she began to talk about what it was that had been the foundation for what she practiced as a lawyer, and later as a Justice. She said to me, "I grew up with the Bible – the message of the Bible, the message of the Gospel – its message of righteousness, truth, law, justice, and peace. I discovered it is worth defending and preserving, and I continue to walk in that new way and that new life." What a compelling testimony it is when someone, in this case a Supreme Court Justice, has the opportunity to preserve a newness of life, integrity, justice, righteousness, and truth. Years ago, Phillips Brooks said, "The great Easter truth is not that we live newly after death, but that we live here and now by the power of the Resurrection. It is not just that we live forever, but that we are to live nobly here and now because we live forever."

If that is true, and it is, then you and I can also walk in a newness of life. It is our responsibility to continue to preserve and defend that which is good, true, just, and peaceful; to continue that effort wherever we can; to seek that peace and accomplish it – in the Middle-East, Ireland, Sudan, the streets of New York City, Cincinnati, or Pittsburgh – Amberson Avenue, Westminster Place, or in our own neighborhood. Wherever we are, it is always worth the effort, and it is always worth the walk.

Fourthly, we walk in the newness of eternal life, victorious life, abundant life – we live as conquerors in life. Jesus said, "I have come that you might have life, and have it abundantly." (John 10:10) "Do not be afraid, I am the first, the last, and the living one. I was dead and am alive forevermore." (Revelation 1:17-18) "Because I live, you too shall live." (John 14:19) Paul wrote, "If the one who raised Jesus from the dead dwells in you, then the one who raised Christ from the dead will give life also to our mortal bodies, through the Holy Spirit given to us." (Romans 8:11)

That is a powerful message, but the world looks at it and often remains very pessimistic, skeptical, fatalistic, and unfulfilled. Jean-Paul Sartre, a French existentialist, had a very dismal and foreboding philosophy in which he lamented, "We are born without reason, we are prolonged in weakness, and we die by chance." Notice the contrast between that and "Because I live, you too shall live." "I am the Resurrection, and the life. Those who believe in me, even though they die, yet shall they live." (John 11:25-26)

The Rodgers family in New England had the habit each evening of gathering around the table where they would discuss particular Scripture passages. They would try to put in their own words what each passage meant in regard to their relationship to Jesus Christ. One night, they were talking about a passage from Revelation, the third chapter, which says, "If you conquer, you will be clothed in white robes and I will not blot you out of the Book of Life; and I will confess your name before my Father, in Heaven." Jimmy, who was seven years old, was the first to be asked to react to that passage and to answer this question: "What do you think that means about being in heaven?" Jimmy said, "It appears to me that God is going to have a big angel meeting us when we get there, calling the names of all who have arrived." The family asked, "Really?" Jimmy said, "They're going to say 'Daddy Rodgers,' and you'll say 'here,' and 'Mommy Rodgers,' and you'll say 'here,' and 'Sue' and 'Mavis,' they'll say 'here.' " Then he took a deep breath and said, "When they call my name, I am so little and so small that I don't want them to miss me, and so I'm going to jump up and shout, 'I'm here!' " The family was amused by that, but a few days later there was a tragic accident. Jimmy was hit by a school bus, injured, and left lying unconscious in a hospital bed. After the family kept a vigil for two days, the doctors came and said that they had done all they could, that there was no hope, and it was just a matter of time. However, the family kept their vigil, late into the night. At one in the morning, they began to notice Jimmy's body stirring a little bit, and his lips seemed to move. The family gathered around the bed and leaned down to hear what he might say, to see if he was conscious. Something wonderful, comforting, and victorious happened, because this little boy's voice, loud and clear, simply said, "I'm here!" and he died. That family knew that Jimmy was in another world and the "big angel" had just called his name.

We can have that same kind of hope and comfort.

> *Death comes and says destruction; Christ comes and says salvation;*
>
> *Death comes and says loss; Christ comes and says gain, abundant life here and eternal life beyond;*
>
> *Death comes and says separation; Christ comes and says reunion;*
>
> *Death comes and says you must leave this earth. But above the voice of death comes a much stronger, clearer voice,*
>
> *The voice of Jesus saying to Jimmy, and eventually to you and to me, "You are but coming to me."*

Easter says we walk in a newness of life. Death has been conquered. Paul wrote, "O death, where is your sting? O grave, where is the victory you had hoped to win; but thanks be to God, who gives us the victory through our Lord Jesus Christ."(I Corinthians 15:55,57) Please notice that phrase is in the present tense; who *gives* us the victory. It is not in the past tense; not who *gave* us the victory. Nor is it future tense; who *might give* us the victory. The present tense in Greek suggests an action which is happening now, and then continues to happen over and over and over again. Thanks be to God, who gives, and gives, eternal life, eternal victory, now and forever. Paul puts this in the present tense; God gives victory. Henry van Dyke in his great hymn, "Joyful, Joyful, We Adore Thee," ends with these lines: "Ever singing, march we onward, victors in the midst of strife. Joyful music leads us sunward, in the triumph song of life."

So we are called to walk in newness of life, in love, in hope, in integrity, in truth, and in life itself. But the message of the newness of life should not end at the door of the Sanctuary as you leave today. It is meant to be continued! Longinus, the centurion guard in John Masefield's play about the Crucifixion, when the weekend was over, came to report to Pilot what had happened. He encountered Pilot's wife. She said to him, "Is He there, is He dead?" Longinus said, "No!" She was incredulous, "Well, where is He?" He said, "He is beyond all that Roman soldiers or foe can do to Him, far beyond, where no one can deter His walk or hinder His truth." You see, for us to leave this Sanctuary and think only of the echoes of what has happened here – the music, the words, the time together, the crowds, the aroma of the lilies – if that is all we have as we pass through the front door with only the echoes behind us, then we have lost the significance of this day. If we go only on the road on Friday to Golgotha, the road which takes us to the calamity of Calvary, then all we are able to say is "Dead man walking." However, if once again we go with the women on Easter morning, and with the disciples, rushing back to tell the others, if we go to Emmaus with those two men and return with them to Jerusalem, we will have another announcement to make: "Dead Man Living!" Jesus Christ is risen! He is risen indeed! Hallelujah!

To Be Continued

Romans 8:1-11
Mark 16:1-8

Mark is thought to be the earliest account of the Gospel. When we first read his report about the resurrection, there are no surprises. It seems very similar to the other accounts. But then something occurs that does surprise us. These women had had enough; too much, perhaps. We are told that once they had seen this empty tomb and heard what the angel had to say, they ran away; they were emotionally traumatized, they were shocked, amazed, and completely silent. The New English version says, "They said nothing to anyone." The Greek grammar isn't exactly correct, but sometimes we can break rules of grammar to make an emphasis. The literal translation of the Greek in that passage says, "They said nothing to nobody!" – they were completely silent!

The second century church was not too excited about ending this particular Gospel at the eighth verse of the sixteenth chapter, so they added to it. They thought something had been left out or forgotten. Consequently, if you look at the various translations of this passage in Mark, you will see two endings; one ending with verse eight, and a longer one beginning with verse nine. In the extended ending, the church pieces together nothing that is totally new, nothing deceitful or untrue, but in taking portions from the other three Gospel accounts, they made the message of Jesus more triumphant and the Disciples more believing. In other words, the church added a lot more hallelujahs.

Quite honestly, I am personally comfortable with ending the Gospel according to Mark at the eighth verse, because it portrays a natural reaction. These women needed time to doubt. After all, the men had time to doubt. Matthew had reported, "They worshipped Him, but some doubted." Luke said, "While we were joyful, we were also disbelieving." Do you see the mixture of belief and disbelief with which they were struggling? In the Gospel of John, Peter said, (paraphrased) "I'm just going fishing to forget about this; I just can't handle it anymore." And later, Thomas said, "Unless I can touch the scars in His hands and His feet, and touch His side, I will not believe." They were dealing with their own struggle. They remained silent, because this was something they had to take time to process for themselves. This is also true for us; we get saturated with news – some of it is good and some of it is bad. No matter how good it may be, there are times when we would just like to get away.

I believe that was what happened here. These women needed to get away from some of these emotionally charged circumstances. They had had enough. They couldn't handle any more. After all, Jesus was dead, and He had been buried. They had cleaned out His closet and given away His few possessions. Now they wanted to go back to things as they were, to routine – blessed routine! Sometimes we complain about the fact that things are very boring and that we are living a very routine existence. But isn't it true that sometimes routine provides more comfort and relief than anything else can do? The way these women dealt with their emotional trauma was to return to routine, to return to the common ordinary things, just to be silent.

They also had to deal with their fear. They were silent because they were fearful. What were they afraid of? Of whom were they afraid? They were afraid of the authorities! Those people who had seen Jesus as a rabble-rouser, as one who had stirred up the simple folk, the worthless riffraff, and who had caused great dissension. They thought also that those little small cell groups that Jesus had developed were huddling together, plotting rebellion. The only way the authorities knew to get rid of this problem was to, in the name of law and order, put Jesus, their leader, to death. These women looked at this and said, "If we go out and say He is alive, these authorities will stomp on us like bugs." The odds weren't very good for these three women. If Josephus, the Roman historian, is correct, at the time of Passover there were probably two million people in Jerusalem; three women against two million people are not very good odds. We know what we would probably have done. We would have said nothing!

Let me put it in another perspective. We are told by the historians that in the first century, there were probably seventy million people in the whole empire, and about forty thousand of them were Christians. Figure that out: a city of seven thousand people would have had four Christians. Let's put it in an even closer perspective: if the greater Pittsburgh area has approximately two million people, and if we use the same formula, there would be only two hundred and eighty-six Christians here. We're not used to being in the minority. We're not used to seeing ourselves as a small voice. Under these odds, perhaps our reaction would have been the same as the women. We would have left that tomb saying nothing.

We know what it is like to be fearful. When someone asks us to be in a play or to read or speak, we're afraid of mispronouncing a word, choking up, forgetting our lines, or stumbling up the steps. Because we are concerned, nervous, and apprehensive about those things, we say nothing. Oh, we'll talk to you about sports, politics, and the weather, but if someone mentions something sacred, we just clam up – we don't want to talk about that! And so, very often, we find ourselves looking for an alternative; we want to find something else to do. We will change a light bulb, we'll paint the wall in the restroom, or we'll rake leaves in the fall, but don't ask us to speak about what we believe. That would be asking too much of us; we might embarrass ourselves. How often have you heard it said, "It is not enough just to talk the talk, you need to walk the walk." I understand what that means, but I think for Christians today that phrase is backwards. We need to look at it the other way. It is not enough to walk the walk (to do the action); we need to talk the talk — to tell the story, to give our testimony, to be willing to show what it is that we believe verbally, through our words.

It is true that one of the most demanding and difficult things we can ever do is to make a positive statement about what we believe in Jesus Christ, as our Lord and Savior. We are willing to build, to bake, to sew, and to paint, but not to testify. Now I am not criticizing those things that are done with great love and devotion in many churches, this church included. I believe those jobs need to be done. But the most important thing we do is to witness for Jesus Christ. We need to claim our story and to be able to tell it. I'm not suggesting that all of us need to preach a sermon or teach a class, but all of us need to be ready to speak. Peter said, "Be prepared to give an account to those who ask of the hope that is in you." (I Peter 3:15) We need to be able to give an account of the hope in us to our neighbors, to our families, to our friends, to anyone who is asking searching questions, and, most of all, to our children and grandchildren. We need to be able to tell that story — the story about our relationship to Jesus Christ.

What about the difficulties we encounter in developing our stories? What should we say? What are our credentials? What is our creed? What can we say to anybody who asks? Are we prepared to say, "This is what I believe?" That is often problematic for us. My wife Vail and I had a friend in one of our churches. He was a surgeon, a wonderful man, whose wife was dying of cancer — a very slow and painful process. We said to him, "David, what can we do for you?" He said, "Pray for her." Now that revealed to me one of two things to me. Either he was telling us how sick she really was, or he was revealing to us that he, in his life, had reached some kind of spiritual milestone. For ten years, I had known David, and during that time he could talk about all kinds of things, but seldom did he talk about prayer.

Most of us don't like to talk about those sacred things because we are afraid of the response we might receive. Suppose if we were told as Christians to go out and share our story – give our testimonies to the world; suppose you were asked to go to the beauty shop, WalMart, a restaurant, or the post office and say, "Jesus Christ is risen; Jesus Christ is alive." What kind of a response do you think you would get? We could easily guess what it might be. The women at the empty tomb knew what it would be, too. They knew the kinds of criticisms they would get. Their responses would have been very similar to the ones you and I still hear today. The world would say that these women didn't have enough to do, they needed something to occupy their time. The world might say, "Perhaps you went to the wrong tomb. After all, the burial was so hasty the day before the Sabbath that you may have buried Jesus in a nearby tomb, to wait for a permanent tomb later. Obviously, you went to the wrong tomb!" Or, the world would say, "One of the disciples stole His body and spread the news that He had been raised." That is the oldest trick in the book. Now you see it – now you don't.

Perhaps people said to the women, and would say to us today, that the burial was premature. For most people who died by crucifixion, it took three or four days. Jesus was only on the cross from nine in the morning until three in the afternoon – six hours, half a day, or less. On that news alone, people would then claim, "They buried Him too soon; He wasn't really dead. When He finally woke up, He left." I really dislike hearing those kinds of arguments, that kind of gossip, those kinds of rumors. For me, those are all specious reasons that water down the Good News – the Gospel of Jesus Christ.

I want to say to you, as clearly and as plainly as I can, that I believe that Jesus Christ being raised from the dead is the ultimate, quintessential Christian message that we have to offer to the world at this time. And as the *Christian message*, it is the corporate Church's witness. It is the individual believer's witness. The Gospel accounts don't tell us of any appearance that Jesus made to the general public. We are told that those who saw Him were the ones that had followed Him. Now that isn't the method that I would have used to announce the Resurrection! I would have had Jesus go to Pilot, put out His hands, revealing the marks on His hands and feet, and say, "There, would you like to give it another shot?" I would have had Jesus walk into the crowds in the courtyard, where the Pharisees, scribes, Roman soldiers, and the hostile crowd were milling about, and have Him walk slowly through the group, in order to scare them half to death. That just shows how small and irrational I am, compared to the great, infinitely wise God. It was God's plan that the followers of Jesus, who knew Him intimately, would tell the story.

Consequently, if the world is ever going to hear the message of the Risen Christ, our Savior and Lord, they're going to have to hear it from us. (Paraphrasing Luke 1:1-4) It is as though we hear Luke saying, "If you talk about the life of Christ, it is a matter of historical record. If you talk about the death of Christ, it is a matter of historical record. But, concerning the Resurrection, we are the ones who have seen it, and we are the ones who will tell it." We can't expect society, or the public, or the government to sustain the real meaning of Easter. It is just not going to happen. It is a Christian world view, it is a Christian commitment, it is a Christian belief system, and if we allow ourselves to be seduced by any other kind of institution or culture at large, or any kind of fad or fashion, or any type of shallow, unscholarly theology that reduces the Christian message to nothing more than myths and midrash, then we have lost the meaning of Easter. We have lost the meaning of what it means to be the "Easter People!"

We need to maintain the message of Jesus Christ, risen and victorious. That is the basic message we have to offer to the world. We have other things to offer, but that is the fundamental message. Paul said if we don't have that, we don't have anything. What happens if the Easter message is lost? It dwindles down and peters out to nothing more than colored eggs, chocolate rabbits, strange bonnets, silly bunnies, spring breaks, and family trips. We need to maintain that powerful message of Jesus Christ, risen and victorious. It is our message, and if it is not given, whose fault is it? It is not the schools' fault. It's not government's fault. It's not society's fault. It is the Church's fault! Our fault – those of us whose "light is hidden under a basket!" If we lose the basic core of what we believe about Jesus Christ, our risen victorious Lord, then we have lost our quintessential, ultimate message.

For me, all of this has much deeper implications for today. When 9/11 occurred, it made people in this country begin to rethink and reexamine the way they were living – their worldview – what was it? For the last several generations, the worldview that has been steadily gaining acceptance is post-modernism. It is as though 9/11 has ripped the scales of post-modernism right off our eyes. What is post-modernism? Martin Kaplan, from the Annenberg School of Communications at USC in California, says that post-modernism teaches this: "Everything is relative, and nothing really matters. There is no ultimate truth or reality or goodness or justice. There are no absolutes whatever." What that leaves us with is nothing more than an indifferent, apathetic attitude toward right and wrong. It is only what *we* think that matters. It is what Joseph Fletcher, years ago, called "situational ethics," so we rationalize everything. We react one way here and one way there, in order to maintain a comfort zone, or to remain "politically correct." In that philosophy, the situation dictates the action, not the truth. We don't care anymore about knowledge and wisdom. We are in the information age – not the age of knowledge and wisdom – just information, entertainment, and amusement. You know the root meaning of amusement; it comes from the Latin, "a" which means "nothing," and "muse" means "to think." So "amusement" literally means "not to think." Too many of us are just "amused."

That is our challenge! We are living right now in this postmodern age. Alan Bloom in his book, *The Closing of the American Mind*, said that in the last two or three generations, students have been more and more reluctant to give their opinion about anything. They have seen people make strong stands for what they believed was true and right, only to see them later proven to be wrong or incorrect, which has resulted in negative consequences. The students have therefore decided that the best defense is to have no opinions at all – they have chosen to live in limbo.

When Ayn Rand, the novelist, was speaking at Yale University, the students asked her, "What is wrong with modern society?" She did not hesitate at all to say, "Never before in the world have there been people striving desperately for answers to critical questions. But, also, never before have they been frantically committed to the idea that there are no ultimate answers at all." When those four planes crashed in September, that worldview was no longer satisfactory. We immediately had to reclaim what is really at the core of who we are and what we believe.

There is another very disturbing phenomenon occurring. Chuck Colson says that in the last several months since September, great numbers of young Christian people have been converting to Islam. It is not my place to question their reasons and rationale for taking this step, but I feel I am well within my right to remind them that the history of Islam has not been peace-loving. There are radical Muslims who have brought about great tragedy and suffering. The problem is that this "conversion" has taken place in students not because they understand and know what Islam is, but rather because they don't know what they believe about their faith – about Christianity. They don't know where they stand.

Whatever the reason for this, we as adults, teachers, friends, and parents need to begin to give our witness as clearly as we can for the Risen Christ; the love, grace, and forgiveness in the Cross, and the power of victorious living as God's People – the Easter People – the Resurrection People. The problem is, for many of us, that we have not shared that message. One of the surveys that has really disturbed me asked a number of college students this question, "Have you ever heard your parents give their personal testimony of their faith to you?" Sixty-three percent said, "No." One girl said, "They only assumed that we understood, and they thought we knew. But they never told us!" Paul says in Romans, "How will they call upon one in whom they do not believe? And how will they believe in one of whom they have not heard, and how will they hear unless someone proclaims the message?" (Romans 10:14) That "someone" is you, and that "someone" is I. How will they hear unless someone tells the story? How will they hear, unless someone gives the testimony of what it is we believe about this Easter message, which we celebrate today?

The question is, How many of us have told that story, and to whom? How have we told it? We must understand very clearly that Sunday school class and confirmation class and youth group are not an end in themselves or exercises to be endured, but rather they are specific opportunities that permit us to experience, with our young people, what it means to have a relationship with Jesus Christ. It is imperative for them to discover, through our testimony and encouragement, what their testimony will be. The Church can no longer run from the empty tomb or from the Easter Service, today, or from any other worship service, and remain silent.

What more do we have to share? We proclaim that God brings

life from death, creation from chaos. Out of nothingness, we are told, God created the world. Jesus was dead, but we believe that He is now alive. Can you share how you experience that? He comes to us, who are dead in our sins, and He says to us, "You can have forgiveness. You can be made new. You can be made alive. You can be born again." He calls us to a new life. "If Christ dwells in you," says Paul in our text, "then He who raised Christ from the dead will give life to your mortal bodies also through His Spirit that dwells in you." Paul also says in Romans, "We know that Christ Jesus being raised from the dead will never die again. Death no longer has dominion over Him. The death He died, He died of sin once and for all, but the life He lives, He lives to God. So you must also consider yourselves dead to sin and alive to God in Christ Jesus."

In the last six weeks of Lent, we have been following a theme, *Our Journey to Jerusalem.* We have now completed that six weeks, walking with Luke through this season together. That part of our journey is complete. We have come to Jerusalem and to the Cross, and now to the Resurrection. Now there is another journey that needs to continue. It will only continue if it continues through us. It will continue only in those who know and trust the living Christ, those who have developed their own personal witness, their own personal testimony, their own story, those through whom the message is "to be continued." The message of Easter is one that we must continue to tell, and we can tell it very simply: Christ is Risen! He is Risen indeed! Hallelujah!

A Time to Remember

Psalm 140:1-7, 12, 13
Romans 8:28, 31-39 (J.B. Phillips)

It goes without saying that last Tuesday, September 11, 2001, was a day that none of us will ever forget, a day that we will continue to remember painfully all of our lives. Each one of us remembers exactly the place and time when we heard the messages: when we heard about the first crash, which confused us; and then many of us saw the second one on television; and then the third in Washington; and the fourth in Somerset; and then that unbelievable, unconscionable thing, the Twin Towers in New York City collapsing. It is impossible for me to define or describe for you exactly how I felt, but I suspect it was very much the same as what you felt. For me it was a kind of *déjà vu* – that empty feeling in the pit of my stomach, that shallow hollowness, that numbed and stunned disbelief and silence – the same that I felt after the assassinations of the Kennedys and Martin Luther King, and the wounding of President Reagan, the tragedy at Oklahoma City, and on and on. Such acts penetrate our lives with intense sorrow and grief. Not simply because of the staggering numbers in the loss of life, but also because all of these things, and especially last Tuesday, have penetrated our core beliefs and the American soul. The billowing

93

clouds of dust and ash over New York City, the Pentagon, and Somerset have erased for us forever the naïve fantasy that we are immune, that we are the richest, we are the biggest, *and we are totally secure.* That has been replaced by the agonizing, shocking reality of our vulnerability.

The brave man who called from the airplane, "We are being hijacked," may have been an omen – may have been a sign for all of us; for aren't we also being hijacked? Someone is taking our lives to where terrorism lives, and now we are checking every shadow, suspecting every noise on the plane, every bump in the road. This morning, shortly after five o'clock, as I was getting today's message in mind, a siren blew in our neighborhood, and I had an ominous and foreboding feeling. We have also been hijacked into thinking twice every time we hear a siren, or plane, or explosion. We are apprehensive about traveling anywhere.

You see the ultimate purpose of terrorism is to disrupt our lives, to set us in disarray, and to destabilize us so that we become paranoid and fearful. That is not where you and I and this country want to go. That is not where we should go, that is not where we must go. We must admit that the memory of days past means that we will never be the same. The ninth month, the eleventh day: **9/11!** I don't think I'll ever hear that emergency call number or dial it myself without thinking about that fateful day, remembering that month and day. It is a day and month that you and I can never, and must not, forget.

However, there are things that you and I as God's people also need to remember, and this is the proper time for us to remember them. First of all, it is a time for us when we must remember the thousands of victims; to mourn for those who have died, and to comfort those who have lost loved ones. That is, after all, our calling. Every one of us here has some connection with this tragedy; some of these are very direct. We heard that morning about the devastating loss of a young woman – a granddaughter and niece connected to our church family. Perhaps we all have known a family, directly or indirectly, who has lost a loved one.

But we are all touched simply because we are part of humanity. On "Good Morning America," Charlie Gibson said, "The tragic process of counting bodies will be very devastating, but even more devastating will be to know that we will never be able to count the number of broken hearts," yours and mine, and countless others. As Christians, if we are to mourn for those who have died and comfort those who have lost loved ones, it is important for us to remember that we have been called to this task. "When one suffers," says the Apostle Paul in Corinthians, "all suffer." (I Corinthians 12:26) There are deep and personal feelings of emotion for us here. Paul reminds us, "We are to bear each other's burdens, and thus fulfill the law (and the love) of Christ." (Galatians 6:2) It is important for us today, in mourning those who have been lost and in comforting those who have lost loved ones and friends, to realize that together we are bearing each other's burdens, to fulfill this new dimension of love, which, "in Christ, God has given to us."

I suggest to you one of the ways we do this: we support each other by physical touch. Because of the news about the death of her niece (a flight attendant on the first plane), there were several embraces in the office before Susie Westerberg, our receptionist, left to be with her mother, Jean Schaefer, and the rest of their family. Later, Cal Wilson and I went to be with the family. When Susie's mother came home and we were all there together, we prayed. Before I left, Susie took my hand and said, "I'll never forget what you said to me in the office this morning." I hadn't said a word! I had just embraced her. Not knowing what to say, I just held her; but it had spoken volumes that I could not possibly have measured! Your embraces, your touch, holding a hand, putting an arm around a shoulder can be so important and far-reaching in sharing our love and concern, and there will be many opportunities to do just that.

That physical touch can be extended even further. We have seen it with a countless number of volunteers, donations of blood, giving of food, and the providing of shelter. On the way home from a service in Michigan yesterday afternoon, we followed a pickup truck. The back of the truck was filled with wheelbarrows and shovels, and there was also a trailer and a small high lift. Attached to the back of the trailer was a sign, "Destination NYC/WTC" (The World Trade Center). It struck me that the license plate was from Montana: a volunteer, willingly, sacrificially reaching out, over long miles to touch others. That physical touch is so important for us. Other people, from as far away as Texas, have been offering skin grafts – an extremely personal touch! There is the wonderful story about the office workers in New York who carried those heavy, five-gallon containers of water from nearby office water coolers to give a much-needed drink to the people in the street who had survived, and also to the rescuers – a cup of cold water. When that kind of touch occurs, we sense a community spirit that, unfortunately, we cannot get any other way. We also have seen flags waving everywhere as a symbol of the patriotic "touch" of our nation.

It is important for us not only to touch physically, but even more importantly, to touch spiritually, through our prayers. How important it is for us to pray, as we have seen happening all around the world – in Westminster Abbey, Notre Dame in Paris, in a synagogue in Berlin, in a mosque in Turkey – people all around the world, praying. This morning, our organist, John Walker, received a message from one of his friends in England, who said their church had celebrated a memorial service for us today in their morning worship. He told John, "All of the churches in England are filled and praying for you." Another message came to John today from someone in France, who said that a politician had announced, "Today we are all Americans. It is important to pray." All around this city for the last several days, there have been prayer services, one here on Wednesday night and another on Friday afternoon. It is important for us to gather to pray for each other, but we must not neglect to pray personally. I was very moved by the story of the woman who is bedfast, a shut-in. For the last several days, every time the name of a victim who has died comes on the screen, she writes it down on her regular prayer list – a pilot, a member of the crew, a passenger, a person from the offices, or someone from the Pentagon. She also records the names of rescuers who are looking for loved ones. She writes them down and then, confined there to her bed, she prays over and over again for all of these persons, *by name*. Her example reminded me of the woman from Oklahoma City who, after that terrible tragedy, said, "I was so comforted every day, realizing that there were countless numbers of people praying who didn't know me and I didn't know them, but their prayers brought me a strength I could get no other way" – the compassion and companionship of Christ. And so, we continue to pray not only personally, but in worship together, in groups, and in our own prayer closet with our families.

Shortly after I came to this church, I mentioned to you in a sermon how important it is as parents and grandparents to pray "with" our children. So often we say, "Let's go upstairs and we will hear your prayers." Let us remember that it is God who hears our prayers. One of the things we can do now to help our children in their questions, as they struggle with their problems, is to pray "with" them, no matter how old they are – not just little ones, but teenagers and college students as well – to pray "with" each other. In that time of prayer, we can begin to understand how we are connected to Jesus and to each other, and in that practice of family prayer, we find hope. Paul says in Romans 8:31, "In the face of all this, what is there left to say? If God is for us, who can be against us?" In the last paragraph of that chapter he says, "I am absolutely convinced that neither life, nor death, nor messenger of heaven, nor monarch of earth, neither what happens today, nor what may happen tomorrow, neither a power from on high, nor a power from below, nor anything else in God's whole world has any power to separate us from His love made known to us in Jesus Christ."

When we touch people physically and with our prayers spiritually, we can instill in them and in ourselves the hope that is ours, which sees a future hope through our tears. Paul wrote a great line in Thessalonians: "We want you to be certain, friends, about those who have died, that you do not grieve about them as others who have no hope. We have our hope. Jesus Christ died and rose again, and this will be the same for those who have died in His name. God will bring them to victory together with Him." (I Thessalonians 4:13-14) Paul says again, in I Corinthians 15:57, "Thanks be to God, who gives us the victory (the hope) through our Lord Jesus Christ!" William Penn said, "Those who love beyond this world are never separated; death cannot kill what never dies." Paul tells us in Romans 5 that through our struggles and suffering, we learn endurance, patience, hope, and "that hope will not disappoint us, because God's Spirit has been poured into our lives."

Our primary role is to remember to mourn those who have been lost and to comfort those who have lost loved ones. Secondly, I think it is vitally important for us today to remember those who are working in search of those who might have survived, or are searching for bodies. There are brave emergency personnel who are totally exhausted: steel workers, fire fighters, police officers, construction workers, volunteers from all over the country, who are literally digging through the rubble with their hands and fingers, ignoring injuries to themselves. Many have developed severe respiratory problems from dust, asbestos, and toxic fumes. We need to pray for them. Ronald Esposito, a police officer, was in a hospital for his injuries. When he was about to leave, he was asked, "Won't it be good to go home now?" He replied immediately, "No, I'm going back to help. I must go back!" There was a fire fighter, with tears in his eyes, who told about his exhilaration when he reached into an open space and took hold of a hand that was not cold – it was warm! Someone was alive! He said he felt a rush, not just of adrenaline, but also of love and of courage down in the depths of his heart, overcoming his exhaustion. We need to pray for the rescuers.

We also need to pray for our President, Vice President, members of Congress, the Cabinet, particularly Colin Powell and Donald Rumsfeld, and other leaders throughout the world. They all need the gifts of wisdom, discernment, and intelligence to take prudent and powerful positive action. Commentator Tim Russert said on television the other day, "It's important for action to be taken, but if it is too weak, terrorism will flower again. If it is too strong, it will anger our allies and, more forebodingly, the radicals in the opposition nations, who will begin to revert to aiding and exploiting terrorism once again." Then Russert said, "There is a need for enormous wisdom; in fact, the wisdom of Almighty God is required."

It is not easy, never easy, but we also must pray for those who harbor in their hearts violence, jealousy, anger, and death – to pray that they might be healed from that hatred. At the same time, in this country, we need to be concerned for those neighbors around us who are Muslims, or who are Arab Americans. We must not profile all of them. Our instinct for self-preservation makes us look at people who are dressed differently, who speak differently, who have different physical features and begin to see them as an immediate threat to us. It is important for all of us to remember that the vast number of Arab Americans in this country are Christians. The majority of these Arab Americans, Muslim and Christian, are peace-loving, law-abiding people. We need to remember the workers, the leaders, and our neighbors.

Finally, this is a time for us to remember our heritage; to resolve that we will engage ourselves in preserving our freedom and our liberty. President Bush said on Tuesday, right after the disaster, "We have been attacked this morning by faceless cowards." Then he said, "This is an act of war." Several members of Congress and several commentators compared the attack on Tuesday to the attack on Pearl Harbor. There are, of course, many similarities, but there are also many differences. The attack on Pearl Harbor was done by a nation against a military target, and the planes were marked clearly with the sign of the nation of Japan. People wore their nationality on their sleeves. They had a face, they had a flag, they had a target. Even though they killed many innocent people, their primary target was military. This group, last Tuesday, had no face, no flag, and their target was *only* innocent people. These terrorists are people who are so cruel, so wicked, so diabolical, and so evil that they pay no attention to any resolutions from any parliament, or any government around the world, or to the United Nations. They are not concerned about trials in the world court, because death is their only language. They have been told that murder through their suicide is a "holy act," and simply a way to guarantee for themselves eternal life and paradise.

It is important for us to find out what went wrong, what happened, but not to point the finger of blame. The worst thing we could do now is to strike out in blind rage just for the sake of doing something – quickly, with revenge. The tool of terrorism is death; the tool of terrorism is fear. But a rational anger – a determined, controlled, intelligent, and measured response – is the ally of the strong. We pray for that. This terrorism, we are told, is the first act of war in the new century. As we agree with that, we understand that these people have been engaged in trying to disrupt us and destroy us in ways that would deny our freedom. Our free society is being challenged. They will win, they will succeed, if we as a free people cower in fear and restrict the freedoms we already have.

We cannot succumb to the tyranny of terrorism. It is important for us to continue to be committed to the rule of law and order, to the justice that we cherish, and to the responsibilities of freedom that are so precious to us. It is important to note that the Bible tells us, very clearly, that governments were established for two reasons: to punish the evil and to reward the good. If sinful humanity goes unchecked, then inevitably the strong will always control the weak; the powerful will always impose their will on the feeble and the frail. Sixteen hundred years ago, St. Augustine, one of our early church fathers said, "In loving God and loving our neighbor, there may be times when we are required to face aggression with force." Over a thousand years later, John Calvin said, "There are times when we need to react against evil with force – but never for revenge, always to achieve redemption, restoration, reconciliation, forgiveness, grace, and life." Jesus says we should not react with "an eye for an eye." I don't know if you noticed it, but a day or so after the trial of Richard Baumhammers, the serial killer of five people in Pittsburgh last April, one of the members of a family who had lost a loved one made this comment on television: "We cannot continue to go on with an eye-for-an-eye mentality, because, if we do, ultimately the whole world will be blind."

The last word for us is not revenge. The last word is Jesus Christ! At our Presbytery meeting last Thursday, our Presbytery Pastor Jim Mead said, "Jesus Christ is the last word." I agree with that. Sin is not the last word. The Cross of Jesus Christ is the last word, the Cross that conquered sin. Revenge is not the last word; redemption in Christ is the last word. Hate is not the last word; love in Christ is the last word. Oppression is not the last word; truth is the last word. Terror is not the last word; freedom is the last word. Death is not the last word; Christ is the last word. Life is the last word; victory in Christ is the last word. Paul asks it this way, "Who can separate us from the love of Christ? Can trouble or pain or persecution, lack of food or clothing, danger to life or limb, the threat of force of arms? No, in all these things we are *more than conquerors* through Him who has proven His love for us." (Romans 8:35, 37) More than conquerors! Some of you have heard me say what that means to me. "More than conquerors" is a strange phrase. Isn't it enough just to win? What does it mean to be more than a conqueror? It simply means that because Jesus Christ is the last word against oppression, sin, revenge, violence, terror, and death, because of *what Christ has done*, we are more than conquerors. Therefore, in the death and resurrection of Jesus Christ, we cannot lose! The old Gospel tune says, "For though the wrong seem all so strong, God is the ruler yet!" – the last word!

In a few moments, our choir will sing a marvelous anthem by James Russell Lowell, written in 1845. In his poetry, there is a struggle of the battle between truth and falsehood. It seems so often that falsehood is "on the throne" and truth is just standing on the side, "on the scaffold." Please listen in particular to the last phrase when it is sung. Watch all the words, but particularly these: "Yet the scaffold (truth) sways the future, and behind the dim unknown, standeth God within the shadows, keeping watch above His own."

"Although the wrong seem oft so strong, God is the ruler yet!"

One hundred thirty-eight years ago, in 1863, Abraham Lincoln gave a speech, perhaps his most famous speech, in a time of tragedy, terror, sorrow, and loss of life in the Civil War: the Gettysburg Address. Please allow me, if you will, in my last remarks to paraphrase that address and bring it up to date for our contemporary time of tragedy!

"Eleven score and five years ago, our forebears brought forth on this continent a new nation, conceived in liberty and dedicated to the proposition that all people have been created free and are of significant worth and value.

"Today, we are engaged in a totally new and different war – a new battlefield – testing whether this nation, or any nation, so conceived and so dedicated, can withstand the assault of hate or survive the threat of terror.

"We come today to dedicate and consecrate ourselves to the goal of peace and freedom. But in a larger sense, we cannot dedicate, we cannot consecrate, we cannot hallow this effort, this time; the countless, guiltless, unsuspecting men and women, who have been martyred in New York City, the Pentagon, and Somerset, have consecrated it far above our poor power to add or detract.

"It is for us, the living, rather to be dedicated to the unfinished work of preserving our freedom and peace. It is for us, who remain, to be dedicated to the great tasks remaining for us, that from these thousands of innocent, martyred loved ones, neighbors, and friends, we will take increased devotion, to highly resolve that these dead shall not have died in vain, and that this nation under God, the Grace of the Lord, and the fellowship and the power of the Holy Spirit, shall have a new birth of freedom, and that this nation, a government of the people, by the people, and for the people, shall not perish from the face of the earth."

All of this – the compassion and the comfort of God, the courage of standing for the right, the commitment to preserve our freedom – is worth remembering. It is a *time to remember*! And dear friends, on this day and forever, *please, never forget*! Amen.

THE TROUBLE WITH HORSES

II Kings 18:13-25
Matthew 6:19-21, 31-34
*"Some trust in chariots, some in horses,
but we will trust in the Name of the Lord."*
(Psalm 20:7)

It was a grim day in Jerusalem. Hezekiah, the king, had already taken all of the money from the treasury and all the gold and silver from the temple to pay to Sennacherib as a ransom. Hezekiah was afraid that his army was too weak, that the Assyrian army standing outside the wall was too strong, and the ransom he had paid was not enough. These Nazis of the Middle East wanted more; not just the wealth, they also wanted the people, the city, the palace, and the power. Hezekiah had two major problems. First of all, he had given away all the wealth, in fact, the entire treasury, and, consequently, he had nothing left to pay for the ransom to buy off this enemy. And, secondly, because his army was so weak, he was depending on support from the army from Egypt – their chariots and their horsemen – to save his kingdom.

Well, this did not impress or intimidate the Assyrian army. Their commander, standing there, began to taunt Hezekiah and his officials. He said to the two officials in the tower and the sentries beside them, "Go and tell your king that he is a fool. You will find him now on the highest window of the palace, looking out across Moab and Edom, looking for the dust of the armies of Egypt he thinks will come and save him. But that will not happen. Egypt is like a bruised reed that pierces any man that leans upon it. The Pharaoh will betray you." And then he called Hezekiah's bluff directly. He said, "I'll make a wager with you. I will give you 2,000 horses if you can put riders on their backs." That was a severe challenge for Hezekiah. The challenge was not so much to acquire the weapons and the money; the challenge was to have soldiers who would involve themselves personally in saving the people of his kingdom.

Perhaps you already see the connection with this obscure story and its relevance with where we are today. For the last twelve days, we have been looking for the need to strengthen our military might, and also to strengthen our economy. Because of that, we have been looking for answers for our "kingdom" – for our situation here in the United States. However, there is a problem, because we are looking not just for quantity of soldiers and money, but also for quality in our national resolve. We want and need people who are committed, who are dedicated, who understand the need to walk in God's way and to be God's faithful servants. The problem is not so much monetary and military as it is spiritual. Who are we? How are we defined by what we say and do? What should we be doing and how should we be doing it? The challenge is obviously there before us.

Twelve days ago, the two symbols of our nation were attacked – the symbols of national defense (the Pentagon) and our strong economy (the World Trade Center). The people who piloted those planes had decided that they were attacking, what Nancy Gibbs in her article in the special edition of *Time* magazine calls, "America's Cathedrals." They assumed that our cathedrals were lodged in those things we could buy and build. But historically, that has not been the true faith of America, or the true soul of America, or the true God for America.

We are dealing now with a spiritual problem that simply goes beyond the weapons, the monetary things, the "horses," if you will,

106

that we now want to ride. God is calling upon all of us to fulfill our responsibility; to ride those "horses," use the weapons that we have, the military might, the economy, all the things that we already have at our disposal. That is true for us all; for individuals, for churches, and for the nation. If it is really true that this is a spiritual problem, and we need "riders for our horses," where do we get those riders? How do we get effective, efficient, competent, capable riders to ride those horses?

I think the spiritual answer is very clear. First of all, we get effective riders because we come willing to repent. The commander of Assyria, standing on the outside by the upper pool, called Hezekiah's bluff. It was a very distinct and clear challenge; he hit him at his point of vulnerability. He asked, "Why are you waiting for Egyptian horses? You say you rely upon God, but have you not taken all the treasury and all the trappings from the temple and given it all away in ransom? And you still have the temerity to say that you rely upon God." Up to now, Hezekiah had been a man who was known for being faithful, at least most of the time. He was a man who had restored the temple, but in this instance, his faith had eroded. His faith had detonated. His trust, his confidence in God had faded away, and he had fallen back upon his own resources – his own answers. That is the point at which you and I need to ask some important questions, to make some very serious personal observations and evaluations.

I have abhorred, as you have, and been offended by the comments of two clergy on television this past week. Pat Robertson and Jerry Falwell claim that all that has happened is a retribution from God because of our sins. The God I know in Scripture is not revealed that way. But I do agree with Billy Graham, who said at the national prayer service on September 14, "You and I need to be more committed, to discover the level of our commitment, the dedication of our faith, how far we would go to make sure that we are not putting

God on the back burner, that we are not being apathetic, that our belief and our trust is consistent and constant everyday, that we have not taken God for granted."

Like many of you, perhaps most of you, our flag is flying in front of our house, along with the flags of our neighbors. It is flying all over the city, and all over the country. I have enjoyed, as you have, either hearing or singing, as I did last night, "God Bless America." Last week, for the closing hymn of our service, we sang together, "America, America, God shed his grace on thee." I love that; I sing that, but I have a concern with that, as well. Think about those phrases, "God bless America" or "America, America, God shed his grace on thee." Those phrases should never be considered as a mandate, a demand for blessing from God. They are really a request that the blessing of God comes not because we demand it of God, but because we have a relationship with God; we are repentant, willing to ask God for His forgiveness, His grace, and His cleansing. The blessing we seek is the result of our relationship. God, through Jesus Christ, will bless America because we have come in humility seeking God's forgiveness. At the same prayer service on September 14 in the National Cathedral, Billy Graham urged us to do this. He quoted from Chronicles, "If my people who are called by my name will humble themselves, pray, and seek my face, and turn from their wicked ways, their apathetic ways, then I will hear from heaven and will forgive their sin and heal their land." (II Chronicles 7:14) I wonder what Hezekiah would have been able to accomplish if he had been able to repent this way, when his moment demanded it. You and I can do it. We can repent of having distanced ourselves from God, of treating God with apathy and indifference, and of not being regular in our faith commitment. And I firmly believe that contrite, humble, repentant people make excellent riders!

Also, if we are to solve our spiritual problem, and go forward from here, we need to keep our prayer life alive. We need to be praying everyday: praying for God's blessing and direction in our lives. That is a given. I don't know about you, but people saying, "Let's have a minute or two of silence," troubles me. I'm not interested in silence alone. Silence, indeed, can be a respectful and, at times, a refreshing thing – to stand in silent respect or reverence for someone or something. But I am not interested in one or two minutes of silence; I'm interested in two minutes of prayer, and more. I'm interested in silence that makes room for prayer in our otherwise chaotic lives. While we may not always be speaking aloud, prayer should be part of our everyday lives, so that we are forming phrases in our minds and in our hearts, meditating, praying for God's direction. We need *at least* two minutes of prayer on a regular basis. We should not avoid what we are called to do; we are called to strengthen our spiritual lives by prayer. September 11 should not be only remembered as a day of national destruction, it should also be remembered as a day when individuals, churches, and nations turned to God, turned their lives over to God again, committing themselves to God in that beautiful, edifying relationship that can be ours through prayer.

Prayer is a unique source of strength for all of us. It is a strength for us now as a church, as individuals, as a nation. Never forget, prayer can always be a source of strength. Elie Wiesel, the great Jewish intellectual, who himself was a prisoner in a concentration camp, spoke about what it was like to be there among the other prisoners. He said, "Most of the time, we all looked the same; we were losing weight, we were starving, we were emaciated, we were gaunt, we all looked alike, except for one clear difference – it was in the eyes. For many of the people who were with us, their eyes were very hollow, aimless, and hopeless; they were very distant and dark. But there were many among us whose eyes remained bold, determined, and focused." Listen to what he also said, "I have become aware that most of the time, if not all of the time, the people whose eyes were bold and strong and focused were the people who had not forgotten how to pray." We need to remain bold in what we do and say; we need to remain bold and strong in what we believe and what we hope for; and we must never forget to pray.

That is what God's people should be doing, that is what we are called to do: to strengthen ourselves spiritually in that very personal, conversational relationship with God, through prayer. Abraham Lincoln once said, "I often fall to my knees in prayer, because it is the only place I have to go." Perhaps we should join in that faithful practice. There is a great old Gospel tune, "It's me, it's me, O Lord, standing in the need of prayer." Faithful people who are regular in prayer, who pray without ceasing – prayerful people make excellent riders on whatever horses we are given.

In addition, we need to be strengthened spiritually by God's strength living in us. God does not do magical, mysterious things in a vacuum, but He will give us the strength to do them. There is a wistful story about a little girl who was asked by her mother to go into the pantry and find a can of soup. The little girl refused because the pantry was very large and dark, and she said that she was afraid to go. The mother said, "Go ahead, because God is everywhere and He will help you." The little girl opened the door, put her head inside, and called out, "God, please pass me a can of chicken soup." Now that is amusing, but it illustrates that we are not called upon to ask God to do those things for us that God has already empowered us to do. In one of His last conversations with His disciples, Jesus said, "You shall receive power when the Holy Spirit has come upon you; and you shall be my witnesses in Jerusalem, and in Judea and Samaria, and to the ends of the earth." (Acts 1:8) In another setting, Jesus also said, "All this I have spoken to you while I am still with you. But the Comforter, the Holy Spirit, whom the Father will send in my name, will teach you all things, and call to mind all that I have told you." And then, immediately, Jesus promised, "Peace is my parting gift to you – my own peace, which the world cannot give. . . . Set your troubled hearts at rest, and banish all your fears." (John 14:25-27) Jesus Christ promises us the Spirit that will strengthen us spiritually; empower, enrich, enliven, and expand us to be able to be the people, and the riders, we are called upon to be!

We need to pray for God's extended blessing in the Spirit, and we need to look at what Paul said in Galatians, about what can happen when the Spirit blesses us. He said, "The fruits of the Spirit are love, joy, peace, patience, kindness, goodness, faithfulness, humility, and self control." (Galatians 5:22,23a) If we pray in the Spirit, if we pray for the wonderful blessing of God's rich power dwelling in us, we will have the spiritual strength to ride all the horses God gives us to ride, whatever they be.

Historically, God has given horses to many people, and he has looked for riders in every age. We have seen this many times at several places. God said, "I gave horses to Babylon. What a power was Babylon! But the hot winds of the desert blew across the shifting sand, which has covered the walls and the turrets, and the archaeologists ask, 'Where is Babylon? Where are the riders?'

"I gave horses to Carthage; what a power! You would thrill at the power of Carthage. But the jungles have reclaimed that city, and the jackals now laugh where men once schemed for dominion and power, and the Arab, who tells you he can find Hannibal's palace, lies.

"I gave power to Rome; I gave horses to Rome; what a matchless power was Rome! But the Coliseum is now a great skeleton – a tombstone for an empire that died for lack of riders."

Then God says, "I have given horses now to you! Perhaps never in as large a number – military, monetary, intellectual, scientific, philosophical, spiritual – perhaps this is the last gift. Do you have riders to ride those horses? The trouble with horses is that you need riders."

We are the ones who need to be the riders. Will we provide the riders? The world will not hear that question until you and I hear it.

The world will not hear any kind of an answer until you and I hear it and give our response, quit playing with religion, repent, pray, seek God's Spirit, and trust in the God who sent the horses, who sent His Son to teach us how to ride, who sent His Spirit to empower us to ride. This is not for just a few people out there who are the leaders of our nation; or a couple of people here or there; it is for *all* of us! The concern is about whether we are willing to ride. The three critical questions for us today are these: If not here, where? If not now, when? If not you, who?

Let us pray.

Lead us, O God, to walk in Your way, to accept Your forgiveness, and Your relationship with us, and Your Spirit and Power, and allow us, thereby, to be Your riders, today, and all the days ahead. We pray in the name of Jesus, Amen.

OUT OF THE SHADOW!

Psalm 23
John 1:1-5
1 John 5:11, 12

A few years ago, Diane Sawyer was interviewing the actress, Candice Bergen. In the interview, she was discussing with Candice her best possible photographic angle – that angle that overcomes flaws and accentuates beauty. Diane Sawyer then asked this question, "What do you fear most about aging?" With no hesitation, the actress responded, "Dying. Often I am haunted by the shadow of death for myself and for others whom I know and love." In trying to emerge from the shadow of death, secular society goes to great length to disguise the reality of death. Why else would we pay so liberally for the cosmetic skills of embalmers, or work so hard to soften our language when we talk about the terminally ill? Why else would we have memorial services instead of funerals; or use those gentle euphemisms ("we pass on, we pass over, we pass away") instead of just saying, "we die?" Our attempts to come out of death's shadow are what Gore Vidal once called, "The heavy burden . . . the foggy shadow of the unintelligible factor of death in our lives."

Even for people of faith facing death, life is greatly influenced by the haunting shadow of death, because, for many of us, it is the last enemy: the enemy of love, reason, and achievement. So, in our attempt to break out of the shadow, if we are willing to talk about it at all, we tend to adopt one of three attitudes that we think will take us out of that shadow and move us beyond the darkness.

The first attitude we attempt to use is escapism. We prefer not to *think* or talk about death. In fact, most of the time we simply *refuse* to think or talk about it at all. One of our ways to escape is to become so immersed in the duties, demands, and pleasures of our present moment that we think we can crowd out of our minds this unmentionable topic that we call death. We try to escape by holding on to the illusion that we are here to stay. Every failing organ can be transplanted; every deteriorating joint can be replaced. Besides, all this talk about death is much too heavy and morbid. Now I agree that to be preoccupied with death is, in fact, morbid. Morbidity by its very definition is a disturbed, unhealthy, obsessive state of mind that is preoccupied solely with death and disaster, and we have seen examples of that. King Philip of Macedon had a slave, who, every morning, when the king came to his throne, would announce, "Oh, King, thou must die someday." Now, that is morbid! Or the poet, John Donne, who in the last months of his life, slept every night in his open casket anticipating his coming death. Now that is morbid! But surely, it is not morbid for us to reflect from time to time on the reality of death and to realize that we cannot avoid it. We cannot ignore it, because at anytime, through an accident, illness, aging, or natural disaster, each one of us must face that reality. We can't avoid it; we can't ignore it. Any attempt to escape it is futile, and so it remains for us, as Emile Brunner once called death, "The inexorable, irreversible, long shadow that keeps moving from the not yet, to the now, to the no longer." Escapism will not work!

Another way we try to avoid the shadow of death is by assuming an attitude of indifference. We move from the shadow of death by saying to ourselves, "I could not care less." John Bailey, in his book,

In the Life Everlasting, says that those who have a disinterest in immortality puzzle him. He suggests that we pretend we could not care less. But surely, we cannot be disinterested or indifferent about the eternal destiny of loved ones in our family, and in our friendships. We cannot be indifferent to that which we experience in the lives of those around us, who are so precious to us. Perhaps for ourselves, we might say we could not care less, but when we think of others, to care less would be a rejection of them; a repudiation; a renunciation. We have no right not to care about those whom we love – whom God has given to us to love. For me, it is a personal testimony to the reality of death when I remember the death of my loved ones and the impact of that reality on my life. When I remember the several hundred funerals I have done for families and friends, I'm reminded that, for me, the not-caring-less attitude is incomprehensible and unforgivable. It doesn't work. From the perspective of my family, it is not an option for me.

Thirdly, we often try to remove or replace the shadow of death by assuming an attitude of agnosticism. We say we don't know what resurrection hope is. We don't understand how it works and so, we are sure it can't be proven. Let us remember that knowledge is not always the last word. We know that Shakespeare wrote much better poetry than our old Uncle Henry. We know that, but we can't prove it. We know that we love our parents, our spouse, our children, and our friends deeply. We know that, but we can't prove it. We know that love is better than hate and that unselfishness is better then greed – we know that, but we cannot prove it. Just how then, can we know something and believe something even if we can't prove it? We know it intuitively; we know it instinctively; what some people would call, "extra sensory perception." Blaise Pascal said, "The heart has reasons the mind knows not of." It is deep within us. Kahlil Gibran, the contemporary poet, says, "Like seeds dreaming beneath the snow, our heart dreams of spring. Trust those dreams," he said, "for in those dreams lies the gate to eternity."

So, agnosticism won't work either. It is at that very point that we are able to move out of the shadow of death, by the light of truth and hope that we find in the Word of God. We find that death is not a goal, but rather a gateway; that death is not a punishment, but rather a passage. A moment ago, we heard the words read from the Twenty-third Psalm. Perhaps the verse that we remember most often is the one in the middle of the Psalm, the verse which says, "Yea, though I walk through the valley of the shadow of death, I will fear no evil: for thou art with me. . . ." The key word in that verse is not "*death*," but "*through*." Death is a passageway – a gateway – to everlasting life. Everlasting life is not something that we have conjured up in our own minds, something that we have created to assuage our fears. It is a gift of God. It is something that is the revelation of God. Immortality, eternal life, is a gift that originates solely in the love of God. In our text today from I John, it says in verse 10, "It is not that we love God, but that He loved us." He also says in verse 19, "We love because He first loved us." And then in I John, chapter 5, verses 11 and 12, we read, "And this is the testimony, that God gave us eternal life, and that is why this life is in His Son. He that hath the Son, hath life." The gift of everlasting life is a gift of God, given to us – revealed to us.

We must remember that eternal life does not begin when we die. It begins when we believe. Every moment, here and now, is nothing more than a transparent example, a foretaste, a first installment of what is yet to come. The word for eternal in Greek is *aiônios*. This word not only refers to length, but also to fulfillment, quality, completeness, enrichment, wholeness, the potential of something more than has already been experienced. If there is no worth or quality in this life, then the promise of "everlasting life" becomes intolerable and unwelcome. But in Christ, God has given us a life of quality, worth, and value. We are not talking about some impersonal endowment of nature here; we are talking about the very personal gift of grace in the Living Christ through His death and resurrection. We have a uniquely personal claim. Many of us can make that familiar lament, "In the midst of life, we are in death," and then turn it around as Martin Luther did, who said, "In the midst of death, we are in life." That, you see, gives us a totally new perspective as to who we are, why we are, and what our purpose is – a new perspective that can give us a worthwhile and hopeful dimension to living.

Dwight L. Moody once wrote to his friends and said, "Some morning, you are going to read that Dwight L. Moody has died. Don't you believe a word of it; for in that moment, I will be more alive than I have ever been anytime." And then he added this, "In 1837, I was born of the flesh. In 1856, I was born of the Spirit. The flesh may die, but the Spirit will live forever. 'That which is born of the flesh is flesh. That which is born of the Spirit is Spirit.' " (John 3:6) When Jesus says, "I am the resurrection and the life. Those who believe in me, even though they die, yet shall they live. . . ." (John 11:25), it is a corollary to the quality of life eternal, the quantity of life eternal, and the confidence of life eternal.

We have a new confidence, a new certainty and assurance. In Romans, the eighth chapter, the Apostle Paul talks about that confidence which is ours. He says, "Nothing can separate us from God's love." There is no circumstance, no failure, no persecution; nothing can take God's love from us. Then he shares this profound thought, "In Christ, we are more than conquerors, through Him who has proven His love for us." I don't know about you, but when I was growing up, the phrase "more than conquerors" used to puzzle me. Being involved in athletics as a participant and later as a coach, I used to wonder what the phrase "more than conquerors" really meant. Isn't it enough just to win? How can one be more than a conqueror? Later in life, I discovered through my faith when loved ones and friends had died, what the phrase actually means, even what it means for my own death. The answer comes to us through the death and resurrection of Christ. That is why Paul uses that phrase. When Paul says that we are "more than conquerors" through Jesus Christ, who has proven His love for us, he simply means that by the death and resurrection of Jesus Christ, *we cannot lose!*

"Thanks be to God who gives us the victory." You notice that phrase is in the present tense. It is not, thanks be to God who *gave* us the victory or who *may give* us the victory; it is thanks be to God who *gives* us the victory. Using the present tense conveys continual, perpetual action. Therefore, He gives it, and He gives it, and He gives it, and He gives it eternally; endlessly, never stopping.

Well, all of this brings us to another question that is clamoring for an answer. What is the nature of this eternal life to which we are called? Jesus, I think, anticipates our curiosity, because in the fourteenth chapter of the Gospel according to John, He said, "Set your troubled hearts at rest, trust in God always, trust also in Me. In My Father's house, there are many mansions, many dwelling places." That simply says to me that this heaven we talk about is not some ethereal place out there; it is a home with rooms so spacious and so vast that it would boggle your imagination and mine. It speaks so invitingly, so graciously, that we anticipate being welcomed into the company of loved ones who have gone before, and even more, we will experience the presence and the nearness of God, the Father, Son, and Holy Spirit. John Gladstone, an outstanding Baptist pastor friend from Toronto says, "Take the best you have ever known in your home, the best you have ever experienced in your home, and the best you have ever dreamed about in your home, and add infinity to it, and you'll have some idea of what Jesus is talking about here."

Jesus also says that the overwhelming nature of this eternal life will be a dazzling, inextinguishable light. John says, "In Him was life, and the life was the light of all humanity. That light shines in darkness, and the darkness shall never overcome it." (John 1:4,5) When we die, it is not as though we have permanently extinguished a lamp; it is simply that if this lamp we have been using is extinguished, it is because a new dawn has come. We will be seeing a new morning, a new dawning that is relentless, imperishable, and will never fade. I've been to the floor of the Dead Sea several times. On one occasion, we arrived before the sun rose. Everything was very dark. However, just a few moments later, the sun rose above the mountains to the east. Awed by this abrupt change, a member of the group exclaimed, "You cannot hold back the dawn!" The darkness on our way there that morning had made us apprehensive – the trip was known to be a dangerous one. But in that moment, as the sun rose, the dawn cleared away any fears or anxieties which the darkness had created. It was true for me physically, and it is still true for me spiritually. In the darkest, most fearful valley of my life, I hear Jesus saying, "You cannot hold back the dawn!" The darkness will never overcome that light. To be in Christ, who is alive forever, is to have stared into the unknown and discovered that it is full of light; full of eternal, unfailing light!

On this day, when we observe All Hallow's Day we name our loved ones who have died in the past year. By recalling all of those who have been precious to us, who are now separated from us in death, we claim victory, the victory that is ours in the Risen Christ. We claim for them, and for us, the promise that He will lead us *through* the valley of the shadow of death. We claim that out of death's valley, Christ will take us by the hand and lead us to the other side, to the warm, welcoming home prepared just for us, to a life of quality – fulfilled, complete, and everlasting. We claim that in His presence there will be a light so bright, so powerful, so imperishable that the darkness will *never* overcome it. That is why we can say for all of our loved ones, and for ourselves, today and for any day, "Thanks be to God who gives us the victory through our Lord, Jesus Christ!" (I Corinthians 15:57) Amen.

EVEN NOW!

When love is young and warm and new,
When there's no thought of end or death,
Then faith and love come easily;
As normal as each pulsing breath.

But when death comes and robs our dream,
And love seems gone – faith hard to find,
Then bitterness invades our souls;
Despair and doubt can cloud our minds.

Yet memories of love are strong,
As we recall what was before,
Amid our loss and tragedy
We find we love not less, but more.

Love thus returned, we claim a hope
At first our hearts could not allow:
A greater love and trust in God,
We claim it now! Yes, even now!

*(Written by William N. Jackson in 1968, the evening before
the funeral of a young man who had been killed in Vietnam.)*

121

Have You Thanked God for Everything?

Job 1:13-22
Romans 5:1-5

Thanksgiving is a very special family time of traditions and stories. One of the favorite stories in our family recalls a time when my daughter was very young. She and I were praying together at night (a good practice, by the way). I began our prayers with some words from Psalm 103, "Bless the Lord, O my soul, and all that is within me, bless His holy name. Bless the Lord, O my soul, and forget not all His benefits." She took that last line to heart, and literally thanked God for everything and everybody; *"forget not all His benefits."*

Accordingly, she thanked God for parents and grandparents, for uncles and aunts and cousins, for pets and toys, for neighbors and strangers; her prayer just went on and on. She even thanked God for her little brother. (I have always been suspicious when our children prayed for each other; were they trying to impress God or me?) But after her long litany of thanksgiving, she ended with this phrase, "And thank you most of all for Jesus, because He lets us know who You are!"

Praise the Lord! My daughter somehow, somewhere, had learned something special about the incarnation; God in Christ, the Word made flesh, God in human form. In her youthful enthusiasm, she had expressed this great truth in an innocent yet profound way. It is some of that childlike faith and trust that I sense in the Apostle Paul as he begins this passage from Romans, the fifth chapter. For here, he is speaking about his faith in an ebullient and exuberant manner: "Therefore, since we are justified by faith, we have peace with God through our Lord Jesus Christ. Through him, we have obtained access into the grace in which we stand, and we rejoice in our hope of sharing the glory of God." For Paul, this was a thrilling revelation and a fundamental promise, that God was not some abstract theory or some distant, remote mystery. Somewhere, somehow, for Paul, God was a living, vital, personal presence. In a personal and penetrating way, God was in Christ, showing those who believed the way of forgiveness, the way of mercy and salvation.

We hope that all of our children, and likewise all of us as God's adult children, would have as strong an awareness and clear revelation of who God is in Jesus Christ, a recognition of His abiding presence. I love the story of the Sunday school teacher who was talking about God in nature. She held up a picture and asked the class, "What is this?" They were reluctant to answer at first, until, finally, one little boy put up his hand. Realizing that he was in Sunday school and that it was important to give the right answer, he said, "Well, it looks like a squirrel, but it must be Jesus." I hope that there is no ambiguity or uncertainty when we see Jesus Christ. I hope when we see the picture of Jesus Christ in the Scriptures revealed by the Holy Spirit, we will see Him for exactly who He is and what He does for us as our Savior. And, therefore, I also hope that our reaction would be much akin to that of Thomas Aquinas, who said, "When I began to comprehend the full measure of who Jesus Christ is – the one whom God has given to us; the one who is not only approachable but accessible; the one who is the source of our love that will not let us go, of our forgiveness, our mercy, our redemption – then I could not contain myself in expressing my joy and gratitude for what God has done for us in Jesus Christ." It is when you and I make that same discovery of Jesus Christ as Savior and Lord that nothing should contain our joy or restrain or restrict our witness.

But look at this text for a moment. Beyond those opening verses, there is something further, something beyond the jubilant doxology that Paul gives about rejoicing in the glory of God. Following that word of gratitude for God's grace, Paul makes a very startling and astonishing statement; astonishing, because it is contrary to the way most of us usually think, speak, or act. Listen to the third verse: "More than that, we rejoice *in our suffering*, because suffering produces endurance, endurance produces character, and character produces hope, and hope will not disappoint us, because God's love has been poured into our hearts through the Holy Spirit that has been given to us." Did you hear what Paul said? Wait a minute! Did he really believe what he said? "More than that, we rejoice in our suffering. . . ." That is just amazing to us, if we really examine it. So often we read right past that line, and we don't realize what Paul has said. But, as a matter of fact, that is exactly the point he wants to make.

Let me clarify, first of all, that Paul is not asking us to go out and look for trouble or to search for crises. He is, however, asking us to face life head on – life in all its reality and in the natural order of things. There is, in the human experience, the relentless revelation of who we are and what life is all about for us. It is obvious that there is much joy and pleasure in life. But it is equally obvious that there will also be inevitable physical pain, emotional pressure, or spiritual stress, no matter who we are. To one degree or another, just because we are human, no one of us is immune!

Consequently, this specific verse, this particular text, is powerful for us today; it is transparently accurate, insightful, and profound, and the key to this is in the preposition. It is there that the impact of Paul's statement can be found. Look at exactly what he says. He doesn't say that we rejoice *for* our suffering, he says, "we rejoice *in* our suffering." In the midst of our trials, in the midst of our struggles, in the midst of the difficulties of life, right at the core of our human predicament, we are able to see God's presence – and His availability – that gives us a whole new context of living and a new perspective.

Let us look at Paul's perspective of thanksgiving. He gives thanks, not merely for pleasures, or the acquisition of material things, comfort, power, prestige, or position. He is also thankful for God's spiritual presence, a spiritual reality that is beyond the ordinary. That is a lesson for all of us, as well. In the midst of our human struggles, confusion, and crises, we can look beyond the moment, beyond the temporary and the transient, to that which is everlasting, eternal and timeless – to a blessing of ultimate significance and lasting value, and to a hope that will not disappoint us, because, as Paul says, "God's love has been poured into our hearts through the Holy Spirit that God has given to us." (Romans 5:5)

If you look at this passage from Romans 5, it is completely consistent; it is completely in character with what Paul says all the way through his writings. Three chapters later, he says, "We know that, in everything, God works together for good for those who love God and are called according to God's purpose." (Romans 8:28) The key thought in that verse is *in everything*. In the very same chapter, he asks, "Who can separate us from God's love; can trouble, pain, or persecution, lack of food or clothing? (verse 35) No, in all these things we are more than conquerors. (verse 37) Nothing can separate us from God's love, made known in Jesus Christ." (verse 39) Then in II Corinthians 4:16, he says, "So we do not lose heart, though the outer nature is wasting away, the inner nature is being renewed everyday. We know this momentary affliction is preparing us for an eternal weight of glory beyond all comparison, for we look not to things that are seen but to the things that are unseen; not the things that are transient, but the things that are eternal." In Philippians 4:11-12, he says, "I have learned in all situations to be content. I know what it means to be abased and what it means to abound. In any or all circumstances I know what it means to have plenty and hunger, abundance and want." Then there is this wonderful phrase in the very next verse (13), "I can do all things though Christ who strengthens me." With Paul, the whole message is consistent: God's presence is with us in good times and bad, in joy and sadness, in success and struggle.

What Paul has clarified here is that there is no difficulty in life, no pessimistic prospect, no devastating defeat, and no stringent demand that can take God's presence away from us. We rejoice *in* our sufferings. That is the key! We have the possibility with Paul to move to an entirely new dimension of thanksgiving, beyond the ordinary, beyond the norm. The first question we usually ask: Have we thanked God *for* everything? For things that are pleasant, or for people who have blessed us? That is relatively easy. The second question is the tough question: Have you thanked God *in* everything? When you and I ask that second question it is the point at which we learn some very valuable and edifying lessons in our life.

This lesson was "brought home to me" in a very powerful way as I began my second year as a student at Pittsburgh Seminary. My best friend from the first year died of leukemia during the first week of that year. This was absolutely unbelievable to me. It was a time in my life when I was becoming more aware of my mortality; but also I was still feeling, as young people often do, invincible, invulnerable, and indestructible. That made my friend's terminal illness even more incredible. This wonderful young man had been full of energy, vitality, potential, promise, and spiritual enthusiasm. How could he be dying? Not only I, but the whole seminary community, went through all the initial stages of grief – disbelief, denial, defeat, helplessness, anger. We struggled through this together.

The thought of Warren dying was incredulous; it was a shock to me. He and I had gone off to work at separate camps that summer. In

August, I got a postcard from him, and all it said was, "Having a good summer, except I saw the doctor and he said I have leukemia, and I have a year to live. I'll see you in the fall." See me in the fall! – only a year to live! My thoughts wandered back to that old television program, *Run for Your Life*, in which a man had one year to live. He raced all over the world experiencing as much as he possibly could, trying to crowd as much as was humanly possible into his last twelve months.

But Warren was planning to come back to seminary! I just couldn't believe that! Why? When he came back and we had an opportunity to talk, I discovered something of the answers to my questions. He said, "My first year in seminary was the happiest year of my life." This wasn't a man who had lived an uneventful, unexciting, cloistered, shallow life. He had already experienced much suffering and sadness on his own. In a hunting accident as a youth, he had lost the four fingers of his right hand. When we discovered that he had learned to write and play ball with his left hand, both of which he had accomplished extremely well, it only increased our respect and admiration for him. He had gone to Sterling College in Kansas, where he had been a successful student and athlete. He had been a missionary in West Pakistan for three years as a volunteer in mission. He had traveled extensively, was a hunter and a sportsman. He had done all these exciting things, and more. Yet, here he was saying to me, "This was the *happiest* year in my life, and I came back here for my last year."

Something of an explanation to all my confusion and questions came in a letter that I was privileged to read, a letter that he had written to the youth group with whom he had worked in Crafton, Pennsylvania. The letter read something like this, "I don't understand what has happened here, I don't know why this is happening, but what I do believe is that *God is working His purpose out*. I am eternally thankful for what God is doing in my life, and that the God I trust will never forsake you and me. He will never forsake me in my dying, or you in your living." Then he paraphrased today's text, and he said, "We rejoice in all of this, because God is giving us patience, character, strength, and a hope that will never die." The effect of this became contagious, not only in that youth group (for I understand from what people have told me, a number of those people grew up into positions where they were in leadership in the church and in youth work), but to me personally, as well as to the entire seminary community. Warren's strong faith had affected the whole student body and the entire faculty as well. His tremendous testimony of faith had a strong effect, almost immediately.

After Warren's death, I had the opportunity to talk to three people from the hospital where he died. One was a doctor who said, "I was overwhelmed by the fact that he prayed for me. It will continue to have a deep effect on my profession, all the rest of my life." A young nurse said, "I never knew anyone who was dying who was so alive in his faith." A second nurse said, "He will never know the impact he had on my life, and I will never forget him." A few months ago, I met a classmate of mine from my seminary days. In the course of our conversation he said, "Do you remember the influence that Warren and his life and death had on all of us?" I said, "Yes, I certainly do." His influence has been felt all the way throughout our lives: not only in that moment at the time of his death during the first week of our second year, but for all of us, all the years since. For forty years, I have continued to claim the great gift of faith that I learned through his life, his faith, his confidence, his strength, which he exhibited even in the deepest of dark valleys, the valley of the shadow of death. I said to my friend, "No, I have never forgotten his influence, and I hope that I never will. I can still rejoice that through his suffering he had taught all of us how to work and play; to win and lose; to laugh and cry; how to live and, finally, how to die." Because of that, every year at Thanksgiving time, the relationship I had with Warren reminds me to be sure to ask those questions. Have you thanked God *for* everything? Have you thanked God *in* everything?

Frances Hunter has a helpful book entitled, *Praise the Lord Anyway.* It is a very short paperback book in which she talks about praising God for the gifts, for the goodness that we have received at His hand. She also speaks about the difficult times, the defeats, disappointments, and the decisions that go bad. Then, she announces in the book her main theme, "Praise the Lord *anyway.*" This is not fatalism, or blind resignation, any more than it was when Job lost all of his possessions, his family, and his servants. Listen to Job's faith: "The Lord gives and the Lord takes away; blessed be the Name of the Lord." Job didn't give up! This was not fatalism, or indifferent resignation – this was recognition of the unfailing strength that God gives, in good times and bad. "Praise the Lord!" Likewise for us, God has permitted many things to be taken away; there have been defeats and disappointments, but because of God's faithfulness in any and all times, we can always say, "Praise the Lord anyway!"

Most of the problem for us is that we don't ask the right question. There is a wonderful prayer by a Confederate soldier; we don't know his name; we only know that the prayer was found in his pocket after he died. I want to recite that prayer for you. Listen carefully to the questions and to the striking answers in this prayer:

> *I asked God for strength, that I might achieve,*
> > *I was made weak, that I might learn humbly to obey.*
> *I asked for health, that I might do greater things,*
> > *I was given infirmity, that I might do better things.*
> *I asked for riches, that I might be happy,*
> > *I was given poverty, that I might be wise.*
> *I asked for power, that I might have the praise of men,*
> > *I was given weakness, that I might feel the need of God.*
> *I asked for all things, that I might enjoy life,*
> > *I was given life, that I might enjoy all things.*

*I got nothing that I asked for – but everything I had hoped for.
Almost, despite myself, my unspoken prayers were answered.
I am, among all men, most richly blessed.*

You and I need to ask the right question. The greatest blessing is not experienced by just looking to see that God has given us what we *wanted*. The greatest blessing is when we discover, when we realize that God provides what we *need*. When we fully understand this fact, we will be able to discern God's strength in the good times, and the bad. In the close of our service today, we will sing that wonderful Thanksgiving hymn, "Now Thank We All Our God," written by Martin Rinkart in 1636, during the Thirty Years War. This hymn was not written in the times of prosperity, pleasure, or peace. This was written in time of plague, death, famine, and destruction, when he was burying as many as thirty to forty people a month, many from his own family. Nonetheless, listen to the faith expressed in these words: "*Now thank we all our God, with heart and hands and voices, who wondrous things hath done, in whom this world rejoices; who, from our mothers' arms, hath blessed us on our way, with countless gifts of love, and still is ours today. O may this bounteous God, through all our life be near us, with ever joyful hearts, and blessed peace to cheer us; and keep us in God's grace, and guide us when perplexed, and free us from all ills, in this world and the next.*"

I hope that anytime we sing this hymn, we will look at the context in which it was written, and the spiritual strength which it communicates. Don't just sing the words casually or by rote; sing those words with trust and confidence. Sing them with conviction. For if we sing with assurance and certainty, perhaps we will discover a whole new dimension of Thanksgiving observance.

I hope, sometime during this season of Thanksgiving, that either individually, as a family, or with friends, we will review all the things for which we are thankful, all those blessings that God has given to us. If you are like I am, that list never seems to end. But, also, before this day is over, I hope that we will be able to ask ourselves both of these questions: "Have I thanked God *for* everything?" But also, "Have I thanked God *in* everything?" Because, when we have asked and answered both questions, then, and only then, can we begin to approach what it means to be totally and unreservedly thankful. Amen.

Jesus Loves Me, This I Show

I Chronicles 29:1-3, 5b, 7, 14-17
II Corinthians 8:1-9
Revelation 3:8a

One Sunday morning in my second church, as the children were leaving the sanctuary after the children's message, and we were singing together, "Jesus Loves Me This I Know," a young woman in the second row burst into tears. The person sitting beside her touched her hand and asked, "Are you OK?" Wiping the tears flowing from her eyes, she said, "I'm alright; but I have not been in church for years, and when they sang that song I felt closer to God than I had ever felt before." There are many of us who can identify with her. For most of us, this childlike hymn – written by sisters Susan and Anna Warner, and William Bradbury – was probably the first one we ever learned. For many of us, each time we hear it, we are reminded of how close we also feel to God.

Historian Kenneth Ashbaugh believes this simple hymn has had the greatest impact of any on the faith of children. For countless numbers of people it has been the foundation for our understanding and recognition of God's love made known in Jesus Christ. Sometimes, even though it is a simple song, there are scholars who feel that it conveys an adequate, comprehensive expression of their faith. In fact, theologian Karl Barth, when he was asked to summarize what he believed said straightforwardly, "Jesus loves me, this I know, for the Bible tells me so."

The hymn has had a broad, far-reaching effect on spreading the Gospel of God's love to the world. It is, in fact, sung in almost every language in the world. Many missionaries use it as a tool for introducing people to Jesus and His love. For instance, during the Cold War, the Christians on the west coast of Alaska would broadcast their worship services and their music to the people across the narrow Bering Strait into Siberia. After the Cold War was over, some of the missionaries went to visit the people in Siberia and discovered them singing very enthusiastically in almost perfect English, "Jesus Loves Me This I Know." After singing, they turned to the missionaries from Alaska and said, "Tell us more about this Jesus who knows us and loves us."

Today we ask about the impact of God's love on us. What should be our reaction and response to God's love? How does the knowledge of God's love affect our stewardship? Quite candidly, if God loves us how shall we then live?

Paul gives some very clear answers to all of these questions in his letter to the Corinthians. In today's text, he is discussing what their reasonable response should be to God's love. He makes his point by dealing with a very delicate and touchy topic: money! Namely, the promise they had made to support the Christians in Jerusalem, a promise they had failed to keep. Right off the bat, he touches a very sensitive nerve by reminding them that all the poor churches in Macedonia had given to the cause which they had neglected, forgotten, or just ignored.

I think that if we had a close friend who had done this, we might go and ask if there was a problem, and then how we might help to solve it. Paul, on the other hand, is much more subtle, indirect, clever – and perhaps a bit sneaky. He appealed to their highest instincts, their sense of honesty, decency, and fairness, and how their failure to keep their promise was offensive to those high standards. This, of course, created a very painful guilt trip for them.

Paul is also very direct. He tells them that they excel in everything – faith, speech, knowledge, eagerness and love, and then says he also wants them to excel in generosity. Then he tells them he is testing how genuine their love is against a background of the faithfulness of others. Then comes the *coups de gras*. He reminds them of how Jesus gave his all, became poor, so that they might be rich, not materially, but spiritually.

This text has immediate implications on our stewardship, on how and what we give. If we know God's love, we should also share it. Jesus loves me *this I know*, and also Jesus loves me *this I show!* There are some very strong lessons about our giving which we can learn from the faithful stewardship of the churches in Macedonia.

First of all, it is apparent that they gave *sacrificially*. To give sacrificially does not mean that we give what is left over, extra. These people were willing to pay whatever it cost to express their gratitude for the love they had known and experienced in Jesus Christ. Sacrifice costs us something. In II Samuel 24, David is offered a gift of wood, an animal, and an altar so that he may make his sacrifice. His classic answer was, "I will not offer to God that which has cost me nothing." That is a good rule.

I am sure that the rich, metropolitan people of Corinth were incredulous when Paul spoke of giving from a combination of abundant joy and extreme poverty. I am sure it just didn't make good business sense to them. Sacrificial giving is a hard lesson to learn.

We have examples of this. Dr. Roy Lauren, a missionary in Korea, tells about a time when several Christians came to visit. As they rode along through the countryside, a Christian businessman in the group noticed just off to the side of the road, a young man pulling a plow while his father held the handles of the plow. The businessman asked

135

why there was no ox pulling the plow. The missionary answered, "They are Christian people, and their congregation was building a new church, so they sold their valuable ox in order to be able to give money for the new church." The Christian businessman, after taking a picture of this unusual sight said, "That must have been a great sacrifice for them." The missionary replied, "No, for them it was a joy and a privilege: they felt blessed that they had an ox valuable enough to sell."

It is obvious that what those farmers did was not good business sense, but the bottom line is that, for them, it made good spiritual sense. For them, there was an even greater purpose. When we think about it, we may discover that sometimes good spiritual sense leads us to a place where it eventually becomes good business sense.

Over the years, I have been richly blessed by visiting Christian brothers and sisters in several villages and towns in Africa and the Middle East. In the majority of these visits I could see that they were very poor economically, especially by our standards, but at the same time they were vibrant and alive spiritually. Most were struggling to make ends meet, to provide essential daily needs for their families, while at the same time exhibiting an unmistakable joy and a contagious hope. Because of rapid growth, several were building new sanctuaries with whatever resources they could acquire and whatever time was available to do the work on their own. Each time I came away with great respect and a renewed understanding of how people can be blessed even while they are making extensive sacrifices. For me, they became living witnesses of what the Apostle Paul describes this way, "Their abundant joy and extreme poverty has overflowed in a wealth of generosity on their part." Their sacrifices cost them something materially, yet at the same time it enriched them spiritually. What an excellent witness! What an inspiring example! What a lasting lesson!

The second observation is this: those in the Macedonian churches who had blended their joy and their poverty together also gave spontaneously. I suggest to you that we often use the word "spontaneous" incorrectly. We think of it as being something accidental, impulsive, or done on the spur of the moment. However, to be spontaneous literally means that something is so much a part of our feelings and our nature, our emotions, our passions, that we cannot help but speak or act. It is spontaneous because it comes from deep within our soul, naturally – it is part of our nature. That is the underlying emphasis in this Corinthian text. Paul did not nag the Macedonian churches. He had said, "They gave without my nagging them." He was not begging from them. They were not cajoled or browbeaten. They gave what they gave cheerfully and voluntarily, *because they wanted to!* Spontaneous giving is giving that comes from deep within us; it is part of our nature. If it is our nature, then it should be and can be given joyfully, generously, and willingly. Something happens when God's love touches our soul.

In Benjamin Franklin's autobiography, he talks about hearing George Whitfield speak on the streets of Philadelphia. It is a wonderful story. About that episode he recorded this: "As Whitfield began to preach, I perceived that very soon he would be asking for a collection. I had several copper coins, four silver dollars, and five gold coins in my pocket. However, I had determined that I, Benjamin Franklin, would give nothing. But as he spoke, my heart softened and I said, 'Well, at least I could give the copper coins.' In a stroke of outstanding oratory, he made me feel ashamed that I was giving so little, so I decided I would also give the four silver dollars." As Whitfield finished, his message had been so inspiring and convincing that Franklin said, "I decided to empty my pockets, gold coins and all. The preacher had touched my soul and it became only natural to respond."

Consequently, over the years I have looked for and studied many of Whitfield's sermons. I've been trying to find the one that Benjamin Franklin heard in Philadelphia so that I could preach it on a stewardship Sunday. While I haven't found that specific sermon in my research and study, I have discovered Whitfield's basic message: *Jesus Loves You*. And he frequently suggested that if we understand that love, we would *want* to respond with our gifts – large or small – with amounts appropriate to our ability to give. The natural result of this would be to show an overflowing expression of our love. It would be our desire to *show* the love we know about in Christ Jesus.

They also gave personally. Paul says that these churches in Macedonia gave voluntarily according to and beyond their means – and then, "not merely as we expected, they gave themselves, first to the Lord, and then by the will of God, to us."

Part of our problem is that we are concerned only about the amount of money and not about our personal involvement. Too often, we make excuses. That was true for Calvin, an old New England farmer. He had gone before the divorce court judge and began to explain his situation. He said to the judge, "Ever since we have been married," he whined, "my wife has hounded me for money – money, money, money, breakfast, lunch, and dinner, and in between." The judge, wanting to be impartial, but also sympathetic, said, "What does your wife do with all the money you have given her?" Calvin said, "I don't know. I ain't given any to her yet."

I think that illustration probably speaks for itself. The easiest thing in the world to do is to make excuses. If we make them often enough, eventually we may convince ourselves the excuses are valid and thereby feel we are released from responsibility. It is then that our stewardship becomes fruitless and lifeless. Let me say this as clearly as I can: The giving church creates a living church, and the reverse is true, as well. When we cease being personally involved, our stewardship is in danger of disappearing altogether. James said in his letter, "Faith without works is dead." (James 2:17) Or saying it another way, "Faith without valid, observable, personal service is useless."

Our witness and our service should be visible personally, a living verification of our faith. Even more strongly, I believe that because of our personal relationship to Christ, we are to be living witnesses of what we say we believe, reflecting Christ in our personality, our relationships, our style of living, and our role as His servants.

Each one of us is called upon to give personal service. I was watching a tennis match not long ago on television. I don't play tennis. Therefore, I pay attention to the commentators on television in order to understand what is happening. While watching, I heard this profound statement: "If your service is broken, you stand a good chance of losing." That is usually true in tennis, but it is totally true in the Christian life. The Bible says, "Those who sow sparingly will reap sparingly; those who sow abundantly will reap abundantly." Those abundant harvests do not come from people from whom we have begged, or from people who have been browbeaten, cajoled, or nagged. It comes from people who have a relationship with Jesus Christ and who know that their hearts – their very lives – belong to God. And it must have been verified with tangible evidence of love and service.

The late Don McClure, a legendary United Presbyterian Missionary, used to tell an inspirational story that occurred while he was serving in the Sudan. A woman had come from the bush country to a service of worship. There, she heard the message from the Gospel about how in Jesus Christ God loves us in a very special and personal way. The person preaching said, "Now God wants you to give something in response to the love of Jesus." They passed a huge metal plate for the offering. But this woman had nothing but what she was wearing on her back. Each person was giving something, putting mostly coins in the plate. When the large plate came to her, however, she put it on the floor and stood in it. When we talk about stewardship, we're not just talking about dollars and cents; we're talking about dedicating ourselves to God and Jesus Christ. As King David said, "God, you are not concerned with the surface, (the gold and silver and wood to build the temple) but of the gifts given from the heart, happily, honestly, and *personally*."

Finally, the Macedonian churches gave promptly. They were aware of the need and the sense of urgency. In *The Music Man*, Harold Hill comes to town to start his band and he meets Marian Paroo, an attractive young librarian and piano teacher. He asks her if she will go to the old stone bridge for a picnic with him. But Miss Marian the Librarian replied, "Not today, but maybe tomorrow." His answer is a classic for those of us who procrastinate. He says this, "We need to be careful, because if we don't act today, we may pile up so many tomorrows we will have nothing left but empty yesterdays." We need to live our life in such a way that it reflects our hope in Christ. There is a proverb from the old Sanskrit writings that says, "Yesterday was a dream, tomorrow is a vision; but if today is lived well, every yesterday is a dream of happiness, every tomorrow is a vision of hope." It is always a good practice to give promptly.

We must never begin taking credit for our giving; our stewardship. We must remember that we are enabled and empowered to do what we do by the Holy Spirit at work in us. In the Netherlands, the Benedictine Order challenges anyone who would join, saying, "If you would enter this Order, you must seek God with all your life; if you would be part of us, you must love God with your whole heart. But you would be wrong if you thought you could gain this on your own, because your arms are too short, and your vision in your eyes is too dim, and your heart and your understanding are too shallow." Our generous giving is, first and foremost, inspired by God. As James wrote in his letter, "Every generous act of giving is from above." (James 1:17) To seek God, you must allow yourself to be found by God, who created us, and be embraced by Jesus Christ who loves us.

"Jesus loves me, this I know, for the Bible tells me so." Surely if we know deep within us what that love of Jesus truly is, we will want to respond intentionally, unreservedly, and cheerfully, to *show* our love to God and to others generously, sacrificially, spontaneously, personally. *Jesus loves me, this I know, and therefore, Jesus loves me, this I show.*

Once we are empowered by God to be good stewards, we must realize that we then have no alternative. Jesus said this in the Sermon on the Mount: "and when you pray, when you give alms, when you fast. . . ." Notice that Jesus does not give us an option here. He does not say, *if* you pray and *if* you fast and *if* you give alms, but "when." Jesus simply assumes that if we are following Him, and trusting and believing in Him, there will naturally be times *when* we will pray, *when* we will fast (involve ourselves in Christian discipline), and *when* we will give alms (our money). We are given that unambiguous mandate from Jesus Christ and also from the Apostle Paul: to share our gifts in the context of love that God has given to us.

Years ago, I heard a phrase used by people who were trying to encourage us to support a worthwhile cause in the Church. They would frequently say, "Give until it hurts." I've come to learn through my own Christian experience a different way of saying that: "Give until it feels good." If we give until it is sacrificial, and spontaneous, and personal, and prompt, until by the power of God it "feels good," then I promise you that we will have discovered an "open door" which no one can close.

For All I'm Worth

Psalm 8
II Corinthians 5:16-21

Several years ago in New York, on a poster just above the windows of a subway car, there was a picture of a beautiful young girl. She was advertising toothpaste with her bright smile and sparkling white teeth. Apparently, someone didn't think she was so beautiful because he scribbled there, "I hate girls." However, he misspelled girls and it read, "I hate grils." Someone else came along and wrote, "It's girls, stupid." A third person came along and wrote, "But what about us grils?" There are times in our lives when all of us, for one reason or another, to one degree or another, feel like grils. There are times when we look at the world around us and we begin to realize that we have not lived up to our own expectations for ourselves. We have a sense of worthlessness, uselessness, or at least a feeling of discouragement.

Sometimes we look at ourselves and ask the same question, "What about us grils?" That is true, especially when we compare ourselves to the vast world around us and discover how insignificant we are when measured against the infinite dimensions of time and space. Can you recall, as I do, perhaps at a summer camp, lying out on a hillside on one of those bright, crystal clear nights, looking up at the sky filled with an enormous number of stars, which seemed to be so close we felt we could almost touch them? It was in just such a setting that I first identified with the observation of the psalmist, "When I look at the heavens, the moon and stars which you have made; who are we that you are mindful of us (or care for us)?" (Psalm 8:3, 4) My question is not as eloquent as phrased by the psalmist. To this day when I look at the awesome panorama of creation I simply say, "What about us grils?" Who are we and what are we worth in the larger scheme of things?

A few years ago, a friend of mine was doing research for a psychology project. He asked seventeen people the same question, "Does the world need another person just like you?" The answer, sometimes in jest, sometimes in embarrassment, sometimes in humility, was always, "No!" *What about us grils?* In 1970, Alvin Toffler wrote the book *Future Shock.* He talked about the paradox of tremendous abundance, wealth, and potential, on the one hand, and the fear and anxiety of being isolated, lost, and alone, on the other. This could happen to any of us at anytime. Therefore, if we are to overcome the feelings of uselessness and worthlessness and the lack of self-esteem, we need to reclaim the promise that we are special children of God. At the time Toffler wrote, he stated that we are moving steadily toward that contradiction. Some people might say that we are already there.

I was once asked to speak at a church-related college, so I called the president to ask what he thought I might talk about. I asked, "Would you like me to talk about belief and trust and faith in God?" He answered, "No, the students believe in God; they just don't believe in themselves." That is a disturbing thought, but it is also very prevalent in the world today, not just among students. Who am I? What is my identity? What am I really worth? We all seek and want to know the answers to those questions. Most of us have a better idea of who we aren't, than who we are. When I was young, I was more aware of differences with others, than I was of my own individuality and identity. I looked at African-Americans, Asians, Italians, Jews, Muslims, and any number of ethnic or religious groups. I knew I was not any of them, but I had not yet discovered who I was, or what I was worth.

A number of years ago, a large group of Christians from all over the country gathered for a conference on evangelism. At the opening session, Lloyd Ogilvie asked each one of us to find someone we didn't know in that large crowd. That was an easy assignment. Then he asked for us to introduce ourselves to each other. Initially, this seemed easy enough, until he asked us to make our introductions without telling our name or our occupation. Consequently, we had to dig deeply inside ourselves to reveal who we were by our interests, values, goals, and dreams. Those of us who did that exercise discovered who we really were, and, perhaps for the first time, that in our unique identity, we were worthwhile. In fact, we discovered that we were individuals who really mattered – to ourselves, to others, and most of all, to God.

Some friends who live in a retirement community once told me that when they first arrived, they felt as though somehow they had been passed over or ignored. They were struggling to find their usefulness, if they were needed, and what they were worth. In the movie, *Pearl Harbor*, some of the soldiers going off to battle wrote this in their journals, "We are not afraid to die, but we are afraid not to matter." We, likewise, are afraid we might not be of some worth; that we might die for no purpose – we all want to have some sense of worth in the world; we want to be a personal memory for someone, somewhere, somehow.

That is exactly the point; that is exactly the feeling that captures the sense of what it means to be "grils." Our text today claims that when we look at the irrefutable, irresistible message of the death and resurrection of Christ, we are able, not only to see that we are infinitely worthwhile, but that others around us are of supreme value, as well. Paul puts it this way: "We now regard no one from a human point of view . . . Even though we once regarded Christ from a human point of view, we no longer view Him in that way." (II Corinthians 5:16) In other words, Christ was not just another man, but the divine Son of God who, through the cross and resurrection, accomplished not only for Himself, but also on our behalf, victory over death and the grave. What Christ did was to say loudly and clearly that, although we were sinners, He felt we were worth dying for. Paul put it this way, "For our sake (for our salvation and for our saving grace), God made Christ to become sin. The one who knew no sin took our sin upon Himself and empowered us, so that we might become the righteousness of God." (II Corinthians 5:21) Worthwhile! This, of course, was emphasized by the Apostle Paul in that powerful phrase, "Anyone who is in Christ is a new creation." Worthwhile! Made new!

But I think we need to caution ourselves that we don't project on God's mind and thought our own personal hopes and desires. That is easy to do. We often want to tell God exactly what we want to be, where we want to go, and how we want Him to bless us by fulfilling our request. When I was growing up, my parents marked my progress on the kitchen doorframe. I decided that because I loved the sport of basketball, and since I was becoming more attracted to the opposite sex, it would be very good for me to be 6'4" or 6'5". Obviously, I didn't reach that. I became 6'1 and ½"; and I carefully measured that ½ inch. (Now I am a little shorter than that, either shrinking, spreading, or both!) Somewhere along the line I had to come to the realization, and resign myself to the fact that what I was – what God intended me to be – was OK! Who I was, and who God made me to be, was exactly what God wanted.

We all need to pray for discernment – wisdom – so that we can begin to understand how our hopes and desires coincide with what

God has in mind for us. Who we are, and what we are becoming, is very special. Each one of us, in our uniqueness and individuality, is very special to God. There is a Muppet character who has helped me to discover more clearly that truth. Kermit the Frog, whom the children all know, has a wonderful song that is very introspective, and with which I identify very closely. The song says this,

"It isn't easy being green, to spend each day the color of leaves, when I would rather be red or gold or yellow – something much more colorful like that. It isn't easy being green. You blend in with so many other ordinary things, because you don't stand out like sparkles on the water and flashing stars in the sky. But green is the color of spring, and green can be cool and friendly-like, and big like an ocean, and important like a mountain, and tall like a tree. When I'm green I wonder – I wonder. Why wonder? But I'm green, and it is beautiful, and I think that is what I want to be."

It is that kind of discernment that you and I need. We need to be able to understand that what God has made of us is infinitely worthwhile; that you and I are something very special. Whatever our uniqueness, whatever our individuality, that is our legacy. Our legacy as God's children is that we have become someone very unique in the plans and purposes of God. God dearly loves and cherishes us. He loves us in wonderful ways with unconditional, unreserved love. God is always reaching out to us; God is always welcoming us. How important it is for us to understand this in order for us to accept our worth.

While we were taking a tour in 1986 of the Hermitage Museum in Leningrad (St. Petersburg), Russia, the tour guide took us down a hallway. At the end of the hallway was a huge picture by Rembrandt entitled *The Prodigal Son*. The tour guide said, "Look at the blind father." And I said, "No, he is not blind! He is seeing better than anybody else has ever seen. He has seen the son who was rebellious, and he has seen the son who is jealous. He has seen them clearly! No, he is not blind!" A number of years ago, I was teaching a class of teenagers about this same parable and I asked the question, "What do you think the father said to the son who came back, and to the son who was jealous?" One teenager gave a profound answer. He said, "I think the father said to both of them, 'I love you, is that OK?' " The father was not blind. He was very open to the kind of love that is a welcoming invitation and an attraction to those who need to know their uniqueness and their worth. Theologian Karl Barth, when visiting Union Seminary in Richmond, Virginia, was asked if he could state his theology in a very brief comment. He simply said this, "Jesus loves me, this I know, for the Bible tells me so." To understand that is to reach through to the mystery and the miracle of that gift in Jesus Christ, which is available to each one of us; to see that we are worth something precious in the eyes of God.

Arthur Miller, the great playwright and Jewish intellectual, was married for a short time to Marilyn Monroe, the sex kitten of half a century ago. In his book, *Time Bends*, he talks about their frantic and sorrowful relationship. He said, "So often, I would look and see her struggle; her desperate struggle with depression and despondency, especially her dependence upon drugs and alcohol." One time, he talked the doctor into one more shot with the hope of getting her some needed rest. As she was lying there sleeping, he found himself staring at her and imagining a miracle. "What if, when she woke up, I could say to her, 'God loves you; you are special.' And suppose she might believe it." But then he said, "How I wish that I still had my faith and she had hers, because I have no mystery or miracle to offer her."

We have that mystery, that miracle to offer in Jesus Christ, our Savior. We are often amazed when we first recognize what is happening to us in the conversion experience. C. S. Lewis once said that Christ did not come just to improve us, but to transform us, to make us new – immeasurably worthwhile. Jesus loves us enough to love us just as we are, but too much to leave us there. We continually grow, attaining the potential that God makes it possible for us to become. I will never forget the man who was going through a conversion experience. In the prayer time at the end of a Bible study, he prayed this, "God, I'm not who I think I am." He repeated that phrase several times, with deeper and deeper emotion. Then he looked up and prayed, "But I'm who you think I am and who, by Your power and grace, I am becoming." We are worthwhile to God – becoming what, in God's love, we can be.

There is a solemn story that occurred during a tragic time in our country's history. Traders went to Africa, took people captive and brought them over to America to become slaves. An old slave trader took a young slave trader with him to a village where earlier they had captured men. As these men came out of the village, they were bent over, physically and emotionally by the weight of heavy chains. However, one young man held his chains up and stood erect, holding his head high. The young trader, who had never been there before asked the old trader, "Who is he? Look at the way he is standing and walking." The old trader knew the family and he knew the village. He answered him, "He is a child of a king, and he cannot forget it." When you and I are bowed down by the weight and the burdens of this life, when we are being imprisoned by sin, or whatever threat that holds us down, we need to stand erect and remember that we are children of the King – brothers and sisters of Christ. We must stand erect and not forget it.

It is important for us not only to realize that we are worth something in God's eyes, but also that we are called to give that gift of affirmation and love to others. Apostle Paul says, "Anybody in Christ is a new creation." He then adds, "All this is from God, who reconciled us to Himself through Christ and has given to us the message of reconciliation. So we are ambassadors for Christ, God making His appeal through us. . . ." (II Corinthians 5:19, 20) The legacy we have received is a legacy we have to give and to share. When we discover that we are worthwhile to God, it is then our task, our mission, to tell that to those around us.

We are frequently surprised when God uses us to share that message. Early in my son's career, he left work at the end of the day and was met by a man on the street who asked for money for food. Jim said that he would not give him the money, but he would go with him to a fast food restaurant and buy him supper. When he checked his cash, he discovered that he had only enough to buy a meal for the man and still have enough for his train fare home. The man ordered his food and then asked if he could also have an apple pie. After checking his wallet, Jim's answer was "Yes." Instead of leaving, Jim sat down at a table with the man and visited with him. The man asked Jim why he had done this. Jim confessed it was because he was a Christian. As they were concluding their conversation, the man asked a question which totally surprised my son: "Do you know what God looks like?" Jim began to use all that he had learned in Church School and tried to explain that we really don't know what God looks like. But the man interrupted the explanation, saying, "No, No, No – you don't understand – God looks like you! You are the first person who ever made me feel worthwhile."

When we become servants, we become reflections of God. Shortly before the Catholic theologian Henri Nouwen died, he spent two years in Toronto, Canada, in Daybreak, a place for people who are mentally, emotionally, and physically challenged. His job there was to talk to and take care of the same six people everyday, seven days a week. He provided their food, their clothing, and their nurture. Henri was a source of love for them everyday. In his book, *In the Name of Jesus,* a book about leadership, he said, "Up to that time, I had been thinking about what it was that made me relevant. I determined it was my education, my degrees, my talent, and my skill. I had a prominent position. After all, I was a professor. All that made me relevant. I not only had a position . . . or at least I thought so, I also had a reputation." But he added, "In this setting at Daybreak, I discovered something totally different about myself. I discovered that my true reputation and purpose was not in my old evaluations of myself." He said, "I had to abandon my preoccupation with power and prestige for the role of love and service." Then he pondered, "In so doing, I discovered who I was; that I was a servant, that I was identified by love. I was measured by compassion, by my service, and I learned who I was, and perhaps more than ever before – what I was really worth." Called to service! Called to be a servant! We are to be servants who allow other people to understand that the God who loves us also loves them. Mother Teresa was asked how she could maintain her dedication to her work for so many long years. She said, "I was empowered by the Spirit, I was identified by love as a servant of Christ."

In today's text, it is demonstrably clear that the Apostle Paul says that God empowers us to be servants through the Holy Spirit. In the Holy Spirit, Paul says that we are blended to become something united with Christ in our service in His name. There is a wonderful story told by Donald Wyrtzen about a concert in New York's Carnegie Hall. Paderewski was the artist performing, and a young woman had taken her four-year-old son to the concert. At intermission time, she stood up to stretch and began to visit with the people around her. Suddenly, she looked down and realized her son was missing. She began to panic. Just before she was altogether overcome with fear, she heard from the stage the familiar, two-fingered melody of "Chop Sticks." When she looked at the stage, there was her four-year-old son, sitting at the concert grand playing "Chop Sticks." Almost immediately, Paderewski came out, sat beside him and, according to the mother, played the most beautiful harmony she or anybody else had ever heard.

You and I may be very ordinary people, but to God we are special; worthwhile. You and I can be average by comparison to the rest of the world. We have our own fears about inadequacies and doubts about our abilities. Perhaps all we can play is "Chop Sticks." Still, whatever our doubts or fears, God can take your tune and mine and make a beautiful harmony, because to others, and us, He continues to say, "You are worthwhile; you are loved."

When we have the knowledge of God's unconditional love deep within our hearts, it never leaves us. If we are indeed worthwhile, if that is our legacy, then we need to persevere; we need to take the risk. James Michener tells a powerful story of the slave trade in New Orleans. A man was on the block being sold. He had belonged to several different families, and somewhere along the line he had been given a Bible. He had read the Bible and understood the message of love in Jesus Christ. Though he knew about that love, he was still a slave, being sold once again. The bidding took place and he was sold for an embarrassingly low price. As his new owner took him off the block and he began to walk down the street, the slave began to sing that old spiritual, "Goin'a Sing My Lord for All that I'm Worth." If you and I listen very carefully to God's love, in spite of the fact that we are human and ordinary, we hear that God's love is unconditional, that it is a miracle, and it is powerful. It is a mystery, *but it is ours* undeniably in Christ Jesus. When you and I begin to realize that the love we have received from Christ has revealed our value and significance to God, I suggest that we might be able to begin to sing our own new song, *"for all that we are worth!"*

Let us pray:

> *Goin'a sing my Lord, for all that I'm worth;*
> *Goin'a sing my Lord, for all that I'm worth, Lord, Lord;*
> *Goin'a sing my Lord, for all that I'm worth,*
> *Goin'a sing my Lord, Lord, Lord, 'til I see your face.*

(Sung by Dr. Jackson)

Strike Three

Psalm 103:1-14
II Corinthians 5:16-21
I Peter 2:8, 10

It was an evening when I had no meetings at the church. I was driving past a field where a Little League team was playing. I was hooked, so I stopped to watch the rest of the game. I found a seat right beside one of those proverbial, stereotypical Little League parents. In just a few minutes, he summarized the complete situation; it was the last half of the last inning, there were two outs, the bases were loaded, and it was a tie score. Just then, he looked up, and, in complete frustration and displeasure as he watched the batter approaching home plate, said, "Oh no, he's already struck out three times, and the last time he cried."

Well, about that time, I began quietly to pull for that young man, hoping that he might do something good, if not something great – at least not strike out. But it really didn't look promising. The guy had a point, because the little fellow who walked up to the plate was very small, his pants were so large they looked like bloomers, and the jersey was so big that it was stuck halfway down his pants, so that the number was hardly seen. The helmet wobbled on his head. He didn't look like an imposing batter at all, and he was reluctantly

153

dragging his bat up to the plate. There was a pat on the back from his coach and a couple of faint cheers (I am sure it was his parents), and then he was all alone in a tense and intimidating moment.

The first pitch was a strike (Oh, no!); the second pitch was a ball (I thought, "Maybe if he waits long enough, he'll get a walk and win the game"); the third pitch was a strike (I thought, "We're in trouble"). However, on the next pitch, he stuck his bat out and the pitcher made a drastic mistake; he hit the bat with the ball. It floated out over the infield, a single, scoring the winning run. I yelled, "Way to go!" But the guy next to me couldn't let it go. He moaned, "Well, he still isn't any Mark McGwire or Sammy Sosa."

I finally felt compelled to say something, because I had just looked at some of the records of those two players. I said, "Do you realize that last year, in 1999, Mark McGwire had 65 home runs, but he struck out 141 times. Sammy Sosa had 63 home runs, and he struck out 171 times. That is two or three times the number of strikeouts to home runs. And by the way, Babe Ruth had 714 home runs, and he struck out 1,330 times; Hank Aaron had 755 home runs and struck out 1,389 times." Well, I don't think I impressed my new friend. From the groan in his voice and the look on his face as we parted, I don't think we ever will be best of friends.

This made me think how often we give so much attention to the home runs that are hit; so much attention to those successes. Later, I went back home and did some more research about some other players I had not told him about. I'm not an avid baseball fan, but I have to admit that there are some fascinating statistics here. Willie Mays had 660 home runs and struck out 1,526 times. Mickey Mantle had 536 home runs and struck out 1,710 times. By now, those of you who are not sports fans are not very excited about this survey, but, if not, just listen to these contrasting numbers. My boyhood hero was Ralph Kiner, who had 360 home runs and struck out 749 times. Willie Stargell, another famous Pittsburgh Pirate, had 475 homeruns and he struck out 1,926 times – four times as many strikeouts. He had the record until Reggie Jackson came along, and he had 563 home runs and struck out 2,596 times – five times as many strikeouts as home runs. (Editor's note: As of the 2002 season, Barry Bonds in his career has 613 home runs and 1,329 strikeouts – better than 2 to 1.)

And it's not just the batters – it's also the pitchers. A Cy Young Award is given every year for the best pitcher in the Major Leagues. It is for the pitcher who exemplifies good pitching, and the award is named for Cy Young because he owns the record for the most wins ever (511). But he also has the record for the most losses (314). Perhaps there should be another Cy Young Award for the pitcher with the most losses. By the way, he also lost the first World Series game ever played. Cal Ripken, who had that incredible record of consecutive games played (2,632), also has a record of the most times hitting into double plays (334). If you think about it, a good batting average in the professional ranks is 300, which means that every time a person bats 10 times, he makes 7 outs. Remember that little guy at the Little League game? He had one hit out of four; that is a .250 average, and that isn't too bad.

We have become accustomed to hero worship, and we have a penchant for winning. "We're number one!" We hear that all the time. If we are human, and we are, we need to realize that we will not always be on top – we will not always win. In his book *Perspectives on an Evolving Creation*, Keith B. Miller, writer, author, philosopher, and theologian, says, "We spend too much time magnifying our successes way out of proportion, and we ignore our failures" – our strikeouts, our mistakes, and our errors.

This kind of contradiction was true even in Biblical times. Sometimes, the Bible is not a very complimentary book. It is, as a matter of fact, very candid and very realistic. Think about the heroes in the Bible. Abraham, the father of our faith, went down to Egypt and said to his wife, Sarah, "Tell the Pharaoh you are my sister, so he won't kill me." That is not the word of a particularly brave, moral, or exemplary person. Moses killed an Egyptian, wandered around in the wilderness, vacillating and making excuses – another strikeout. As for David, all we have to do is mention Bathsheba and we know his strikeout. James and John came along with their mother and asked to have the prominent position in the kingdom, to be seated at Christ's left and right. That, of course, was not what Christ was looking for. Peter denied Christ three times and Saul (Paul) persecuted the Christians. If you add up the last five people mentioned, there are seven strikeouts.

That is what we see in Scripture: people with whom we can identify who are thought of as winners but who also have their share of strikeouts and mistakes. We can sometimes identify with these Biblical heroes. For instance, Jerome Hines, the late opera singer, said, "When I read the Scriptures, so often I begin to discover that my name is in the script. My name is on every page. The Bible is not simply describing those personalities, but also revealing my strengths and my weaknesses, as well." What is the point of this today? The point is this: We need to deal with trying to find the balance between our successes and failures; our victories and our losses. Once again, if we are human, and we are, then we need to realize that no one of us is immune from making mistakes. All of us – rich, poor, young, old, male, or female – we all make our mistakes. There is no one who is free from that situation. We will not always be winners, and neither will we always be *Number One*!

So today (if this is all true, and it is), we need to discover the singular, significant lessons for us to learn in all of these examples found in Scripture. The first lesson is this: God knows exactly who we are. God knows our problems. God is very much aware of our strengths and our weaknesses – all of it. He knows our good days and our bad days. As we heard from Scripture, the last verse in the Old Testament text today, "As a father pities his children, so the Lord pities those who revere (or fear) Him." In Romans, Paul says, "All have sinned and come short of the glory of God." God knows our weaknesses and He knows our mistakes. In spite of that, the highest purpose of God, the deepest desire of God, is to save us and to redeem us. God has our best interest at heart.

I love the story about a man who called a home and a little boy answered in a whisper, "Hello."

The man on the phone said, "Is your father there?"

The little boy whispered, "No, he is busy."

"Well, is your mother there?"

"No, she is busy."

"Well, who else is there."

"The police."

"Could they come to the phone?"

"No, they're busy."

"Who else is there?"

"The firemen."

"Could they come to the phone?"

"No, they're busy."

"What are they busy doing?"

"They are looking for me."

The good news of the Gospel, the good news of the Scripture, the good news of Jesus Christ is that in the midst of our frazzled, fragmented, broken world, God is looking for us – each of us, all of us. God is reaching out to us in Jesus Christ, not to punish, but to change us, to redeem us, to make us new.

We often talk about self-development. That is a good word. And self-esteem – that is also a good word. After all, self-development is very laudable and self-esteem is very valuable. But God is not just interested in self-development programs or the enhancement of our self-esteem. God is most interested in transformation, redoing our whole life – creating in us a new sense of who we are and a new sense of purpose in our living. How does God accomplish this for us? He accomplishes it for us in the victory that comes to us through what God did for us on the Cross. He sent His Son for us!

When I was a kid growing up in Western Pennsylvania, we had a lot of kids of all ages who liked to play baseball in the vacant lot – next to the church. We had a rule there that if you were under eight years of age and had two strikes, you could pick one of the big kids on your team to take your last pitch. Good rule! It is, in fact, the kind of thing that happens for us through Christ, but in a much stronger way. Jesus Christ, our elder brother, has taken the last pitch for us, and, more than that, He did not strike out. He won an ultimate victory. Paul says, "God chose the one who had no acquaintance with sin at all, and made Him to become sin," to take the last strike for us, "so that we might become the righteousness of God." When the psalmist talks about that, he says, "As the heavens are high above the earth, so great is God's love toward us; as far as east is from the west," and that is a long way. "So far, He has removed our transgressions from us." Paul simply adds, "Anyone who is in Christ is a new creation. The old has passed away (the old sins and old "strikeouts" have passed away), behold the new has come."

Because this is true, because God has done this, then we are free to admit our humanity. We are free to admit our mistakes, our errors, our strikeouts, and that is essential. Dr. Roy Menninger, of the Menninger Clinic, says that the one thing he deplores is people saying over and over again, this old myth: "I must always be strong." He said, "First of all, it is impossible. Because we are human, sometimes we are strong, and sometimes we are weak." And then he said, "It is no sin to admit our vulnerability." Now, when we admit our dependency and our vulnerability, this does not demean our humanity. It is simply setting the stage for us to have a new beginning, a new start, a new time at bat, if you will. We must remember that every setback can be a prelude to a comeback.

When we discover that new beginning, then we not only have the forgiveness that we receive from God, but His forgiveness makes it possible for us to forgive ourselves. An old friend of mine is a very good golfer and, when he makes a bad shot, he simply walks up to the ball, looks at the ball and says to himself, "I forgive you for that." Then he looks at the rest of us and says, "Watch my recovery." That is exactly the position that we need to take when we have made errors. We need to recognize our strikeouts and our errors, accept them, and begin to look in a new direction, to step back up to the plate. The little guy at the Little League game didn't want to be there. The fan who sat next to me didn't want him to be there either. However, the best thing he did after his first three strikeouts was to go up to that plate, and, with a little encouragement from his coach and a couple cheers from his parents, do his best. That was the very best thing he could do.

A reporter in a locker room was interviewing Pelé, the great soccer player from Brazil, and asked the question, "How often do you think about the great number of wins that you had? You have been so successful. It is a tribute to the kind of person you are." Pelé's answer was this: "The real measure of any player is ultimately how well he plays the first game after he has lost."

Paul says, "Forgetting what lies behind, and straining forward to what lies ahead, I press on toward the goal of the upper call of God, in Christ Jesus." That suggests that we can begin to learn some lessons from our mistakes. God does not call us to be successful. He calls us to be obedient and faithful. And when we are obedient and faithful, then we begin to learn some very precious lessons.

Michael Jordan is known by most people as the greatest basketball player who has ever played. He has an unusual record, as well. Twenty-five times, he has made spectacular last-second shots to win games. But he also acknowledges that in his career he has had about as many bad shots at the end of games, if not more so. Those were terrible shots, which he said were so bad that they were not reported on the sports page. He said that he has learned two lessons in all of this, "I've learned how to win graciously, and to be a good sport, and to win with good taste. But I have also learned that many of my best lessons come from my failures; to inspire me to improve, to practice, to be disciplined, and to be the best player I could possibly be."

"Forgetting what lies behind, and straining forward to what lies ahead, I press on. . . ." – to the next step, beyond the strikeouts, beyond the mistakes – to become the best person we could possibly be.

In the New Testament, Jesus said, "Be ye perfect, even as your Heavenly Father is perfect." (Matthew 5:48) Remember, that word "perfect" does not mean without mistake, or without error or blemish. It really means, "be complete in yourself, even as God is complete in Himself." God is asking us to be the best that we can be; to use the gifts that we have been given. It is then that we discover one of the best ways to overcome these problems of ours that occur in our faith – walk within the Body of Christ, where we are surrounded by our sisters and brothers in faith, who can give us encouragement – motivate, energize, and affirm us. This kind of love can lead us to become something that we can become no other way. It is exciting to see what happens when someone is strongly and properly motivated. Exciting things happen – extraordinary and impossible things happen.

Perhaps you have heard about the man who was walking across a cemetery one cold and rainy night, and fell into an open grave. He was trying to get out, but he couldn't make it because he was so wet and it was too slippery. He finally gave up and sat down in the corner, put his coat around him and said, "I'll just wait till morning until someone comes to help me out." Not long after, another person came along and fell into the other end of the grave. He also tried to get out and was having great difficulty. The first man, whom the second man had not noticed sitting in the far corner with his coat wrapped around him, said, "You'll never make it."

He did! When we have the proper motivation, all kinds of exciting things happen – impossible things.

One of the best motivations for us in the community of faith is to love each other. The informal definition I like to use of *agape* love in the Greek New Testament is to "desire the best possible thing in the other person." To understand and experience love that way is to encourage others to become the best they can be. When we begin to motivate each other with that kind of love, desiring the best possible thing in the other person, then all kinds of exciting things happen. When and how do we begin to motivate others with our love? We always need to think about the Christian imperative. The question is asked, "When is the best time to plant a tree?" The answer is that the best time to plant a tree is twenty-five years ago. The second best time is today. The Scripture says, "Now is the acceptable time, now is the day of salvation." Now is the time to motivate each other, to energize each other, to affirm each other in the love of Jesus Christ – "desiring the best possible thing in the other person."

The great lesson here is that our strikeouts don't always defeat us. The best example of that is the Apostle Peter. Peter denied Christ three times and, after Christ rose from the dead and was with the disciples in the Sea of Galilee, He said to Peter three times, "Do you love me?" We are told his answers but we can only guess what his internal reaction was in that moment. But we know what Peter said later on. Listen to what he writes about having learned from that conversation with Jesus."You are a chosen race, a royal priesthood, a holy nation, God's own people, that you may declare the wonderful works and deeds of Him who called you out of darkness into His marvelous light. Once you were no people, you were defeated; now you are God's people. Once you had not received mercy, now you have received mercy." (I Peter 2:9-10) He could only write that if his denials had been forgiven. He could only write that if his strikeouts had been exonerated. He definitely had three strikes, but he was not out.

I want to suggest to you that when we look at the struggles of life – our defeats, our mistakes, our errors – sometimes it can be very painful, but it is not fatal. Dave Dravecky was a talented pitcher with the San Francisco Giants. At the height of his career, a tragedy occurred. He developed a tumor in his pitching arm, and, after some treatment, it was decided to operate and take the tumor out. His arm was very weak, but, after some rehabilitation, he tried to pitch again. His second game back, as he threw the first pitch, his arm broke. Not long after that, it was necessary to amputate his arm. Dave and his wife, Jan, were on television several times talking about how they were adjusting to this personal tragedy. They talked about the ongoing treatments and the pressure they were experiencing, but they also clearly and convincingly witnessed to their faith.

I knew Dave when he was in high school playing basketball in Boardman, Ohio. I watched him play both basketball and baseball. I knew he was a very strong person then, but I know that, because of his faith, he is even stronger now. I wrote to Dave to thank him for his witness on public television, where all could hear about his courage and his faith. He wrote back, "The first strike was when I discovered the tumor and had the surgery. The second strike was when the arm broke, and the third strike was when the arm was amputated." Then he added, "Even with these three strikes, although painfully disappointing, it has not been fatal. I've had these three strikes, but I'm not out. I still have my faith, I still have my family, and I still have my future with God." At the bottom of the letter he simply wrote "II Corinthians 4:16-18." If you look up those verses, you will see they give the foundation of his faith and the reason for his courage. They read, "So we do not lose heart, though the outer nature is wasting away, the inner nature is being renewed every day. So we know this temporary affliction is preparing us for an eternal weight of glory beyond all comparison, because we look not for things that are seen but the things that are unseen. Because the things that are seen are

162

temporary, but the things that are unseen are eternal." It was clear to me that what Dave was saying was that his experience of losing his arm, losing his career, was painful, but it was not fatal. Three strikes, but he was not out!

The lesson for us is very much the same. You and I realize that we will have the opportunity for many victories, many successes, and many achievements. Measure those; be thankful to God for those. Praise the Lord for those. But also remember in light of what God has done for us in Jesus Christ – redeeming and saving us in the power of the Cross and Resurrection, that it is also very true that even if we have three strikes against us, we still don't have to be out. In fact, we can be "more than a conqueror," which means that in Christ Jesus, ultimately, we cannot lose!

Imagine That!

Philippians 4:4-9

Late in his life, Wilbur Wright was asked, "What was the most difficult challenge of your life?" Surprisingly, he said, "It was before Kitty Hawk." Before the flight he had planned with his brother, he had shared his dreams, hopes, and desires with family and friends, and they all reacted by saying, "It's all in your imagination." He said, "That was so devastating that it almost disturbed me enough to keep me from attempting to fly." People were telling Wilbur they thought that it was not realistic, and it couldn't possibly be done.

Have you ever noticed how often we use the phrase, "It's all in your imagination" negatively? It can have a severe adverse impact on certain people, especially when we are insensitive, uncaring, or callous when we use it. The hypochondriac tells us that he or she is sick, and we say, "It's all in your imagination," forgetting that imagined pain can be just as unbearable, and just as unpleasant as the real thing. Or, a child calls out in the night that she sees images on the wall, shadows in the room, and she is frightened, and a parent, frustrated by a busy day and the repeated calls from her child, says, "It is all in your imagination – go back to sleep."

165

In his book *Between Parent and Child*, the late Haim Ginott, a child psychologist, said that kind of turn-off with children not only increases fear, but also curbs creativity. I agree with author Ursula K. Le Guin when she said, "I doubt that imagination can be suppressed. If you truly eradicated it in a child, that child would grow up to be an eggplant." Then, of course, the skeptics and cynics look at our faith and say, "It's just a crutch, it's just something to get you through life," forgetting that for us, in the middle of the usual unpleasantness and uncertainty of life, we have a living, real relationship, a powerful personal message in Jesus Christ by which we live. Still, they challenge our faith by saying, "It's all in your imagination!" Sometimes we say it to each other – we say things are not possible, or not realistic, or not true; it's all in our imagination. It's just fantasy!

However, there's also a positive side in using this phrase. One question we ask when ordaining our Deacons and Elders is: "Will you seek to serve the people with energy, intelligence, *imagination*, and love?" Well, we can handle most of that: energy, we are willing to extend ourselves and work hard; intelligence, we promise that we will study; love, we feel that we know what it means to love and to be loved. But imagination? That is often beyond us.

The late Louis Evans, Sr., who was pastor at Hollywood Presbyterian Church for a number of years, said, "The problem for many of us is the difference between religion and relationship." He said, "So often, we read the Scripture with no more feeling than we do the timetable in the airport, with no more regularity than we would the full works of Shakespeare. Sometimes we go through all the actions and activity of worship and the Sacraments just in repetitive routine; it's only something that we do, perhaps by rote, or as a traditional ceremony." But that is just religion. Let us not forget that the most important reason you and I come here to worship is because we have a relationship with Jesus Christ through the power of the Holy Spirit. Dr. Evans also suggested, in a very positive way, that we need to be open to the Spirit and allow the Holy Spirit to liberate us from the legalistic restrictions and old habits. We need to seek to have the spirit consecrate us and enable us to "dream new dreams and see new visions" – in other words use our imagination. Furthermore, in the relationship, we have the possibility of having a new power. Christ said, "I will give you power when the Holy Spirit has come upon you." That means that our thinking can be transformed, our lives can be empowered, and our hope can be realized.

I suggest to you, also, that to say "Imagine That" is not simply conjecture and speculation about the future. There is a lot of rush to judgment these days about prediction, with people guessing what they think may be found in a new year, or a new millennium. I know there are many things for which we might like to have advanced warning – the possible failure of our computers; the lack of light, heat, and water; a job success or failure; or the possible disruption of airline traffic. As it has often been throughout history, there are many people who are spending an inordinate amount of time looking for signs and examining significant events, and then trying to predict the end of time. The Scripture says clearly we shouldn't spend a lot of time doing that, wasting valuable time trying to calculate when that end time will come. Christ said, "We don't know . . . we just need to be ready." But people go on with this thinking, feeling they need to predict the future, and it all becomes a frenzy of unproductive activity, scrutiny, and wasted pointless analysis, which in the end becomes, what a professor friend of mine once called, "the paralysis of analysis."

Imagination, in its primary function, is the recognition of the power and presence of God in our lives, believing that God can and does do miraculous things. We see evidence of that in Scripture. Ezekiel had a great vision of God. He saw burning fires, creatures flying, wheels within wheels, and bright precious stones ablaze with color. After he had that vision of God, later he saw this valley full of bones and he said, "Can these bones live?" (Ezekiel 37:3) What imagination! The imagination of Ezekiel was that even that which has died could be raised to new life. Ezekiel acquired an imagination through this vision he had through the Spirit of God.

Isaiah also had a vision; he proclaimed, "I saw the Lord high and lifted up." Then in his imagination, he began to see himself as a sinner against the background of God, and the world around him as sinful people. So he lamented, "Woe is me, for I am a man of unclean lips and I dwell in the midst of a people of unclean lips." And then, because of his contriteness and confession, he found cleansing, forgiveness, and new hope, so that when he heard God asking, "Whom will I send and who will go for us?", he answered with his unparalleled example of commitment, "Here am I, send me." When you and I read stories like Ezekiel and Isaiah, it's not just to review the record and read or reread it over and over again. It's to inspire us, to summon up within us the readiness and the willingness to use our imagination to "dream new dreams, and to see new visions."

Jesus talked in very picturesque and imaginative language. At one point, he sent seventy disciples out on a mission, two by two, and they came back raving about what had happened. They said, "Even the demons are subject to us, in your name." Jesus didn't reply by bringing out a corporate portfolio or the promises of a politician. Nor did he come with the instruction sheet as big, thick, and complicated as the IRS instruction sheet. In fact, all that Jesus said was, "I saw Satan fall like fire from heaven. Do not rejoice that the demons are subject to you, but rejoice that your names are written in heaven." That kind of response created a vivid imagination in his disciples that, somehow, someway, sin and evil would eventually be conquered – overcome – defeated!

Most of us would like to have the Bible be a nice ethical handbook, which would give us a checklist, telling us how we are to speak, what we are to say, and how we are to live. But it is not that way. Jesus generates imagination in our minds by implying what possibly could happen. For instance, He tells a parable about a Samaritan; we call him a "good Samaritan," knowing full well that in those days, because of racial prejudice and injustice, people felt that there was no such thing as a "good Samaritan." However, this Samaritan did something noticeably good; something the self-righteous religious people never anticipated. He unexpectedly stopped to help the stranger who was hurt and dying, while a priest, a Levite, and a Pharisee, all religious people, walked on by. Jesus told that story and then asked the disciples, "Who is your neighbor?" Can you fathom the imagination that sprung up in their minds as they heard that question? Or, perhaps, even to us as we hear that story told to us today from Scripture?

Jesus doesn't give us the scientific description of botany and then say, "Here's the foundation in the science of creation. This is what a leaf looks like, and here's how it is made. Now that you've observed this scientific process, you should believe and know that God really cares about you, because He has created you and all of these things of nature." Jesus says it much more imaginatively, "Consider the lilies of the field . . . they neither spin nor toil, but I tell you they are in more array than Solomon in all his glory." As a result, our imagination increases and expands within, when we see that God cares not only about infinitely small things, He even cares about us. We might call that "sanctified imagination." It is all in our imagination!

Jesus also comes to the Last Supper with His disciples, takes a simple piece of bread and a cup, and says, "This is my body broken for you; this is my blood poured out for you." Just imagine the impact on those disciples, and, I hope, on us every time we share in the Last Supper. In that communion service, we see and feel, in the power of the incarnation, the strength of the Cross, and the hope of life abundant and eternal, which never fails. It is our imagination! This all moves by way of imagination to an unremitting, inexhaustible experience of life in Jesus Christ.

Jesus gives us the power to imagine that our life can continue to grow, attain, and expand. The famous jurist, Oliver Wendell Holmes, once said, "Life in God is like a Japanese picture that does not end with the margins." For us as Christians, our life in Christ is the same kind of picture, one that continues to grow, expand, and enlarge. The picture of our life does not end with the margins, it is never complete; it is always growing. We are carried by our imagination to "new dreams" and "new visions," which we could see no other way.

St. Augustine said, "Let the love of God wash down upon me, the Spirit of God flow through me, and the revelation of God touch my heart and life, that I might be able to see the incredible power and presence of God, and praise and serve God with my heart, soul, mind, and strength, and then discover in all that my part and my place in God's Kingdom." That was a meaningful prayer, for him; it can also be your prayer and mine – to see the "incredible power and presence of God wash down and flow through my life and yours, completely enabling us to praise and serve God with heart, soul, mind, and strength; thereby, finding our place and our part in the Kingdom of God." Through our imagination, we believe it can and does happen to us and through us.

George Bernard Shaw wrote a play about Joan of Arc, called *St. Joan*. In the play, the grand inquisitor is asking Joan about her visions. He says, "These voices that you say you hear, isn't it just in your imagination?" And St. Joan answers in the play, "Certainly it is in my imagination, but how else can God speak to us except through our minds, our imagination." I think that is true for us, as well; I know it is for me. When God touches our lives, it is in our minds and hearts. He touches our imagination. How else could God clearly and personally speak to us except in the depths of our hearts and minds? The writer of Proverbs says, "Where there is no vision, the people perish." (Proverbs 29:18) When people are apathetic, indifferent, insensitive, or uncaring, the people perish; when there is no imagination, they perish, too.

Malcolm Muggeridge, the great author and philosopher, became a Christian late in life. He began his life as an agnostic. One time, reflecting upon how he became a believer, he said, "The reason I remained an agnostic so long was my lack of imagination. I think that is true for any agnostic or any atheist. They can't break out of that narrow feeling because they have a lack of imagination." He said that it is often all too easy to remain in our nice, little, protected world that we can control and manipulate, and with which we are satisfied. We are then tempted to say "Don't stretch us; don't challenge our thinking." Muggeridge said, "We need a firm *release on life* to break out of that shell that holds us in – and that release comes from God's gift of imagination."

That is exactly the point at which Paul addresses us today, to all of us who claim to be part of the community of faith. Paul speaks to us in a very special way about the gift of imagination. He says in Philippians, "Rejoice in the Lord always, again, I say, rejoice. Let everyone know your forbearance. The Lord is at hand. Have no anxiety about anything, but in everything by prayer and supplication let your requests be made known to God. And the peace of God, which passes all understanding, will keep your hearts and minds in Christ Jesus." (Philippians 4:4-7) There is an imagination in the Spirit that goes beyond the ordinary life by which we live. Paul says to let the peace of God dwell within us in order that we might go beyond what the world expects, and what we expect of ourselves. When we do this, we discover the imagination that comes when we are walking in God's way. Finally, in a glorious crescendo, Paul puts it this way, "Whatever is true, whatever is honorable, whatever is just, whatever is pure, lovely, gracious, winsome, if there is any excellence, anything ever worthy of praise, *think about these things*." I think it is also proper to translate that last phrase by simply saying, "Imagine that!"

Imagine what could happen in our lives if we would allow God, through His Spirit, to move us beyond the ordinary to that which He is calling us individually and corporately to be. We can see the imagination in Ezekial, Isaiah, Joel, Amos, Paul, Peter, and John, and, of course, in the marvelous, picturesque language of Jesus. But let us not forget that we can still see this gift, His imagination in people around us today, in the contemporary world in which we live.

About fifteen years ago, I met a woman from South Africa named Sheena Duncan. Sheena is a white woman who was the president and chairperson of a group called Black Sash. This group's plan, under her direction, was to help to break down apartheid – the terrible division of the races in South Africa. That was her mission and that was the way in which she felt she was called to go. I asked her, "How did you have the courage to do that, to stand as a lone white woman in that kind of struggle and culture, making that kind of courageous challenge?" She answered contemplatively, "Every morning after my devotions I stop and *imagine* what it would be like to see justice, equality, fairness, openness, unity, and reconciliation, blending together in our land." Then she said, "One time, as I was imagining all of that, I also began to imagine what I might do to help to bring that all about." I think it could be very profitable and productive if we let imagination be part of our devotional life. I know that after apartheid was broken down, Sheena Duncan continued to make the new racial equality work because she kept on with that same imagination and courage with which she began. I imagine that God is calling each one of us to something special. God has uniquely created and equipped us for a special life of service.

About ten years ago, I met Evgeny Yevtushenko, the Russian poet (at that time it was the Soviet Union), who had come to Chautauqua, New York. One afternoon, he read his poetry in broken English. While he did not mention the name Christ in anything he read, there was an obvious Messianic hope in what he read to us that day. He sold books of his poetry, and for one of my friends, he inscribed the book this way: there was the symbol for humanity, the hammer and sickle for communism, the star for democracy, and the cross. Then he wrote above his name, "In love of Jesus, who was also betrayed." A Messianic hope! A few days later in conversation with him, we asked him about what he had written; about his ideas and what he had said. He answered, "Wouldn't it be lovely (he perhaps meant well or good) if all of us would think about, imagine what Jesus really said, and then take Him seriously." Imagine that, really pondering, considering, meditating upon what Jesus Christ has said, and then *to take Him seriously*. It is a powerful message for all of us, whatever our role in this church or in this life.

There is a positive attitude that can come to us as we share, even through the valleys. I was talking recently with the officers of this church about mountains and valleys in their lives and what they do when challenges come. Where do they find evidence of blessing and strength when the valley is very deep? Well, I suggest to you that it can come in unsuspecting ways. Two years ago, I called on a shut-in and I asked, "How do you feel today?" She answered, "Confident – hopeful!" What a great answer! She was at home alone and, although many people came to visit, she was still lonely. She was old, her infirmities were very serious, and she was in constant pain. Yet, in that moment, when I asked how she was feeling, she said that she was confident – hopeful. As I was pondering that, she began to sing the Gospel tune, *"Turn Your Eyes Upon Jesus*, look full in His wonderful face, and the things of earth will grow strangely dim in the light of His glory and grace." Imagine that! – that kind of strength that can come to us in any and all of life's circumstances.

Jimmy Carter recently spoke about his work with Habitat for Humanity. A writer for a Detroit newspaper, having heard his speech, made some interesting observations. He wrote, "Jimmy Carter has given being-a-former-president a good name. Here was a man who had genuine humility, a passion for people, a desire to serve, and an uncompromising vision for hope." Continuing his musing, he wrote, "Wouldn't it be a good idea for us to have all those same qualities?" Wouldn't it be a good idea for us to think about what he said? "Imagine that!" – humility, passion, desire, hope, a vision for goodness!

The problem for many of us is that we just don't focus on what we are attempting to do for God in Christ. Sometimes we just need to concentrate on our call. It is very easy to get diverted or distracted. A couple of years ago, I was sitting in the airport waiting for my plane. A man sitting beside me was reading a magazine and, after he closed the magazine, we began to talk. He said, "What do you do for a living?" Usually, I try to avoid answering that question. I sometimes say, "A salesman," or something diverting like that. However, on that day, I admitted the truth, "I'm a clergyman." He said, "Oh!" and with embarrassment he began to apologize because he was reading *Playboy* magazine. He didn't have to apologize to me. Then he said what we've heard from a lot of men over the years, "I wasn't really looking at the pictures, I was just reading the articles." Isn't it interesting how we focus on things that take our attention – things that are inane, that aren't any great value; we focus on those things. Hopefully we can begin to see the need to focus on that which is good and true. Too often we hear people defending the conflict and violence on TV, and in the world in which we live. We hear them protest, "Well, its just entertainment." I have a hard time believing that the three minutes that invite me to buy designer jeans, or a sweet soft drink, or something that I can wear in the summer can influence me, but the next twenty minutes of anger, violence, selfishness, and self-centeredness *cannot* affect me. To me, that doesn't make sense.

Where are we focusing as a nation? Where are we focusing as a people? I was blessed with a grandfather who was a deeply spiritual man – he died at ninety-five. He was very vital until the last three months of his life. He was a very well-read man even though, because of family circumstances, he never went beyond the eighth grade. He was not naïve or uninformed. He knew what was going on in the world and was involved in the community where he lived. But as I began to know him better and better, I discovered something about his daily routine. In the morning, before he made breakfast for the family (which he always did), he had his devotions; he prayed for all of us, and then after he made breakfast, only then would he read the paper and listen to the news. In the evening, rocking slowly in his favorite chair he would listen to Lowell Thomas at seven o'clock and Gabriel Heater at nine o'clock. Then he would gather all the family together and say, "We're going to have devotions now." We would read Scripture and we would pray The Lord's Prayer. (To this day, I remember as a child thinking that prayer ended this way: "For thine is the kingdom and the power and the glory. Amen. And all who want to go to bed can go to bed." That was the way he ended the prayer. And, as a youngster, I thought it was in Scripture!) When I think back on it, he didn't begin his day with *Good Morning America* and end it with *Night Line*. He began and ended his day with the Lord, and that affected everything he heard in the news the rest of the day. It was a way in which he came to understand what it meant to be God's person – focusing on God's word and promises – beginning and ending his day with the Lord, which put everything else in perspective.

Well, what about us? What about those of us in the Church? What about those who accept positions of leadership in the Church as lay people and pastors? What about all the people of our congregation? Where and how is it that we can imagine God's presence in our lives? Perhaps we can begin to think about a ministry to the homeless, or this church's involvement in Habitat for Humanity, and do whatever we can to make that a vital and vibrant mission. Or, how about the hungry; or the people in the shelters for women and for men? Perhaps we could be more involved with people and their needs, and not just give money, leaving all the work to the officers of the church. We have here a calling ministry on shut-ins (The Samaritan Ministry). Some of the best callers in my churches have been devoted laypersons who have made calls on people with specific needs, and have empathized with them, based upon their own similar struggles. Some had experienced the death of a spouse or of a child, and they could identify with, and spiritually support, others experiencing the same loss.

Imagine that! Imagine what could happen in our church if we would think seriously about education for our adults and for our children, and allow that to expand and grow. It is so easy for us as adults to worship and let the kids go to church school. Too often the kids don't go to church and the adults don't go to church school. Imagine what could happen if we were a church of true stewardship using all that God has provided. God has given all of us gifts that are to be used to honor and glorify God.

And what about evangelism? Remember, evangelism is not simply getting people to join the church in order to put numbers on the roll. Evangelism in Greek literally means, "to tell the good news." Imagine what could happen if you and I were able to tell our story, to give our own personal testimony about our relationship with Christ and about what Jesus means to us in our lives, opening the door for conversation about all that Jesus Christ can do. Imagine that! Imagine what might happen in your life, with your family, your spouse, your children, your parents, your neighbor; imagine what kind of relationships could be developed in your lives.

Paul spoke to the Philippians, and through the mysterious working of the Holy Spirit, Paul is also speaking to us today. Let us think of the words of our text today as special words for us, as Paul says them one more time, "Finally, whatever is true, whatever is honorable, whatever is just, whatever is pure, whatever is lovely, or gracious, if there is any excellence worthy of praise, *Imagine that!*" Amen.

Let us pray. O God, speak to us through our minds; increase our awareness of who You are. Brighten our imagination, that we might see who we can become, once we identify who You are to us. O God, open to us the power to be Your servants with great imagination, and with great courage, and with great hope, as we serve and walk in Your way. We pray in Jesus' name. Amen.

Now That's the Spirit!

Psalm 139:1-12, 23, 24
John 14:15-19, 25-27
Acts 1:8 and 2:17-19a

"Now that's the spirit!" This is a phrase which is very sentimental to me, and it is also very nostalgic because it was one of my father's favorite phrases – he used it all the time. In fact, he was known by that phrase; it served as identification for him, not only with his family, but also with many friends and colleagues. As a young boy, I can remember when my brother and I would come home from school, having done well in an athletic event or a musical performance, and he would say with great joy, "Now that's the spirit!" Conversely, if we had a bad day and had a disappointment, the phrase then became a word of encouragement so that we would try again; and he would say, "Now that's the spirit!" When he came home from the church, where he was the pastor, when things had gone well, or it had been an exciting day, he would exclaim, "Now that's the spirit!" And when his beloved Pittsburgh Pirates won a game, or Ralph Kiner hit a home run (and in those days, Kiner hit more home runs and they won games), he would say, "Now that's the spirit!" When my brother and I got involved in a spat and we showed a willingness to forgive each other, he'd say, "Now, that's the spirit!" When he looked out at the world around him and saw positive racial, social, and spiritual attitudes and behavior, he'd say, "Now that's the spirit!" Every time I hear it, it is a pleasing, fond, and tender memory.

I suspect that when I was a young man, I didn't think too much about that phrase because I heard it all the time. He said it almost every day. When I became older, I began to realize that for him, it was not a cliché; it was an expression of his faith. It captured the way he lived out his faith. His great desire, his intense prayer, was that his family and friends would be "in the spirit" – that their hope would become a reality by being in tune with the Spirit of God.

In the text today, Jesus makes a very clear statement about what it means to be in touch with God's will and in tune with the Spirit, when we are alive in the Spirit. "Because I live," said Jesus, "you too shall live." (John 14:19b) In Galatians, Paul talks about living in Christ as being the separation of the flesh and the spirit. To be "in the flesh" is to be at the mercy of our human nature, involved in the sin and frustration of the world, and impotent because of the control of pride, passion, lust, and ambition, which is the direct result of being self-absorbed and self-directed. To be "in the Spirit," on the other hand, is to be in the unlimited power, control, and focus of God, to be open to the promise, hope, possibility, and potential that can be ours – available to us all in Jesus Christ.

"Now that's the Spirit!" We celebrate the Spirit on Pentecost. It is not just the birthday of the Church, but that event in Christian history that signifies the radical change that can take place in our lives when you and I are open to that Spirit, which is available to us everyday. Naturally, we would like to be able to see the clear, undisputed evidence of the Spirit, which is always helpful and empowering. Perhaps you have heard about the man who was brought with others to a police lineup in order to discover who had robbed a local store. Each person in the lineup was asked to step forward and say, "Give me your money or I'll shoot you." The first three men did that. When the fourth man stepped forward, he said, "But that is not what I said." The clear evidence there, of course, was that he was the guilty man. We are looking for clear evidence that can come to us in Jesus Christ, through the Holy Spirit . . . evidence that comes to us as we seek to know God's presence among us today.

That evidence, I think, is all around us. First of all, it is in people whom we know where the Spirit has come alive. With the school-shooting tragedy just last week in Georgia, I cannot forget what happened the month before in Littleton, Colorado. Cassie Bernall was a believer, a young lady who had just recently been converted to the faith, and very active in the school and church. She had just transferred from a Christian school to the public school, where she felt she might be able to have a more effective and productive witness. When she faced down the barrel of a gun, she was asked, "Do you believe in God?" She answered, "Yes, I do," and she was shot and killed. Rachel Scott, who wanted to be a missionary, was confronted by one of the same gunmen outside the school and was asked the same question. She answered, "You know I do," and was also killed. Valeen Schnurr, a Roman Catholic girl, was asked the same question, and as a result of her positive affirmation, she too was shot. She was not killed, but she still carries nine bullets and shrapnel pieces in her body. Thank goodness most of us will never face that kind of threat, fear, anxiety, or challenge in our lives. I can only hope that if we ever face that kind of challenge or threat, or if ever we are asked that kind of question, *"In whom do you believe?"* that we could say, *"I believe in God, the Father, through Jesus Christ, and the Holy Spirit."* What tremendous courage and power that profession of faith can give us. What a great example and a great promise it is to us; "You shall receive power when the Holy Spirit has come upon you . . ." (Acts 1:8) – the spirit of power and of courage.

The spirit also comes to us in prayer, intercessory prayer – the prayer that we share together with and for each other. When I was a young man living outside of Pittsburgh, two doors down from us was a couple who had no children, Lou and Nancy Dykes. They were very active people in the community. She was an elementary school teacher and he was a semi-retired businessman. Almost every time I participated in an athletic event or was in a public performance, speaking or singing, my neighbor Lou Dykes was there. When she was able, his wife came along with him. At that time, I just thought they had school spirit. After all, they had grown up in the same school where I was attending. Ten years later, after I graduated from high school, Lou Dykes died. I went to the funeral home to call on his widow. She said, "I want you to know that all through your high school career when Lou went to see you, it was part of his special affection for you. He had a prayer list, and every day your name was near the top of the list. You were like a son to him." Next to my own parents praying regularly for me, his prayers were very important. When we learn that many people are praying for us without our knowledge, we begin to discover something of the power of the spirit of prayer – a power that is good for the church, the home, the individual, and the community. There is a rich common blessing that comes to us when we share in the *spirit* of prayer.

What is more, we acquire a spirit of humble, sacrificial service. About fifteen years ago, I was at a meeting in Canton, Ohio, where Mother Teresa was scheduled to speak. I was sitting in the middle of the auditorium with a friend of mine. All around us there was great anticipation and excitement. People were talking about her arrival, wondering what she might say. Suddenly my friend and I realized that behind us the noise had subsided. We looked over our shoulders and saw people standing, not speaking. Just then, we looked off to the right and there, coming up the aisle, with that easily identifiable headdress, was a woman who was just tall enough to be seen over the people who were still seated. As she passed each row, people stood and became quiet. By the time she got to the stage, the whole auditorium was standing in absolute silence, out of deep respect and admiration for this wonderful servant of God. The president of the college was somewhat taken aback, and, for the moment, seemed frozen in his tracks. Mother Teresa walked over, and because of her short stature, pulled the microphone down to her level. She spoke softly to this respectful, quiet crowd, "In the name of Jesus Christ and in the power of the Holy Spirit, I thank you." I just realized that I had seen before me the example of a strong, Spirit-filled servant of God in this very humble, gentle person: Mother Teresa.

I wonder about our spirit of service when we are urged by Christ to hear His promise in Scripture, "The greatest among you will be the servant of all." (Matthew 23:11) We hear of the innocence of a childlike spirit. We are told to be "childlike" – not childish, but childlike – in our faith. We are to have the trusting, dependent faith of children. As Paul says in Romans, "Those who are led by the Spirit of God are children of God." (Romans 8:14) In the Gospel of John, we hear an intriguing description of power, which says, "Those who believe are given the power to become children." (John 1:12) (The power here is the innocence of the spirit that comes through childlike trust and faith.)

Leonard Sweet tells a wonderful story about a little boy who was going across the commons of an apartment complex to see his grandmother. He had just been to Sunday school that day, and he had been taught that whenever we give something to someone else, perhaps we will see Jesus. As he was going across the courtyard, he saw an older woman who was seated on a bench alongside the pathway. He stopped to sit beside her. Thinking about what he had learned in Sunday school, he offered her some of his M&M's. She took them and smiled, and because she looked so happy, he offered her some more M&M's. She smiled even more broadly. They sat, not saying very much to each other, and then, as he got up to leave, she stood and they hugged each other. He thought that was appropriate.

She did, too. After that, he went on to his grandmother's house. His grandmother noticed that he was smiling happily and she asked, "Why are you so happy? You seemed happier than usual when you arrived here today." He, thinking of his lesson from Sunday school, said, "I have just seen Jesus, and she is really beautiful." At the same time, the woman went to her sister's home, and she also was happy. The sister asked her, "Why are you so happy? You seem so upbeat." She answered, "I have just seen Jesus, and he is younger than you think." The innocence of a child – the sharing, the hope, the hug, the opportunity to give, that spirit; if we would involve ourselves in that kind of innocent spirit, I think we might be surprised whom we might see.

There is also the spirit of forgiveness. Perhaps some of you heard the late Corrie ten Boom speak, with her contagious and powerful witness. She was a Dutch woman who as a child, along with her sister, was taken to The Ravensbrük, a concentration camp. They were there for at least three years and, during that time, spent long hours lamenting how, in prison, they felt they were no longer able to be effective servants of God. After the war was over, Corrie went to several cities in Germany to express the word of forgiveness to the people of Germany. She gave the same speech repeatedly. I once read her description of one of those meetings. "My regular message was, 'I forgive you for what happened to me. When our hearts are contrite, when we are really sorry, God takes all our sins, throws them into the deepest ocean, and then posts the sign that says, *No Fishing Allowed.*' " When her testimony was over, those very staid and stoic Germans would stand up quickly, put on their wraps, smile, and walk out the door. However, one night, after she had given her speech, as everybody else was leaving, she noticed one man pushing his way through the crowd to speak to her. When she saw him, there was a startling flashback. He had on a distinctive old brown coat and a ragged brown hat; the all-too-familiar, frightening uniform the SS guards had worn during the Second World War. The more she stared, the more familiar he looked. She closed her eyes, and for a moment, in her mind's eye, she felt herself transported back to a large room with a light bulb at the end of a single wire, swinging back and forth. She remembered who he was – one of the prison guards! She also remembered the meals, the watery soup and the hard bread, and the piles of clothing and shoes. She remembered what she felt when she and her sister, Betsie, were forced to walk naked, embarrassed and dehumanized, past the guards as they leered at them. She remembered how frail her sister looked.

Then she opened her eyes and he was still coming toward her. She first felt a sense of bitterness, anger, and resentment and she prayed, "God help me. Help me to reach out to this man's hand as he comes to meet me." She closed her eyes again and began to remember the words from her speech she had just given. "If we are contrite, God is faithful and just to forgive us our sins." Then came these words from the Lord's Prayer, "Forgive us our sins, as we forgive others who sin against us." She also remembered the words of her mother, "It is better to forgive and to forget, than to resent and to remember." So, she reached out her hand toward the man, and as she did that, she felt a warm feeling going down her arm and out of her hand to him. As he grasped her hand, she felt that warm feeling all through her body. He didn't recognize her because there had been hundreds of people in the prison camps, but she had definitely recognized him. He said, "I've become a Christian, and I needed to hear exactly what you had to say tonight. Thank you for that message of grace and forgiveness. I needed to hear it from someone who was there; I needed to hear it from the lips of someone who had been in that camp where I was a guard." She responded, "Brother, in the name of Jesus Christ, I forgive you." Afterwards, she began to ask herself, "Where did that strength come from in that moment?" Then she remembered, it came from the power of the Holy Spirit, which,

Paul says, never disappoints us – the spirit of grace and the spirit of forgiveness, the spirit of vision and adventure.

Peter said in that great speech at Pentecost, "I'll pour out my Spirit on all flesh, and your sons and your daughters will prophesy. Those who are young will see visions, and those who are old will dream dreams" (Acts 2:17) – of vision, of adventure, and of risk, reaching out beyond the ordinary!

Every step of faith demands a risk. I found the following poem in a book by a friend, David McKechnie: *Let's Start Over*. The anonymous author of these verses has captured the essence of being empowered by the Spirit to venture into untried territory – testing one's self, trying new things, being vulnerable, standing up for one's faith, trusting and accepting new challenges in the name of Jesus Christ.

> *To laugh is to risk appearing the fool.*
> *To weep is to risk appearing sentimental.*
> *To reach out for another is to risk involvement.*
> *To expose feelings is to risk exposing your true self.*
> *To place your ideas, your dreams, before the crowd is to risk*
> *   loss.*
> *To love is to risk not being loved in return.*
> *To live is to risk dying.*
> *To hope is to risk despair.*
> *To go forward in the face of overwhelming odds is to risk*
> *   failure.*
> *But risk we must.*
> *Because the greatest hazard in life is to risk nothing.*
> *The person who risks nothing does nothing, has nothing, is*
> *   nothing.*
> *One may avoid suffering and sorrow, but he cannot learn,*
> *   feel change, grow, or love.*
> *Only a person who risks is totally free and totally alive!*

Stepping out in faith, courageously and confidently taking risks for Christ's sake, is a fundamental part of what it means to trust in the promises, power, and presence of the Holy Spirit.

Well, where is this Spirit? How is it available to us? The psalmist said, in the passage we heard today from Psalm 139, "Where could I go to escape your Spirit? Where could I flee from your Presence?" – a rhetorical question, which he also answers. "If I ascend to heaven, you are there. If I make my bed in Sheol, you are there also. If I take the wings in the morning and dwell in the uttermost parts of the sea, even there your hand shall guide me, and your right hand shall lead." So, when the psalmist asks us the same rhetorical questions, "Where can we go to flee your Spirit? Where could we go from your presence?", we can join him and respond with a confident, decisive answer: "Nowhere!" – God is always present with us!

Likewise, in John 14:16,17, Jesus makes a promise to His disciples, "I will pray to the Father, and He will *give* you an Advocate (or Helper) to be with you forever. This is the Spirit of Truth. . . ." God is the "Divine Giver!" As B. B. Warfield has said, "The fundamental fact in all revelation is that it is a *Gift from God!*" God's Spirit is a *gift*, which is always available to anyone who sincerely seeks Him.

Because the confirmands are here today, I want to tell a story that I heard from my friend, Tom Long, who is a professor of homiletics at Candler School of Theology. He spoke about a confirmation class in a church where the young people had about eight weeks of training. When the class was over, they came and stood in front of the sanctuary facing the congregation. The teacher of the class asked a question of each of the class members. On this particular day, the question from the teacher was, "Jimmy, who can separate you from the love of Christ?" Quoting from Romans 8, Jimmy said, "I am absolutely convinced that neither death, nor life, nor messenger of heaven, nor monarch of earth, neither what happens today, nor what may happen tomorrow, neither a power from on high, nor a power from below, nor anything else in God's whole world, has any power to separate us from His love, made known to us in Jesus Christ our Lord." Jimmy smiled, his parents smiled, and the people smiled. The teacher went to the next person, and the next and the next, always the same question, and each time the answer given was the full quotation from Romans 8. Then the congregation became somewhat anxious, because down at the end of the line they saw Rachel. Rachel had an easy grace, a very warm smile, and genuine kindness. However, Rachel also had Down Syndrome. The congregation knew that. Everybody there knew that there was no way in the world that Rachel could ever memorize that passage of Scripture from Romans 8. The closer they got to the end of the line, the more anxious the congregation became, because they didn't want this little girl to be embarrassed. Yet the teacher went right ahead and asked the question. "Rachel, what can separate you from the love of Christ?" There was a brief hesitation, and then with that genuine, warm smile on her face, Rachel just said, "Nothing." *Now that's the Spirit!*

WHAT HAPPENS WHEN WE PRAY TOGETHER?

II Corinthians 1:8-11
Job 42:1-10

Have you noticed how dependent we have all become on the "remote control?" Many of us have become listless, and way out of shape. In fact, I recently heard someone ask this question; "How do you get men to do their exercise?" The answer was, "Put the TV remote control between their toes, so that at least they will do a few sit-ups." That might seem a little silly and frivolous, but when was the last time that you can recall actually getting up to walk across the room in order to turn on the television set or change the channel? Oh, you may have done it when the battery died in the remote control and you were forced to manual operation. It seems as though most of us like to have a special button that we can push from across the room, across the field, or across the office, which would give us remote control over whatever is happening.

The truth is that we live in a world of remote control. There is a remote control for almost everything: TV's, VCR's, stereos, model airplanes, car doors, personal computers, telephones, electric fans, camcorders. That all seems somewhat silly and trivial. However, the silliness disappears immediately when we begin to realize that our desire for a remote control style of living is found not simply in

189

electronics, but frequently finds its way into the way we treat each other and, perhaps, even in the way we relate to God.

One reason we like remote control so much is that it puts us in complete control. The operative word there is "control"; we have control about what we want to watch and hear, and we love that. The troubling issue here for us, however, is that we have a desire for remote control in our spiritual living, as well. I think that sometimes we use prayer as a device to get the proper channels that we seek, the programs that we want, the selfish desires that we long for. Has the phenomenon of remote control become so much a part of our lives that we have become so accustomed to it that we have lost the relevance and the significance of prayer – personal prayer, the power of prayer, reality of prayer, or intimacy of prayer? Nowhere is the power, reality, and intimacy of prayer seen more fully and more clearly than in intercessory prayer: praying for others, interceding for others, praying for and with others, praying together. The theologian, P. T. Forsyth, says, "The intercessory prayers of Jesus in the Gospel accounts are, for me, more significant and more impelling than the wonderful miracle stories."

What we have in this text from II Corinthians is a description from Paul of intercessory prayer, and the need for it. He talks about a great affliction that he and the others had in Asia. He wants the people to know how difficult it was there. They almost despaired of life itself. They felt they were under a sentence of death, but God had rescued them. And then, Paul makes this personal plea, "Please join us in helping us by your prayers, that through the prayers of many, we might rejoice together." He was inviting them to join in intercessory prayer, praying for and with each other, "Praying Together."

The basic question for us today is what is this prayer? How does it work? What happens when we engage in intercessory personal prayer? I suggest to you, first of all, that when we pray together in

190

intercessory prayer, something happens *to us*. It has a very definite impact. It has a very recognizable effect upon us. We hear from the last chapter of Job about his repentance from his sin – how he humbles himself. He is then able to forgive his friends who had wronged him, and he begins to pray for them. That is the point at which God gave him a double portion of all that he had possessed before. Please notice here, that the answer to Job's prayer was not because he whined, or begged, or was angry with God, or accusatory or critical of God. The reward came because Job prayed for his friends. Something happened to Job because he prayed a prayer of intercession for his friends. The spiritual reward was that Job was able to be more forgiving, gracious, and faithful than he had ever been before.

Arthur John Gossip, the great Scottish preacher, once asked a woman who prayed extensively for members of the parish if there was time to pray for herself. She replied modestly, "No, but it must not matter to God, for I have been regularly blessed beyond my imagination." Something had happened to her when she prayed for others.

When we pray together, and we pray for each other, something happens to us. This unselfish, generous, genuine prayer has its own special reward, in and of it itself. It is not a material reward, or the offer of power or position. It is, rather, what happens *to us* within our souls. Our minds are transformed; our attitudes are changed – ill will becomes friendship, dislike becomes love, indifference becomes compassion, and exclusion becomes acceptance. Do you have anybody that doesn't really like you and, perhaps, you don't like them – somebody who irritates you, who is hostile towards you, who has accosted you? What do you do with people like this? Well, let me suggest to you the best thing to do for people who irritate you, with whom you have difference of opinion, who dislike you and you dislike them. The best thing you can possibly do is to *pray for them*!

Years ago, on a work-camp mission trip in Booneville, Kentucky, we met a family who had been living there all their lives. We met the man who was head of his household. He told us that they lived in the lower end of the holler. At the upper end, there was another family. These families had a feud that had gone on for years. They didn't speak, and if they did speak, it was only in anger or with threats. Then he said, "But now we are friends; we are good neighbors." We asked, "Well, how can that be? What made the difference?" He said, "Because we began to pray for each other." Then he said something I have never forgotten, "Something happened to us when we began to pray. It's hard to hate somebody you pray for."

That is really true! It is hard to dislike someone you pray for; it is hard to be angry with those for whom you pray. Jesus said, "What good is it for you to pray just for the people who love you?" If that is all you do, you'll never learn, you'll never grow. In fact, Jesus told us that we need to pray for our enemies. Mother Teresa said, "When you have intercessory prayers as a part of your devotional life, listen very carefully, because you may well discover that something may be happening to you and through you; you may actually be the answer." Something may happen *to us*!

In intercessory prayer, when praying for others, praying with others, praying together, something happens *to us*. But also something happens *to others* for whom we pray. We find them receiving healing, hope, joy, and confidence. I don't want to suggest that we always get all the answers that we expect – the things that we want, exactly as we ask for them. But I do suggest this to you, that if we are obedient, patient, observant, and perceptive enough, we may begin to discover answers that we could find no other way.

There is an example of this in the medical world. Dr. Leonard Dossi wrote an article called "Healing Hurts." He was being interviewed on television about his article and he made this comment, "There is an astonishing number of articles in medical journals, all around the country and all around the world, about the therapeutic value of prayer with suffering patients." The example he gave was Dr. Randolph Byrd, a cardiologist from San Francisco, who is also a professor at the Medical School of California. In his research, Dr. Byrd discovered some very fascinating facts. He talked to two groups of people who had been his patients. First, he spoke to those who had received regular pastoral care (calls from pastors and people in the church). They were people who had a personal prayer life, and who had people praying for them from afar. He also had another group to whom he spoke, who said they had little or no pastoral care. They didn't have a personal prayer life, and they were not aware of anybody praying for them.

Sometimes we are skeptical about the scientific value of this kind of research. It wasn't very broad; however, the facts are fascinating. Dr. Byrd's research revealed that the group that had been prayed for had required far fewer antibiotics. There was less development of pulmonary edema. They had little or no need of ventilation, had the lowest number of deaths in that period of time, and were usually released much sooner. Well, how do we assess this? What is the credibility of this type of research? One answer came from Dr. William Nolan, a surgeon, who had once written an article debunking faith healing. However, after seeing this research, he said, "It sounds like this study stands up to scrutiny." Then, he confessed a change of heart, "Perhaps the doctors should write more regularly on the order sheets for their patients, 'Pray three times a day.' " The Apostle Paul puts his prescription this way: "Pray without ceasing!"

We have evidence of this kind of successful prayer. We can see it all around us, every day. However, sometimes when prayers are answered and we see the results, we say that it must be a coincidence. I love what William Temple once said, "When I pray, coincidences happen. When I don't pray, they don't happen anymore." We can pray honestly and openly *because we expect things to happen.*

Some people have said it is arrogant for us to pray for others; it's self-righteous and judgmental for us to pray for others. Let me say this to you: If we really believe that God hears our prayers, if we really believe that God answers our prayers – provides unexpected answers different from what we have asked – if we really believe, then the only thing that is arrogant and self-righteous and judgmental is *not to* pray for them.

Something happens to us when we pray for others, and something happens to them. But also, finally, something happens *with God*. Notice I didn't say "to God." Something happens "with God." Please notice that. Prayer is not some kind of religious scheme that manipulates God into our way of thinking. Prayer is not some kind of ceremonial, ritualistic scheme, nudging God in our direction, getting God's attention, inducing God to think and act like we want God to act. Prayer is not taking a shopping list to God for all the things we want. Leave that for Santa Claus and the Easter Bunny!

Prayer for me has something to do with the intimate companionship I can have with God – the God who is "with us." Last Tuesday night, I spoke to a group of students at Kent State University in Ohio. One of the students said that, early in his life, he began to think that God was simply the creator who had made the world, and then sat up in a big celestial balcony to watch it all work out. But then he testified, "Now, as I have come to know Christ, I have discovered, through my prayers, that God is a vital presence in my life." Let me suggest to you that is exactly what prayer is for me, and I hope it is for you. Sometimes we are so egotistical that we act as though we think we know what God wants. We just need to remind Him about what our wants are. As one person said recently (and I hope somewhat facetiously), "I'm only doing and saying what God would do and say, if He knew all the facts."

Prayer is not a scheme, nor is it a scream. Prayer is having personal conversations or dialogue with God. It is being in companionship with God. It is being in tune with God. It is sensing the presence of God. When we have that kind of experience of prayer, when we sense we are in the presence of God, we are open to growth, to a very rich, powerful, spiritual experience. We become different people. We become more willing to trust God in what He says. We become more willing to love our neighbors more openly. We become more willing to forgive irrational, angry, hostile behavior, and refuse to hold a grudge. We are more concerned with redemption and reconciliation than we are with revenge. We are more willing to recognize and identify the needs, hurts, sufferings, and pains of others, and more ready to respond in a genuine, authentic, tangible way. We become more willing to be vulnerable, to sacrifice for others, and lay our lives on the line for them. We are more interested in reading God's Word and discovering what it says to us on a daily basis. We are more disciplined and persistent in our prayer life. We are more confident in what it is that God is making possible for us to become – "new creatures in Christ." We are more open to those broad "channels" of love and those wide "programs" of God's grace and power that are not "remote" or separated from us, but are with us. Those "programs" and those "channels" never need to be changed.

When we have that kind of relationship with God, we begin to develop a childlike trust, a conviction, a confidence, a hope that God is at work in our lives – a sense of God's presence. Several years ago, my wife and I were visiting in a home where they have three children. After dinner, the parents said, "Time to go to bed. Go up and say your prayers." The two boys ran up first. The little girl was a bit more deliberate. Halfway up the stairs, she stopped, turned around, looked at us, waved her arm and said, "Anybody need anything?" Oh, for that kind of childlike innocence, insight, instinct, intensity, and awareness of God's presence in life, to be able to pray with that kind of confidence, and that kind of assurance. The great hymn says, *"What a friend we have in Jesus, all our sins and griefs to bear."* Even though it doesn't work with the meter and the music, I'd like to sing it this way: "What a *presence* we have *with* Jesus, all our joys and cares to share. What a privilege to carry everything to God in prayer."

When we are praying for each other, when we are praying with each other, when we are praying together, something happens *to us*, something happens *to others*, and something happens *with God* in His presence with us. That is our calling; that is our duty as disciples and our challenge in the Church of Jesus Christ, whether it is this congregation or the Church in general. God is calling us to a life of intercessory prayer.

Charlie Shedd, the great pastor, preacher, and author, came to our church in Flint, Michigan, a few years ago. After speaking for a two-day seminar, the next morning he came to our staff meeting. He had an enlightening and encouraging conversation with all of us about what might happen in our church program. He also shared what was happening in his own life and in his own church. At the end of our conversation, one of our staff members asked, "Charlie, what is it that you 'said' to bring about all of this success; what did you 'say' to be able to achieve your dreams and goals in your church and in your own life?" Charlie paused for a moment and then answered, "I guess it was, 'Let us pray.' "

When I think of the world in which we live, with hunger and homelessness, depression and despair, uncertainty and anxiety, the fear of terrorism, and the threat of war; when I think in terms of the Church, and particularly this church, when I think of the present situation in which we find ourselves as we look for growth, for healing, for mission outreach, for education, understanding of God's Word, for a sense of presence and an awareness of who we really are; when I think of our need as a church for a future, for the vision, for what can and must take place here, for the gifts God will provide to help make things happen; when I think of all that, I often wonder what would be the best thing I could say to help facilitate it all. And then I think of Charlie Shedd and remember that he was absolutely right. The best thing for all of us to say is "Let us pray!"

IT'S ALL ABOUT ATTITUDE

Genesis 50:15-23
II Corinthians 4:7-18

To me, it seems like a very long time ago, perhaps to you as well, that we were completely captivated by, and mesmerized by, the drama unfolding in Somerset County at the Quecreek Mine. Nine miners were trapped 240 feet beneath the surface, and the drama, which went on for three days, not only captivated us, but also people all around the world. Perhaps, as I, you stayed up part, or all, of the night to see the outcome; what would happen. Shortly after eleven o'clock, we heard the good news: "All nine are alive!" Nine for nine! Then at 1:30 a.m. and 2:30 a.m. and 3 a.m., we watched until all nine had been brought to the surface; all of us experienced an overwhelming sense of relief. It is something we will never forget.

The next day at the press conference, at Conemaugh Hospital in Johnstown, the trauma surgeon was asked about the conditions of these nine men. He said that, for the most part, they were in very good shape. Eventually, someone asked how they had survived this ordeal. He said that the pumping of the water out of the mine, and the opening of the six-inch line of air that was sent down immediately, were crucial steps. He also added that it was their training that had taught them to do exactly what they needed to do. They found a lunch box floating that still had a small lunch in it and a thermos of Mountain Dew. They parceled it out as long as they could, so that each one would have some small, regular amount of nourishment. They huddled around each other to keep warm, tying themselves together so that they would not be lost in the darkness. They shared two small headlamps, turning them on only occasionally to preserve the batteries. Then the surgeon said, "But most important of all, it was their attitude." And then, as an aside, he added, "After all, it's all about attitude."

We seem to talk frequently about our attitude – what is our attitude? The word "attitude" can be very neutral, or it can be very negative. We look at someone who has been very egotistical and self-centered, and we say, "*She* has an attitude!" Or we observe someone who has been greedy, has deceived and misled other people around him, and we say, "*He* has an attitude!" There are times in Scripture when we see people with a poor attitude; an attitude that is not positive or hopeful. For instance, Elijah, who had conquered the prophets of Baal, cries in fear, "I am totally alone, forever." Moses says, "It would not be wise for me to go to free the Israelites from Egypt, because I can't speak well. Send someone else instead of me." The whole Book of Lamentations is a series of bad attitudes and bad feelings. Jesus, Himself, said, "Woe to you scribes, Pharisees and hypocrites because of your bad attitude, your greed, your jealousy, your judgmental way, and your legalistic way." (paraphrase)

We must not forget that in Scripture there's the positive view – a positive attitude which is the bottom line of Scripture; all the way through the Word, we find a positive message. I think in Proverbs, the writer is speaking positively, when he says, "As we think, so we are." Speaking for the Lord, Jeremiah says, "I know the plans I have for you, plans for good and not evil, to give you a future and a hope." Jesus makes it clear in at least two instances: one, when He says, "With God, all things are possible." (Matthew 19:26); and, again, in

Mark 9:23, when He reminds a father of a sick son that, "Everything is possible to one who believes." The Bible encourages us today to think in ways that give us that positive attitude – to think positively. Norman Vincent Peale proclaimed that message throughout his whole life: "The power of positive thinking," which he interpreted directly from the Scripture. Now Robert Schuller has a similar phrase, "Possibility thinking." Both preachers remind us of Scripture's direction to think positively.

Our thoughts are part of our lives – twenty-four hours a day; there is no question about that. The late Carl Menninger said that our thoughts are part of our lives all the time; whether we are resting or working, or dreaming, or playing; they are always with us. In fact, he said that ninety-three percent of life is thought-directed, and our thoughts can have either a good or bad effect on us. Sometimes we are unable to recover from illness because we have a negative attitude. We also know that when we are beginning to heal from an illness, it is often because our attitude has improved. The color of our thoughts reflects the way we live.

The prevailing message in Scripture is that we have a choice. Scripture makes it clear that we can make choices as to how we feel, how we behave, and what we do. Paul makes it very clear in Romans, when he says, "Do not be conformed to this world, but be transformed by the renewing of your mind (your thinking); that you might prove what is good and acceptable and perfect; the will of God." Paul, who, himself, faced all kinds of difficulty and hardship in travel, imprisonment, persecution, chains, and criticism, maintained this strong positive attitude. Our text today reflects this positive attitude of the Apostle Paul and the positive attitude, which should be for each one of us. In II Corinthians, the fourth chapter, beginning at verse 7:

"But we have this treasure in clay jars, so that it may be made clear that this extraordinary power belongs to God and does not

come from us. We are afflicted in every way, but not crushed; perplexed, but not driven to despair; persecuted, but not forsaken; struck down, but not destroyed; always carrying in the body the death of Jesus, so that the life of Jesus may also be made visible in our bodies. For while we live, we are always being given up to death for Jesus' sake, so that the life of Jesus may be made visible in our mortal flesh. So death is at work in us, but life in you. But just as we have the same spirit of faith that is in accordance with Scripture – 'I believed, and so I spoke' – we also believe, and so we speak, because we know that the one who raised the Lord Jesus will raise us also with Jesus, and will bring us with you into His presence. Yes, everything is for your sake, so that grace, as it extends to more and more people, may increase thanksgiving, to the glory of God."

This positive attitude, which we are instructed to have, which we are invited to have in our faith, can lead to positive consequences, giving lasting effects; giving us a very optimistic, edifying dimension to life, and a direction for the life which we are to live. We find this attitude in several areas, which I think are revealed directly and indirectly in this passage today.

First of all, our positive attitude should begin with the element of forgiveness, grace, and reconciliation. Paul says, "As grace extends to more and more people (as forgiveness extends to more and more people, as reconciliation and redemption extends to more and more people), it may increase thanksgiving to the glory of God." As we extend our forgiveness and offer reconciliation, we increase thanksgiving to God's glory, in us and through us. This is not easy. When someone attacks, threatens, or insults us, there is an inclination for most of us to engage in retaliation or revenge. It is much easier for most of us to carry a grudge than it is to carry a cross. But, we are called to forgive! Most of us have heard the phrase, "I'll forgive, but I won't forget." Quite frankly, friends, if we haven't forgotten, we haven't forgiven. God forgets. God wipes it away! God says, "As far as the east is from the west, so far have I removed your transgressions from you." (Psalm 103:12) It is wiped out! When Christ gave us forgiveness from sin, it was wiped out. It is not held to us any longer. We are no longer guilty, because, as Paul says, Christ, who could have condemned us, instead, "died for us, prayed for us, rose again for us, and reigns in power for us." We are forgiven unconditionally and completely.

When we refuse to forgive others, and sometimes even ourselves, we are denying the cleansing power of the cross that can change us. When we forgive others, our mood is changed and it brings about reconciliation with those who have offended us. When Steven Spielberg, the successful movie director, was a little boy, he was a very frail child who wore big glasses and was the smallest in his class. One of his hobbies was to make movies with an old wind-up 8-millimeter camera. One day, his mother even allowed him to skip school, going with him out into the Arizona desert to make a home movie. Being a small and frail child, he was often the object of teasing and torment by bullies in the schoolyard. One day, a particular bully came up to him and began to push him around and threaten him. Steven's response shocked his tormentor: "I'm going to make a movie, and I want you to be the star." I am told that to this day, Spielberg and that bully are very good friends. In fact, I have been told that the bully now works for Steven Spielberg.

What happens when we forgive; when we take the initiative, go on the offensive and give forgiveness and bring about reconciliation? There is a radiant change. When Abraham Lincoln offered to pardon all those Southerners who had left the union, one woman attacked him and said, "That is not your job as President. You are not supposed to forgive them. You are supposed to destroy your enemies." Lincoln's thoughtful, profound response was, "Have I not destroyed my enemies when I have made them my friends?" What an amazing attitude – in fact, it is an awesome example of "Amazing Grace."

The story in the Old Testament of Joseph and his brothers is also helpful. After he had helped them, they suddenly realized who he was and they remembered what they had done to him, sending him off, selling him to the merchants of Egypt. And now, here he was in charge of their welfare, their security, and their lives. They became fearful and apprehensive, wondering what he might do to them. "Please forgive us!" they pleaded. That is when we hear that gracious, forgiving response of Joseph, "You meant it to me for evil, God meant it for me for good; therefore, fear not." As a kid, I used to romanticize about that story because it was one of my favorites. I used to ask my mother to read it over and over again, about Joseph and his multi-colored coat, and the brothers, who, in jealousy, sold him to traveling traders, and how he later became an assistant to the king. At first, I found myself identifying with Joseph's magnanimous phrase: "I'm going to forgive you." However, as I became older and more realistic, and perhaps a little more mature, there were times when I could also identify with the brothers, remembering what it is like to receive forgiveness. That immediately improves and broadens my attitude; I'm not just the giver, I am also the receiver of forgiveness.

How we need that gift of forgiveness in our day! Last April, on our way to Malawi, we stopped in South Africa. We visited Soweto, where the great battles over apartheid occurred. We saw the bullet marks on the walls of Nelson Mandela's home. Since returning home, I've looked up some of Nelson Mandela's speeches. I found this statement, which he made after his inauguration as president. He stated, "Without our enemies, if we do not include them, we can never come to a peaceful and hopeful solution to our dilemma. We need to have them. The reason the world has opened itself to South Africa is because we have brought ourselves together with our enemies, those who oppose us, and we have said, sitting down together, 'Let us stop the slaughter so that we may begin to talk and live in mercy, peace, and unity.' " O that the spirit, which was accomplished in South Africa and is still being accomplished there, could find its way into the Middle East. But not just there – it is easy for us to point in that direction. O that the spirit of being together, talking, forgiving, sharing, and having dialogue would appear when we have struggles in our domestic situations; in our homes, in racial crises, in political disputes, in those times when our class separation between the wealthy and the poor makes us a little too proud – or possibly, a little too disengaged. *It is all about attitude,* the attitude of forgiveness, grace, redemption. "As grace increases to more and more people, extends to more and more people, it increases thanksgiving, and it increases glory to God."

Secondly, we need the positive attitude in overcoming difficulties – to have persistence and perseverance. We have heard these words many times, but please, hear them again; "We have this treasure in earthen vessels to show the transcendent power belongs to God and not to us. We are afflicted in every way, but not crushed; perplexed, but not driven to despair; persecuted, but not forsaken; struck down, but not destroyed; always carrying in the body the death of Jesus, so the life of Christ may also be visible in us" – who we are and what we do. How reassuring it is to realize that we have the possibility of having an attitude that can overcome any difficulty, any struggle, any sorrow, any disappointment, or any defeat we face. We have the possibility of coming out of the valley into a new light, a new hope. We just need to dare to dream, to dream beyond where we are when things in life get very heavy.

What kind of dreams do you have in terms of your life where you are right now? Where would you like to be in your dreams? Where do your dreams enhance the work of the Kingdom of God? – the work of God? – the purpose of God? I encourage you to dare to dream because your dreams are important to you. What is your dream? What is your attitude about times of defeat in your life? What is your willingness to sacrifice and stretch in new directions?

There are many examples of people who have been willing to sacrifice and stretch. Rudyard Kipling's first works were rejected because the publisher said he didn't know how to use words well. George Orwell wrote his book, *Animal Farm* (which, by the way, had nothing at all to do with animals), but the publisher in this country said, "We can't use that here because animal stories don't sell well in the USA." Walt Disney's first editor at a newspaper fired him because he "wasn't creative." Michael Jordan was cut from his high school basketball team. Dr. Seuss submitted his works to a publisher twenty-three times before they were finally accepted. How popular they have become! Someone asked Thomas Edison if he became discouraged because he had tried 1,011 experiments before finally making the first light bulb. He answered, "No, I just found 1,011 ways not to make a light bulb."

We need to make those kinds of positive choices; the choices that move us forward in a positive direction. The late James Malone, a friend who was bishop of the Catholic Diocese in Youngstown, Ohio, told me about going to a church where he was asked to do the children's sermon. He was caught off-guard. He hesitated, because he was not accustomed to doing children's messages. Remembering he was the bishop, he asked, "OK, children, what does a bishop do?" The children looked at him for a moment, and finally one little boy said, "They move diagonally." We must not move diagonally, or in reverse, but straight ahead – forward – making our choice to step ahead with God, in the right direction.

I can attest to you, as I am sure you can also to me, how in times of great defeat and great discouragement, it would have been very easy to feel self-pity, and grovel, and become depressed. But with God's help, our attitude can overcome our struggles. Ken Medema, the blind piano player, composer, and singer who has worked with Billy Graham, and on several television programs, recently said on Robert Schuller's *Hour of Power* broadcast, "Very often, a very deep setback can merely be the prelude to a strong comeback." What an attitude! *It is all about attitude.* We don't stop playing because we have grown old; we grow old because we stopped playing. We don't stop dreaming and daring because we have grown old; we grow old because we don't dream anymore; we don't dare anymore. I dare you to pray if you are in a difficult time or in a difficult struggle. I dare you to reach out to find that positive attitude, that strength, and that power, which God can give you. The late Karl Barth, the theologian, said that when we clasp our hands in prayer, it is the beginning of the discovery of a new attitude, which can overcome any struggle in the world. *It is all about attitude!*

Thirdly, there is an attitude of hope. We have hope. Paul said in the same passage, "So we do not lose heart, though the outer nature is wasting away, the inner nature is being renewed everyday. For this slight momentary affliction is preparing us for an eternal way to glory, beyond all measure, for we look not to things that are seen, but the things that are unseen."

Sheila Weinberg, in her book, *Healing the Heart: Healing the Planet*, tells about a friend of hers who has an Aunt Margaret. As Aunt Margaret became older and older, she began to lose the ability to speak. Finally, she could only say three words. When you engaged her in conversation or asked her a question, her first response would be either *temporary* or *unexpected*. Sheila and her friend began to realize how accurate that was. She may not have been able to say a lot of words, but she still knew what life is about. Life is very temporary. We can easily see that life is transient – temporary. Much of life is also unexpected. We don't know what will happen next. Life is what happens when we are making other plans. But she also had a third word, and that word was said always with a smile. It was *hope*. Life is very temporary, life is very unexpected, but for those of us who believe, it is also filled with hope. For Paul says, "We look not to things that are *temporary* (unexpected), but to things that are

205

eternal (hopeful). For the things that are seen are temporary; the things that are unseen are eternal."

Victor Frankl, who was a prisoner in a concentration camp, once wrote this, "We, who lived in concentration camps, remember the small numbers of people who would go from hut to hut, bringing comfort and small portions of the pieces of their own bread to share. Their numbers were small, but they were significant proof of the evidence that people can take everything away from us, except one last thing. That one last thing is the human freedom to display, exercise, and use our attitude of hope, in spite of the circumstances." Everything can be taken away from us, except the freedom to exercise and express our attitude of hope. That is an enormous comfort. Paul said, "If we live, we live to the Lord; if we die, we die to the Lord. So, whether we live or whether we die, we are the Lord's." What an attitude! – an attitude of forgiveness, cleansing, perseverance, and hope!

Edward Mote wrote the hymn that we will sing at the last part of the service, "My Hope Is Built on Nothing Less." He wrote it in 1834. He wrote it in the morning, and later in the afternoon he met a certain Mr. King, a neighbor and friend. Mr. King asked him if he would kindly visit with his wife in their home because she was quite ill and very depressed. Edward Mote had a regular habit of visiting shut-ins. He would always sing a hymn, read some Scripture, and have a prayer. That day, when he went directly to the home of Mrs. King, he didn't have his hymnbook or his Bible. However, in his pocket he had the words of the hymn he had just written. It was not the tune that we sing today, but he sang those words to her, "On Christ, the solid rock, I stand, all other ground is sinking sand. . . ." After which she said, "Your words have given me a new attitude for my life" (a solid attitude of hope, forgiveness, persistence, and perseverance).

In the film *Gandhi*, Ben Kingsley portrayed the lead character, Mahatma Gandhi, the Hindu religious leader who, through his strong advocacy of and commitment to non-violence, achieved independence for India from England. Through the miracle of make-up, Kingsley was an exact likeness of the revered hero of the Indian people. One day, when the crews were setting up lighting and camera angles, Kingsley, in full costume, wandered off. A few moments later, he found himself on a lonely back street where he encountered a very old man. When the man saw Kingsley, he came to him, dropped face forward, weeping, and wrapped his arms around the actor's ankles. Kingsley was dismayed, and just slightly embarrassed. He immediately drew back attempting to explain, "No! No! I'm not who you think I am!" The man rose up on his knees and looked up, still with tears in his eyes, and said, "Oh, I know who you are. I just hope that somehow, through your story, you can help us all regain the attitude of peace and freedom and love."

Obviously, it is not good to have a "Messiah Complex." The world knows that we are not Jesus. However, if we are obedient and faithful, if we are open to the working of the Spirit in our lives, we may be able to reflect His message to the world in which we live! Paul says that when we pray, "we do not lose heart," because we are focusing on the things of Christ, which are eternal. We discover what it means to be a Christian – a positive, hopeful servant and messenger for Christ – reflecting the attitude and love of Christ. In Christ, we can be empowered to be a forgiving, graceful, reconciling people; we can be a people courageous enough to walk through every deep and threatening valley to accomplish our dreams, and faithful enough to maintain an attitude of confidence and hope, no matter what the circumstances. "It is, after all, all about our attitude," our attitude with and for our Savior, Jesus Christ. As I ponder about that promise, I remember that my hope (my attitude) is built on nothing less than Jesus' grace and righteousness. Amen.

(The congregation then sang the hymn "My Hope Is Built on Nothing Less than Jesus' Blood and Righteousness.")

SIGNIFICANT PURSUIT

Colossians 3:1-4, 15-17

Most of you are familiar with the game that began twenty some years ago called Trivial Pursuit. It is a game that involves answering one unimportant question after another until the players discover that somebody has answered most of the inconsequential questions, achieving some kind of dubious victory. When I've played that game, I found that the answers were not only trivial but also, at the same time, somewhat enigmatic. Questions like, "How many fingers did Anne Boleyn have? – What vegetable provides the most poundage per acre? – Who among the movie stars was a distant cousin of Lady Di? – What was Hitler's favorite movie? – What was the score of Super Bowl Nine?" (That is not so trivial to me because Pittsburgh played in that game). What I discovered in playing the trivia game is the fixation that many of us have when we become preoccupied and obsessed with minutia. People have become so obsessed that they write books about it. The television programs *Who Wants to Be a Millionaire*, *Jeopardy*, and *Wheel of Fortune* are all based upon answering trivial questions. I heard of a woman who, when the game

Trivial Pursuit first came out, read all the cards in the game, with the hope that when she played the game she would remember enough of the trifling answers to win.

Pondering this phenomenon, I recall the words of T. S. Eliot, when he asked these poetic questions, "Where is the wisdom that is lost in the knowledge? Where is the knowledge that is lost in the information?" That is exactly the point. When we become so obsessed and preoccupied with trivial things, we discover that we run the danger of having lots of facts and very little wisdom; an abundance of information with no knowledge. Paul Tournier, a Swiss psychologist/psychiatrist, said that when we emphasize and concentrate on the trivial, there is usually a noticeable lack of standards and values in our living. This produces a situation where we have developed a bargain-basement philosophy, ideology, or theology. You know what a bargain is. A bargain is something that you can't use, that has a price you cannot resist. It is not worth anything!

If all of that is true, we need to evaluate ourselves, to be reflective, in order to see what our top priorities and primary pursuits are in life. One anonymous poet asked this question, "If there were dreams to sell, what would you buy?" When we look around, we see that we have an abundance of possibilities, a great diversity of opportunities, a plethora of possibilities that are fully available to us. The questions remain: What are we willing to buy? To what will we give our greatest efforts and exert our greatest energy? What will we give of ourselves to make that life which we are seeking significant? What would we buy if the dreams are actually for sale, especially when we look at some of the priorities toward which we drive ourselves?

I would suggest to you that one dream for sale is materialism, a preoccupation with possessions rather than things intellectual or spiritual. That is very easy to do because we are naturally inclined to possess things, to own them. Ten years ago in the *Houston Chronicle* newspaper, there was an article about Robert Lee Blaffen II – known by his initials, R.L. It was said in the article that he had died of a self-inflicted gunshot wound. Everybody in the community knew that he was the grandson of the founder of Exxon and the great-grandson of the founder of Texaco. He was known as a recluse who was unemployed most of the time. His only accomplishment mentioned in the article was that he spent his life collecting, buying, and selling Mercedes and other valuable cars. That is sad and disturbing to us, when we think of all the potential he had. He had a great heritage, was an heir to a vast fortune, and owned a large estate. Yet with all that potential, he did not give his life to anything meaningful, comprehensive, or productive.

How disturbing and unsettling it is to hear a personal history like this. However, it challenges us to stop and think about the philosophy by which many of us live. Recently, I saw a well-worn bumper sticker, which promised, "The one who has the most toys when he dies, wins." That would be funny, if it weren't so true. We try to accumulate many things, because that has become *the goal* for many of us – how much do we possess? How much can we own? I found it very perturbing, not long ago, on the front page of one of the sports sections, that there were more articles about the amount of money that the professional athletes were making, than there were articles about the games they were playing; more emphasis on, and interest in, the millions they acquired, rather than in their athletic achievements; more interest in possession, than on performance. In spite of all the money that is there, in spite of valuable cars and the amount of toys we collect – all of which may seem very important at certain times in our lives – it is still very true that, in the great scheme of things, all of that which we consider our possessions, our belongings, is very trivial. Perhaps that is why Jesus spent so much time in the Gospel accounts talking about money and possessions. He confronts us with the need to see where we concentrate our energy; He reminds us, "Where your treasure is, there will your heart be also."

We often overemphasize the goal of success and personal fame, the accolades of people around us. We want to succeed, and that becomes the preeminent driving force in our lives. Claire Booth Luce, for a number of years, was a congresswoman from Connecticut, later becoming the ambassador from the United States to the Vatican. She was also a playwright; a truly brilliant woman with an ebullient, gracious personality. At seventy-five, someone asked her if she had any regrets in her life. She replied, "When I was fifty-six, one of my very best friends was dying of a brain tumor. She asked me three times to come and visit, but I was always too busy 'succeeding.' When the news came of her death, I was chagrined, embarrassed, humiliated, and mortified, because the opportunity to minister to my dear friend had been squelched, and passed me by. I began to realize that all the things I had been doing were very trivial – everything else didn't matter." Searching for success always comes in second place, when measured against that which is eternal.

What about winning? That is another one of our dreams. We like to win. We like to hear that we're number one. It is certainly OK when a team is undefeated to say, "We are number one." But sometimes, even if our team has lost six games in a row and then has won the seventh game, we still claim to be number one. It is quite an interesting phenomenon. We are number one! We like to win! The late Vince Lombardi, who was the popular coach of the Green Bay Packers, often used a phrase which was attributed fairly or unfairly to him: "Winning is not everything, it is the ONLY thing." Now that may be a very good phrase for motivating one's team, but if we take that philosophy to the bottom line, we see exactly what it is suggesting – when winning is the only thing, it means that sportsmanship, fairness, and the rules of the game do not count. We try to win at any cost – the end justifies the means. Wanting to win, to be in first-place, becomes our primary preoccupation and motivation.

There is another dream we are too willing to buy into, and it is that life is merely about the pursuit of pleasure: having fun. If there is one negative commentary on the last half of the twentieth century, it is hedonism, the doctrine and lifestyle that seeks only what is entertaining and amusing, and which seeks only pleasant consequences with no pain. The mantra is, "If it feels good, do it."

One actress in Hollywood said, "I would do anything, as long as I could have fun!" Anything? Does that mean that we are free to hurt someone else, or to disregard human values, just so that we can have fun? Does it mean just giving up all high moral and ethical values and standards, rationalizing anything, just to have fun? Having made that assertion, the actress added, "It says, after all, in one of our documents (she wasn't sure which one), it is our right to have happiness." She was wrong! In the opening of the Declaration of Independence, it says that "the *'pursuit'* of happiness" is the *"right"* we have. It is so easy for us to want only pleasure, to love only those things that are fun, and, as a result, miss that which really brings happiness and joy into our lives, the adventure of *pursuing* that which is good, true, and of divine value.

Many of us are in such a hurry navigating our overloaded schedule that we find ourselves constantly struggling to save time. As a result, often we move beyond the things that endure, those things that have lasting beauty or value. When we were in the Soviet Union in 1986, our first stop was in Leningrad, which has now been renamed St. Petersburg. We had the opportunity to visit the celebrated Hermitage Museum. Because of scheduling problems, we had only forty-five minutes in that fabulous museum. The tour guide incredulously said to us, "Don't stop to look at anything, because, if you do, you will miss everything." I've been thinking about that for fifteen years. "Don't stop to look at anything, because, if you do, you will miss everything." It is disturbing to realize that is the way a lot of us live.

Our goal is to keep busy, keep moving. In his book, *Time Wars: The Primary Conflict in Human History*, Jeremy Rifkin says, "It's ironic that this culture, which is so committed to saving time, feels increasingly deprived of the very thing that we value." The historian Will Durant says, "The person who is always in a hurry is not quite civilized." We do need to value time better.

Paul says in the Ephesian letter, "Be careful in the way you live, not as unwise people, but as wise, making good use of your time." (Ephesians 5:15,16a) I love the King James translation, which says, "Redeem your time." Bring it back, make it useful, and give it quality. Methuselah, the person in the Bible who lived the longest, is mentioned six times in the Bible, and every time it has to do with some genealogy in which he is listed with the people of his family. The only time anything else is said about Methuselah, besides his ancestral line, it says, "Thus Methuselah lived 969 years, and he died." That is all it could say; "969 years, and he died." But, what of his quality of life? His productivity? His service? – 969 years, all that time, and nothing to say but, "and he died." We need to look at the time that is ours to live and concentrate not just on the length of time, but on the God who gives us the time. I love the story about a little boy who was asked to spell love, and he replied, T-I-M-E. We need quality of time for ourselves and for the significant others God has put into our lives.

We frequently lack standards and commitment in our lives. Forty-five years ago, Pierre Berton, a newspaper columnist from Montreal, Canada, wrote a book called the *The Comfortable Pew*. The book challenged us to see how we are often satisfied to make the whole religious experience comfortable, easy, and palatable. As long as there are no demands or strict requirements, we are willing to live with it. It is comfortable!

In light of that, I saw a cartoon a couple of years ago filling a full page. It showed the front of a church with a big billboard, and it said at the top, "The Lite Church." You know, like Lite potato chips, Lite beer, Lite soda, and Lite cheese. Then, on the bulletin board, were the requirements of this Lite Church. It promised, "24% less commitment; forty-five-minute services and five-minute sermons." It also announced, "We request only a 7.5% tithe; we only require penance for four out of the seven deadly sins. You only need to be concerned about eight of the Ten Commandments; your choice." At the bottom it said, "The church you always wanted, and less."

Pondering that, I am struck by the contrast between the Lite Church, which is so appealing to many of us, and what Jesus says in the Scripture, "If you come after me, deny yourself, and take up your cross and follow after me." (Matthew 16:24) The cross is a costly thing. It requires more than just nonchalant compliance to make us happy and comfortable. When I consider to whom I have committed my life, or what is my highest desire and ultimate goal, I think of the Apostle Paul, who said in Philippians 3:10, "All I want to know is Jesus Christ and the power of His resurrection. . . ." In Colossians, our text for the day, he says, "If you have been raised with Christ, seek the things that are above, where Christ is seated at the right hand of God." In other words, because we are the Easter people, since we have been raised with Christ, we are enabled to *seek the things that are above.* "When Christ, who is your life, is revealed, you will also be glorified with Him," revealed in glory with Him; that's what Paul is saying to us. He is not saying that we need to put away all material things – they have a place. Success has a place. Winning has a place, and pleasure has a place. Time, requirements, and commitment all have a place. All he's asking is that we evaluate in every dimension of life what is of most value and significance.

Jesus gives us the best answer when He challenges us to see our life's priorities. In Matthew 6:25, He says, "Do not be anxious about what you will eat and what you will wear; for is not life more than food, and the body more than clothing?" At the end of that paragraph is that great text, "Seek first the Kingdom of God and His righteousness, and all these things will be added unto you." (6:33) Years ago, someone gave me a paraphrase of that verse, which says, "Seek first the Kingdom of God, Jesus Christ, His righteousness; and all these things of life that seem so important to you will be put in their proper place and perspective." The materialism; the success; the winning; the pleasure; the time; the requirement; our commitment – all in their proper order. "Seek first the Kingdom of God." As we seek Jesus Christ, we honor Christ.

Paul also says in our text today, "Put on peace, let the peace of Christ dwell in your heart . . . let the Word of God dwell richly in you. Sing psalms and hymns and songs of praise to God." Then this great line, "Whatever you do, in word or deed, do everything in the name of Jesus Christ. . . ." Years ago, we visited Assisi in Italy. There was a young priest from Baltimore there for the summer, who was taking American tourists around the church. As part of his tour, he read this line for us from a person who had lived in the town of Assisi, when St. Francis was there as a priest. "Whatever St. Francis said, whatever he did, it was as though Jesus Christ was standing right there beside him." That is what Paul is saying to us even today – whatever you do, in word or deed, do everything against the background of Christ, as if Christ were standing right here beside you.

What a magnificent task that we have been given! I would suggest some questions for us to consider as a result of Paul's challenge to us. Do the words that I say, does the language that I use, glorify the name of Christ? Are my words edifying, inspiring, encouraging, spoken in the name of Christ? Do the contracts that I draw up and sign honor the righteousness and virtue of Christ? Do the promises that I make and keep reflect the justice, honesty, and truth of Christ? Do the people around me see in me the sensitivity, compassion, concern, sacrifice, grace, peace, and love of Christ? Am I willing to forgive others, as God in Christ has forgiven me? Would Christ consider my judgments to be unprejudiced, unbiased, and fair? Would my witness be seen as a portrayal of selfish pride, or an exhibition of humility in Christ? Paul is asking us to consider those questions and many more like them. Whatever we say in the words we use, whatever deeds or actions we take, whatever we say, whatever we do, let us do it all against the background of those questions. What are you pursuing? What is the most important thing in your life?

Lest you think I have forgotten, those of you who are involved in trivia: Anne Boleyn had eleven fingers; the vegetable that provides the greatest poundage per square acre is cabbage; the movie star who was a distant cousin of Lady Di was Humphrey Bogart; Hitler's favorite film was *King Kong*; and the score of Super Bowl Nine was sixteen to six, in favor of Pittsburgh. (To me, as a Steeler fan, that was not trivial – I can dream, can't I?)

As long as you play that game of Trivial Pursuit, I hope that you will enjoy it, have fun, let it entertain you and inform you. However, when you *live your life*, think about what Paul said: "Whatever you do, do everything in the name of Christ . . . If you have been raised with Christ, seek those things that are above, where Christ is." Think also of the words of Christ, "Seek first the Kingdom of God, and all these things will be put in their proper place." If you follow those commands, then on this day, in the beginning of the New Year, the first of the new millennium, all of your pursuits will be significant. To God be the glory in Christ Jesus!

To Dream the Possible Dream

Luke 9:37-43
Mark 9:21-24

In Thomas Wolfe's novel *You Can't Go Home Again,* there is a man who is caught between the Depression, on one side, and World War II, on the other. He buys property and begets his children. He is a mystery to his neighbors, and his only enjoyment seems to come from cheating them. From cradle to grave, he seems never to notice the obvious things in the world that are beautiful and of great importance. The description of him says this: "He took everything for granted; he has no consciousness of things eternal or immortal; and he has lost the ability to dream." To me, that is one of the real poverties, if not *the* real poverty in life. Poverty is not just when somebody is broke, hungry, or homeless. The real poverty is when we have lost our ability to dream. That is why, for me, these texts today from Mark and Luke (also found in Matthew) are so appealing. In this conversation between the father and Jesus, there are valuable lessons for us about what it means for us to dream.

First of all, this father dared to dream. It's tragic when anybody loses that impulse – to dare to dream. A young lady came into my office and, by outward appearances, everything was positive. She was attractive, intelligent, articulate, and personable. But a very few moments into the conversation, it became evident that she was very troubled. Her father was dying of cancer. She had a real passion for the concerns of the world; she was anxious about pollution (pollution of the environment and in politics). She was deeply disturbed about the problem of greed and avarice; she was concerned about the depletion of the ozone layer, and the increase of the poverty level. She was concerned about the rising number of people addicted to drugs and alcohol, and the low number of people concerned about morality and integrity. Yet, most of all, her trouble was personal. She was a college graduate and she had a master's degree. She was well-prepared for her field; but because she was so well-educated, people had repeatedly told her she was over-qualified. So, she was working as a waitress, totally discouraged and totally disappointed. She looked at me with dark, sad, tear-filled eyes and said, "At this point, I don't even dare to dream."

In both texts, in Luke and Mark, we are told that this father dared to dream. In spite of his discouragement, his disappointment over his son's affliction (the convulsions, foaming at the mouth, being cast into fire and water, endangering himself and others), this father still dared to dream. He dared to dream that someone, somewhere, somehow would help them. Even when the disciples refused his request, he still dared to dream. This conversation between the disciples and the father must have been very discouraging. Likewise, when you and I are daring to dream, very often there is someone, many times several people, trying to deflate our dreams. There's always somebody who says that what we are doing is fruitless and hopeless; it is something that can't be done; it is silly, impractical, impossible, and unthinkable. When someone tells us that there is nothing we can do, we need to remember that old cliché that "if we shoot at nothing, we usually hit it."

The solution is this: we need to recapture and reclaim our passion for what we really believe. The Danish theologian and philosopher, Soren Kierkegaard, made a very poignant and telling remark. He said, "This age will die not from sin, but from the loss of a passion for what they believe." That is a challenge for you and for me, as the Church and as individuals. If there is a death of our spirit, our age, our Church, and our faith, it would probably come, not so much from sin, but from the loss of passion for what we believe. That is why the Proverb writer says, "Where there is no vision (no dream), the people perish."

One of the ways to recapture and reclaim our belief, and the passion for our belief, is to develop and maintain a positive, productive attitude.

A little boy visited his grandmother. She admonished him that he was allowed to go and look at the swimming hole, but he was not under any circumstances to go in. A half hour later, he came back and his hair was drenched. She said, "What happened?"

"I fell in," he replied.

Then she said, "But your clothes are dry; I need an explanation."

He said, "Oh, I took them off. I had the feeling I was going to fall in."

When we anticipate something is going to happen – especially if it involves the "positive thinking" of Norman Vincent Peale or the "possibility thinking" of Robert Schuller – we must move beyond our reticence and reluctance, and take an aggressive, proactive approach, and not only dare to dream, but also to act upon those dreams, as well.

Nineteen months ago, my third sermon here was entitled *"Imagine That."* I used a passage of Scripture from Philippians: "Whatever is true, honorable and just; whatever is pure, lovely, and gracious; if there is anything excellent, anything worthy of praise, think about these things." I translated that last phrase, "imagine that"; in other words, "dare to dream."

However, it is not just a matter of daring to dream. There is an urgency about our faith, there is an imperative about our faith. What are we dreaming? What are we willing to do? This father not only dared to dream, and to desire an answer for his dream, he also dared to act. Overtly, deliberately, he brought his son to the disciples, and when they refused his request for help, he took his son directly to Jesus. Sometimes, we shy away from taking action because we are afraid of criticism; we are reticent and reluctant simply because, deep down, we're not really sure things will work. I don't happen to believe that this is God's will and plan for you and me – or for the Church. God intends for us to take prompt action.

A little over two weeks ago, many of us probably made some New Year's resolutions – personal dreams: to diet (it seems that everybody just wants to take off ten more pounds); write a letter to a friend; take a regular day off; exercise; spend time with family; or just relax. We know what happens to most of those resolutions. The author Charles Sheldon once said, "Dreams and resolutions are like babies crying in church. They should be carried out immediately."

We are called to do something; we are to act on those things that God has called us to do. It is an imperative for us, and something should happen right now – something beyond our fantasies; beyond just what we are thinking about. Tomorrow is Martin Luther King, Jr. Day. Those of us who are old enough remember, very vividly, his great speech in 1963 on the Washington Mall, "I Have a Dream" – a powerful, significant speech. I am told that as he was leaving the platform on his way to his car, one of his admirers called out, "I loved your speech. I can hardly wait until your dream comes true." It is reported that King gave a terse and succinct reply: "You don't have to wait. Our dreams are within reach right now. We have already begun to work them out, right now, and you should join us."

222

We are also told that his favorite spiritual was "Precious Lord, Take My Hand," *lead me on, let me stand.* I once heard him describe why it was his favorite spiritual. He said, "It is a plea for God to take my hand, *now*, lead me on, *now*, when it seems to be impossible to go on any further, when the bend in the road seems to go around to nothing, even then, take my hand and lead me on, *now.*"

Sometimes we just need to take a risk, overcome our fears. When I was about twelve, we were visiting my uncle in Colorado. He lived there his entire adult life – seventy years plus. He was a typical Coloradoan; he would drive down those narrow mountain highways with one hand on the wheel and the other pointing around at things he wanted us to see. That didn't excite me a whole lot, especially driving near Canyon City on a road that was so narrow. It was obvious that we couldn't turn around on it. There were no guardrails, and I was very frightened. If that wasn't enough, as I looked ahead, I saw a place where the mountain came down from the right, and it looked as though the road bent around to nothing. I was relieved when I saw a huge sign. I was sure it was going to say, DANGER, STOP, BACKUP; I knew it wouldn't say, "turn around" because there was no room. However, imagine my surprise when we got to the bend, the sign read, YES, YOU CAN! KEEP GOING. "Take my hand; keep going; dream; act upon those dreams."

Finally, when we dare to dream and act upon those dreams, we discover another promise that God gives to us. There is more we haven't seen yet! There is more possibility! Potential! Perhaps when you saw the sermon title you thought of that Broadway musical, *Man of La Mancha* and its most popular song, "To Dream the Impossible Dream"; "this is my quest, to follow that star . . . to reach the unreachable star." Certainly that is an admirable trait; to reach out for the impossible, to extend to things beyond our reach. This is very admirable and Jesus understands that. He doesn't deny it, but He simply says, "The unreachable and the impossible are only for human beings, but for me, all things are possible to one who believes." (a paraphrase) He takes the unreachable and the impossible, and it becomes possible for us.

In the very insightful and perceptive conversation with Jesus, in our text, the father says, "If you are able to do anything, have pity on us and help us." When I read that Scripture, I can almost see Jesus smiling, when He responds, "If you are able?" (he's able), for then He says, "All things are possible to one who believes." He doesn't say all things are guaranteed, but He says, "All things are possible...." Because all things are possible, we are willing and able to reach beyond where we are, to discover more, to dare to dream, to act.

Jesus urges us to look beyond the things we can only see, touch, and taste. Have you noticed how frequently we use the phrase, "Seeing is believing." That is very valid and true. We rely on visual proof. But if sight is the only measurement we use, then our life is greatly limited. One of the things I love to do, when I am at the seashore as I walk along, is to stop occasionally and look out across the water to the place where the ocean meets the sky, that line we call the horizon. Do you know what the horizon is? It's nothing more then the limit of our sight. Through study, experience, testimony, and travel, I have learned that beyond that horizon, there is something more. I believe it is there. I know I can't see it, but I believe it is there. The conclusion is this; not only is seeing believing, but, sometimes, the reverse is true. Believing is seeing. There are certain things that we never fully understand, never fully grasp, until we first believe them. For instance, we believe in Jesus Christ, and then we begin to understand and see the power of and the reason for the Cross. We believe in resurrection hope, and then we begin to see and understand the full dimensions of life; its purpose; its meaning; its value. There are many times when believing is simply the avenue into greater understanding, greater knowledge, and greater possibility. I love the statement of Robert

Frost when he spoke about his love for his wife. He said, "I believed it into fulfillment."

Seeing is believing; believing is seeing. Jesus said to this father, "All things are possible to one who believes." Listen to the man's reply, "I believe, help thou my unbelief." That is one of the most powerful prayers in all of Scripture. I don't know about you, but it is my prayer daily. "I believe, help thou my unbelief." I believe this much, and therefore I want to be enabled to see much more. Please help me in areas that I haven't yet believed, so that eventually I will see how much more there is to see. Help me to believe. I'm still daring to dream – on my way throughout life.

Back in 1963, at the Junior Miss contest, Catherine Marshall, the author of *A Man Called Peter* (Peter Marshall), was one of the judges. She also spoke to the contestants, and she said this, "In the future, I want you to discover and use your gifts; do your best; keep dreaming, and you will discover a reward." The winner of that contest was Diane Sawyer, now a commentator on ABC News, in the morning for "Good Morning America" and evening for "Prime Time." She said, "I listened to those words, and I began to try to follow them; I used my gifts, I tried to do my best and kept dreaming. I kept looking for the reward, but the reward seemed to remain an illusion. I never quite got to the place where I thought I had found the reward." Then she said, "Only a few years later did I begin to realize, in a revelation that came like a bolt of lightning, what Catherine Marshall was saying; the reward is not the destination; the reward is to be on the journey, to be on the way." All things are possible on the way for those who believe. We often discover that much of life, the possibilities of life, are fulfilled by being believed into fulfillment. "I believe, help thou my unbelief."

What is it *today* that you and I as faithful servants and good stewards believe for ourselves, our children, our community, our Church? I encourage you to dream about those things not yet seen that you are still reaching for. I'm talking about both big dreams and small dreams. The size of the dreams, of course, is relative. My big dream may not be your big dream, and vice versa. Whatever the size, as my friend, David McKechnie says, "I want you to dream holy dreams." A "holy" dream does not mean self-righteous and sanctimonious dreams. By holy, I mean that which is unique, which is what the word "holy" really means. It means to be radical, distinctive – in tune with God, and with the Spirit of God.

And so, we dream Holy dreams. I do, and I hope you do, too. I dream for healing – the healing of people who have emotional problems, such as depression, or people who are suffering physically. I dream of the enrichment of individuals to recognize and use all of their gifts and talents; for single persons, for married persons, for families. I dream that people can be energized in their emotional life, spiritual life, and physical life. I dream about acts of reconciliation, when people are brought back together after they have been estranged. I dream about renewal, when someone has lost the passion or desire to live or serve. I also dream that the Church – this Church – will discover a significant mission, and that means not only financially, but personal involvement, participation, and engagement – a hands-on ministry. I dream that the church will also have a relevant voice in the secular community ministry, standing in protest against all wrong, inequities, and injustice; empowering those who are weak; encouraging the human spirit; affirming the gifts, strengths, and potential that we all have. Most of all, I dream that we will focus with high energy on that titanic task: to bring all persons to full commitment in the holy life that has been revealed for us in Jesus Christ. That is my prayer. My prayer also continues, with one more step. May you keep on daring to dream, keep acting out those dreams, and continue to believe that in Jesus Christ, for all those who believe in Him, *everything is possible*! Amen.

THE SPIRIT IN A GREAT SPACE!

Luke 4:14-21
John 14:15-19, 25-27
Acts 1:8 and 2:17, 18

Yesterday we observed the quadrennial celebration in our nation's capitol: the inauguration of a new president. Along with the pomp and circumstance – the dining and dancing, the parades and parties – it occurs to me that those who are discriminating and thoughtful, who are genuinely concerned about the future, the welfare, and the prosperity of this country, were more concerned about something beyond the merriment. You and I were concerned, I hope, with the inaugural address; listening to what was said; thinking about it; analyzing it; dissecting it; measuring it; judging it; so that we could begin to see what the plan and purpose – the agenda – of the president really is. For me, and I hope for you, what was important, was the spirit in the president's speech. Beyond that, I looked to see where and how this speech was inviting, engendering, and encouraging us – uplifting our spirit.

I suggest to you that in our text today, from Luke, the fourth chapter, we find another inaugural address. This one, however, was not just for four years; it has been important for two thousand years, and will continue to be for eternity. This address by Jesus at the beginning of His ministry was given as He came to Galilee. Luke says: He came filled with power in the Holy Spirit. He went to the synagogue, as was His regular habit. There in the synagogue, the scroll was handed to Him and He read from Isaiah: He outlined His agenda based upon the prophecy of Isaiah. Reading from the prophet gave authority and authenticity to what Jesus said – "to preach good news to the poor; release to the captives; recovery of sight to the blind; free those who are oppressed; and pronounce and proclaim the fulfillment of the Kingdom, the acceptable year of the Lord."

As we were yesterday with the president, Luke was concerned about the spirit of what was said in the synagogue. What was the spirit? Luke clarifies the matter by telling us the source of the spirit. He tells us that Jesus came, "Filled with power and the *Holy Spirit.*" Then Jesus further clarifies the matter by quoting Isaiah, "The Spirit of the Lord is upon me." It is God's Spirit. This implies that the Spirit of Jesus is being given to us as He fulfills that agenda, in and through us. How important that is for us as we hear that message today. Where is the Spirit now? Jesus says it has been given to us: "I will call upon the Father to give *you* an advocate; the Spirit of truth, who will be in *you* and be part of *you.* These things I have spoken to *you* while I am still here with *you*, but *your* comforter, the Holy Spirit, whom the Father will send in my Name, will call to mind all things that I have told *you.*" Then, that wonderful commission Luke records in the beginning of Acts, "You shall receive power when the Holy Spirit has come upon *you*, and *you* shall be my witnesses. . . ." There is an obvious connection there with what Jesus said at Nazareth. We also hear the quote from the prophet Joel, which Peter used in the Pentecost sermon, "In the last days, says the Lord, I will pour out my Spirit upon all people. . . ." The Spirit is always available to us, in us and through us – a gift from God!

For the last seven years, this church has had an exceptional program called "Music in a Great Space." I applaud and am grateful for the talent and skill that is provided here in that exceptional series. Perhaps you notice the close connection here between that title and the title of this morning's sermon, "Music in a Great Space" – *The Spirit in a Great Space*. I am convinced that you and I need to be thinking about the Spirit more than anything else here in our space. While the music that echoes and reverberates here is stimulating and inspiring, I am also convinced that what makes this space, and this place, great is not the architecture, acoustics, traditions, or symbolism, all of which have their own importance; what makes this space great is the presence, power, and promises of the Holy Spirit! To me, the Holy Spirit is God in the present tense; God living in us and through us; God living as part of our lives, every day. I suggest to you that if we are to be a "great space," if we are to be a great church, we need to have that "present tense" of God's Spirit in our lives. We need to be a Spirit-filled church, and especially now as we work together during the interim period and the time of these four weeks of study. I think it is important to think about what it means to be a Spirit-filled church.

First of all, I suggest to you that a Spirit-filled church is one that has the quality of humility and love. That word "humility" is so often misunderstood. "Humility" comes from the Latin word "humus," which means, "ground," or, literally, "down to earth" – that which is natural. It is not self-deprecation; it is not cringing or groveling; it is not obsequiousness. It is rather the willingness, in all openness and honesty, to acknowledge our human condition; our finiteness; the limitations of our human condition; to admit our weaknesses and confess the sin of our lives. At the same time, we need to acknowledge the transcendent, quintessential, sufficient nature and promises of God's gifts, which He also gives to us to meet our human needs.

The humble person is not someone who is seduced by adulation, praise, or admiration. The humble person does not give in to the myth of infallibility and does not cherish unrealistic illusions. The humble person is teachable and resilient; open and willing to change. Humility allows us to become the new creatures that God says we can be. God can accomplish that. I love the little limerick of Nipsey Russell, the comedian, who says, "If you go off to college and gather some knowledge, I hope you go all the way through; for if they can make penicillin from mold, they can make something special of you." If you are humble enough to learn and listen, God can make you a special person.

When we talk about humility, the first person that comes to mind is Mother Teresa. I want you to listen to the description of this saint written by Malcolm Muggeridge, the English author, lecturer, and theologian, when she was alive. The book is titled *Something Beautiful for God: Mother Teresa of Calcutta.* He describes some of the qualities that defined the humility of this special person. He describes her as unselfish – not petty, self-seeking, or boastful; as teachable – open-minded, flexible, and eager for new life and truth; as penitent – aware that we all fall short and fail; as open to the forgiveness we need – to the grace and mercy, which renews and restores us; as gracious – showing compassion and unconditional love to all in need, to those who are hurting; as having a sense of humor, not taking herself too seriously, yet, at the same, time remaining totally committed, disciplined, and dedicated to becoming what God called her to be. Muggeridge summarizes by saying, "This saint of God takes light to a godless world and brings to the world's darkness, a clear, well-defined dignity." True humility and true dignity always go together. One cannot read the New Testament without observing right away how Jesus condemned arrogance, conceit, and false pride.

Jesus said, "Whoever will exalt self, will be humbled; but whoever humbles self, will be exalted." One cannot miss in the New Testament that Jesus Christ dignifies humility and love. In the Beatitudes, "Blessed are the poor in spirit – the humble – for theirs is the Kingdom of Heaven." "Blessed are the meek – gentle, loving, mild – for they shall inherit the earth." This space, this church in which you and I worship; this space, which holds the Body of Christ, is in great need of the qualities of humility and love.

Furthermore, a Spirit-filled church is one that has the quality of integrity and character, a church that attempts to live by the high standards and high values that Jesus Christ has given to us by word and example. Jesus strongly condemns hypocrisy. He said, "Woe to you, Scribes and Pharisees, hypocrites. . . ." I think we need to be very certain what the word "hypocrisy" means. It does not mean failing to do the right thing. That includes us all. Hypocrisy means acting as though we are doing the right thing; pretending to do the right thing, but not *really* doing it. That describes the person who really lacks integrity. If the Spirit of Jesus Christ is real and authentic in our lives, then our commitment to honesty – and truth, justice, and righteousness – must be unequivocal, unwavering, uncompromising, and without pretense!

Sir Isaac Newton was one of the most influential people in all of history. He is the one who discovered the law of gravity and also wrote a famous scientific treatise, *The Principia: Mathematical Principles of Natural Philosophy*. Later in his life he put all of his scientific pursuits aside and was appointed to be the warden of the Mint – the treasury. In 1697, a man came to him and offered him a bribe of £6,000 (which probably would have been $20,000 to $25,000 in our money). When Sir Isaac Newton refused, the man said that this offer was from a very distinguished lady, a duchess, who wanted Newton to have this money. In response, Sir Isaac said, "I desire that you tell this woman that if she were to come in person and offer me this bribe, I would ask her to leave my home, even as I am asking you now to leave." When he was asked for an explanation of why he would not just quietly take the money, Newton answered, "What I did was consistent with the spirit of integrity and character that I learned from my childhood in the community of faith." Harry Emerson

Fosdick, who told this story, said, "No blow, fair or foul, not materialism or politics, could get past his spirit of integrity, the foundation of faith, the shield of character that was in the quality of life that he had learned in the Body of Christ." In this day in which you and I live, when there seems to be such a lack of integrity – people disrespecting and misrepresenting the truth, ignoring honesty, and rationalizing or making excuses for their sin – I think it is vitally important that the people of God, you and I, who are the community of faith, need to hold on to the spirit of integrity and character, so that nothing fair or foul, nothing materialistic or political, will ever compromise us. May you and I, in this space, in the life of this church, have that spirit of integrity and that shield of character that will prepare and empower us to go from this place and live in such a way that we show our integrity and character to the world, and to thereby honor Christ!

I suggest to you that this spirit of humility and love, this spirit of integrity and character, will not be effective or influential unless we take on the overt, unambiguous spirit of service; the act of obedience as we follow the Lord. Jesus admires and commends all those who are God's faithful servants, when He says, "The greatest among you will be the servant of all." When we become God's servants, we are energized, able to run with endurance and perseverance. I want you to note that this is not just enthusiasm and interest God is asking for. We can initiate a lot of good enthusiastic starts, but we need to follow through. I love the comment by Zig Ziglar, who said, "I'd rather have one person who is committed than a hundred people who are only interested."

James writes in his letter in the New Testament, "Faith without works is dead." He is not saying that our works will earn our salvation. He is simply saying that if you and I claim to have faith, and claim a relationship with Christ, there had better be some action, works, and some service that verifies what we say and believe. That is absolutely essential to make our space here great. "Faith without works is dead."

Faith without verification is ineffective and lifeless! Jesus also gives us a high standard when He says, "I came not to be served, but to serve." The Apostle Paul tells us that God's Spirit is blended together with our spirit. Listen to what Paul says in the eighth chapter of Romans: "For all who are led by the Spirit of God are children of God. For you did not receive a spirit of slavery to fall back into fear, but you have received a spirit of adoption. It is by that very spirit, bearing witness with our spirit, that we are children of God, and if children, then heirs, heirs of God and joint heirs with Christ." Our spirit is blended together with Christ as God calls us to be included in the family of God.

David H. C. Read tells a wonderful story about a military chaplain. This chaplain knew a young lieutenant who, once when he was on active duty, had failed miserably on his assignment. In the battle, he had endangered his life and the others around him. He was court-martialed and thrown in the brig. Several weeks later, when his commanding officer returned to duty, he learned about what had happened to this young man and said, "We cannot lose this person. We cannot reject him; this young man is too good. If he has paid his debt, if he is truly contrite, I will reinstate him to his rank and to his office. And he is to be trusted." That completely surprised everybody in the troop. Within a month of his reinstatement, in a similar situation – almost exactly like the one in which he had failed – he was so daring, brave, courageous, and competent that he won a promotion for gallantry on the field. Later, he received other honors, as well. When asked about this, the young soldier said, "What else could I do? My commanding officer knew that I failed; he forgave me, he trusted me, and my only way to honor him was to serve him with my very best." We have a Savior just like that, who knows that we have failed, fallen short, and sinned, and saves us anyway. Yes, He knows we have fallen short and, yet, He offers to redeem us and restore us. What else can we do for this One, this Savior who trusts, saves, redeems, and restores us, except to serve Him with our whole heart? As John writes in his first letter, "We love because He first loved us." We can also reverse that: because He first loved us, we love – because He first served us, we serve!

The spirit of service, obedience, and commitment is exactly what we need to be talking about in the life of the church. That is so important as to be essential. One of the best remembered lines from an inaugural address was the quote John Kennedy paraphrased in 1961, originally attributed to Oliver Wendell Holmes in a Memorial Day speech in 1884: "Ask not what your country can do for you, but what you can do for your country." I think we need to say something similar in the spiritual sense. "Ask not only what God can do for you, but ask what you can do for God" – what you can do to honor and glorify God by your faithful spirit of service and obedience. For a long time now, I have been drawn by these words of Albert Schweitzer: "I do not know what your destiny will be, but one thing I know, the only ones among you who will be really happy are those who have sought and found a way to serve."

Finally, we need the spirit of prayer. The church at its best, as far as I am concerned, is a praying church. Whether you are praying individually, in small groups, or here in worship publicly, the church at its highest and best, is a praying church. I believe the greatest malady in the church is not theological stagnation or social apathy. The great malady with which we must deal as the Body of Christ is prayer paralysis. Twenty months ago, my first Sunday here was Pentecost. My sermon title that day was, "Now That's the Spirit," based on one of my father's favorite phrases. I was talking in that sermon, in the present tense, about the idea that God is giving us His gift of the Holy Spirit – giving us the gifts, giving us empowerment to be His people. That's the spirit I prayed for then, and that's the spirit that I pray for today. I pray it for myself, for you, and for this church. I pray that we will have the spirit of humility and love, and the discernment to understand what all of that means. I pray that we will have a spirit of integrity and character, and the courage to live by that standard. I pray that you and I will have the spirit of service and obedience to honor Christ, and our faith in Christ, by what we do and say. When those prayers are answered – today, tomorrow, and every tomorrow – then we can say wholeheartedly, and with great confidence, that we have been filled by *the Spirit in this Great Space!* Amen.

Keeping in Touch

Mark 1:40-45

It was about 3:30 in the morning. The telephone rang, and the voice on the other end said, "This is Shirley." I said, "Shirley, what is wrong?" and she said, "Well, I needed to be in touch with you – I needed to make contact because I just can't sleep." I said, "What can I do for you? May I pray with you or perhaps read Scripture?" She said, "Whatever! But if you would just keep talking, I know I would probably fall back to sleep." This is probably not the best story for a preacher to tell at the beginning of a sermon, because I sincerely hope that you will stay awake so that together we can hear what God is saying to us today – to discover how God is touching us, and how in Christ's name we touch each other.

For the last two years, through the miracle of email, short-term missionaries Jonathan and Sara Partee have kept in touch with us at Shadyside. They have also kept in touch with other congregations, with many families and friends, sharing their inspirational and effective mission work in Ethiopia. The letters and emails they have sent have revealed to those receiving them that they know exactly why they are there. First of all, it is because of their desire to keep in touch with the people of Ethiopia; to share the good news of the

Gospel of Jesus Christ, the life and hope and love that is found in Christ. They are also there because, as they share their testimony with others, it helps them to keep in touch with their own relationship with Jesus Christ, and their response to God's call. *Keeping in touch!*

Julius Fast has written a book called *Body Language*, in which he suggests that our communication is not only with words, but it is also, frequently, eloquently, and effectively done with body language – with a gesture, our posture, the way we walk or sit, a frown or a smile, extended arms instead of folded ones, open hands or a clenched fist. This body language often conveys much more than we are expressing with our words. Faust strongly emphasizes the significance and value of touch. In his book, he says, "The swiftest and most effective style of body language is the language of touch." A touch of a hand, an arm around a shoulder spells out a message more vividly and directly than a dozen words. Often it is touch that interprets our words. If words and touch are given concurrently, in the right moment and context, the entire message can be greatly magnified.

Today's Scripture reading, from the Gospel according to Mark, conveys just that kind of alliance of touch and testimony. It's the right moment, context, and message. In this miracle of healing of the leper, one of the first miracles that Jesus did, we see early evidence of the ministry and style of Jesus. From the very beginning, it was abundantly clear that Jesus intended to keep in touch with the hopes and hurts, with the successes and sufferings, of all those people with whom He came in contact. And still, we are moved to ask today, what is the touch of Jesus? How is Jesus touching us? You and me? What is the impact of that touch upon us as we attempt to keep in touch with what God is calling us to do and be?

I suggest to you, first of all, that the touch of Jesus is a touch of indignation. When this leper came to Jesus, in spite of all the prohibitions and restrictions (a person of leprosy was not to speak with or come in contact with anyone), this overt act of his coming to

Jesus moved and touched the Savior's heart. Our text says today, "Moved with pity, Jesus stretched out His hand and touched him." Several other translations say, "moved with compassion. . . ." At least two say, "moved with moral, warm indignation. . . ." And one says, "moved by anger. . . ." Indignation and anger would surprise us; we are not comfortable with those words, especially when we think of Jesus. Anger and indignation do not register in our minds as positive and constructive emotions.

For us, these are much misunderstood emotions. Most of us think of anger as one of the seven deadly sins, one that we must avoid. So, if indignation is truly one of the translations here, then the essential question is this: At whom, or about what, was Jesus indignant or angry? Jesus certainly wasn't angry with this man because of his infirmities, and certainly not because of his audacity to defy superstition and come and speak to Jesus. I'm convinced that Jesus was indignant and angry at the system. Society was ignoring, excluding, and isolating this man, refusing to lift a hand or heart to help him. This is the point at which this indignation of Jesus becomes justified. The theologian would call it, "righteous indignation." There is a place for righteous indignation in our lives as we stand against that which is evil, that which is hurtful or demeaning to others.

There was a nun who worked several weeks with Mother Teresa on her first assignment. When the assignment was completed, she said to one of the other nuns, "What surprises me and what puzzles me is how, when Mother Teresa is with these people on the street, she seems so angry." The other nun replied, "Remember, she is not angry at the people who are suffering, she is angry at the conditions that have caused their pain. She is also angry at the people and the society who lack the integrity, fortitude, and resolve to do something about it."

If Jesus has touched our lives, the question is: Who are the people we are willing to touch? What are the prejudices, patterns, prohibitions, fears, and forces that keep us, as God's people, from fulfilling our obligations as Christian brothers and sisters? Are we angry enough at the injustices, inequities, and unrighteousness in the world around us so that we reflect the righteous indignation of our Savior and Lord Jesus Christ? Are we *keeping in touch?*

The touch of Jesus is also the touch of identification – which is what the incarnation is all about. That is what it means to have the Word made flesh: Emmanuel – "God with us." Paul says, "Jesus did not count equality with God a thing to be grasped, but emptied Himself, taking the form of a servant, being born in human form." (Philippians 2:6, 7) God's gift to us in Jesus Christ was the incarnation. Jesus took upon Himself the pain, pressure, and problems of human existence. That is the way in which He was able to identify with us. Jesus was able to identify with people around Him, whatever their situation, reputation, station in life, success or failure. When Jesus saw this leper, He anticipated His own suffering on the cross and identified with his pain. When Jesus saw this leper standing before Him, He anticipated His own rejection by the scribes and the Pharisees, and identified with the rejection of the legalism and the prohibitions of the people of that day.

That was typical of Jesus; that was His common style of action. He identified with the people He saw. He identified with the woman at the well and her need for water – spiritual, as well as physical. He identified with the disciples who needed to have their feet washed, so that they would understand what it meant to be servants. He identified with and praised the children for their humble, trusting faith. He identified with those who were blind, who could not see – opening both their physical and spiritual eyes. He identified with the thief on the cross and with Lazarus in the tomb. In the Garden of Gethsemane, He identified with our feelings of desolation and uncertainty. On the cross, He identified with our Sin. At the Easter tomb, He identified with our victory. If we have been touched by

Christ, the question for us is, "With whom are we willing to be identified, for Christ's sake?"

The touch of identification leads us to the next touch of Christ – the touch of compassion. Compassion combines companionship and passion; it is feeling deeply alongside people who are suffering. Jesus said, "Take my yoke upon you . . . join together in compassion for one another." Sometimes compassion is the most effective way of expressing our love and the love of Jesus Christ.

The late Bruce Thielemann, who was the pastor at First Presbyterian Church in downtown Pittsburgh, was an acquaintance of mine in college and seminary. We became closer friends when he and I began to share ministry at conferences, churches, retreats, and seminars. In this sharing, we began to admire and respect each other more and more. Bruce was an exceptional communicator of the Gospel – one of the best I have ever known. The last time he visited our church in Michigan, he told a very powerful and poignant personal story. When he was pastor in Glendale, California, one of the young men from his church participated in a civil rights protest, during which he was attacked, beaten, and left in a coma. His family called Bruce, even though the parents were not members of his church. They even admitted later that when this tragedy occurred, they were not believers. However, they had heard, through their son, of this man, Bruce Thielemann, and since they were at a loss for what to do, and so helpless, maybe this pastor could bring some word of comfort and assurance – they desperately needed someone to help.

With that, Bruce came. He said, "When I walked into that room and saw that boy lying on that gurney, and when I heard those people tell their story, and saw their tears, all I could do was weep with them." This great communicator said, "I stumbled for some kind of eloquent words to say, but they did not come. I said something, perhaps glibly, about God and suffering. I gave a very brief and halting prayer, and then I left." He said, "I was so discouraged, disappointed, and depressed, because I felt that this pastoral visit had been a complete failure." Later, after the boy had recovered, the whole family joined the church in Glendale. When they gave the testimony of their faith, they said; "Our faith began with a gentle, genuine touch of compassion." It was by a man of God who simply gave the touch of Jesus through his tears and through his touch.

John Henry Jowett, a Victorian Scottish pastor, said, "We cannot heal wounds we do not feel." He added, "Tearless eyes will never be the heralds of the compassion that we need to reach beyond where we are to others." To see beyond to others, Henri Nouwen says we must be "wounded healers."

While today's gospel story is very inspiring, as we see Jesus touching this leper, we become aware that the narrative takes a sudden and surprising turn. I have always been puzzled by how Jesus said sternly to this man, "Go away and see that you say nothing to anyone. . . ." Perhaps that has also puzzled you. The only explanation I have for this is that first century people were looking for something spectacular or sensational, much like we do. However, Jesus had another purpose in mind. He was more interested in a profession of faith than popularity with the crowd. He was more interested in testimony than titillation; more interested in confession than a carnival. Consequently, He said, "Go and show yourself to the priest, and give whatever you offer for your cleansing. Do what Moses commanded you to do, as a testimony to the people." Jesus wanted this person to "go and show," not simply a man with a changed body, but also a man with a changed heart.

This man, however, could not resist. Before you and I condemn him, let us recognize that if something like this had happened to us, we couldn't remain silent either. It would have been impossible. When Jesus really touches our lives, we want to tell that message as quickly and powerfully as we can. *Empowered by Jesus!* Henry Martyn, a theologian, said, "The Spirit of Christ is the Spirit of Missions, and

the nearer we get to Him, the more intensely missionary we become."
We become empowered by Jesus. One of my favorite hymns while
growing up was the well-known hymn by Elizabeth Prentiss, "More
Love to Thee, O Christ." We sang and harmonized it together as a
family. That hymn remains for me very meaningful, but for an
additional reason than just the nostalgia of having sung it with my
family. One summer at a church camp, one of the speakers based her
message on that hymn. She said that to show more "love *to* Christ" is
very important. We definitely need to do that, but there's another
perspective, which we can find in that hymn, if we simply change
one word: "More love *through* Thee, O Christ." When we are
empowered by Christ, and Christ's love is living through us, then
our witness becomes uncompromising, unequivocal, unmistakable,
and effective!

Richard Selzer, retired professor at Yale Medical School, has
written several books. One is a book of essays called, *Mortal Lessons:
Notes on the Art of Surgery*. He tells of standing at the bedside of a
young woman upon whom he had just operated to remove a tumor in
her cheek. Across from him, on the other side of the bed, was her
husband. Dr. Selzer said that he watched them both very carefully.
This woman's mouth was twisted because he had cut a nerve and one
of the muscles during surgery. Her mouth was now permanently
twisted. He looked at them and said to himself, "I don't know who
he is or who she is with this twisted mouth that I have created with
this surgery. But I discovered who they were as I watched them
looking tenderly and lovingly at each other." Then she said, "Will
this mouth always be twisted?" The surgeon said, "Yes, I had to cut
a nerve and a muscle, and I can't repair that. It will always be twisted."
He watched as the husband took her hand and smiled, and said, "I
like it, it's cute." Then the surgeon wrote, "I knew immediately who
was there, and I bowed my head because I'm never bold when I have
a spiritual encounter." He continues, "I watched as he bent over, and

I was close enough to see how he twisted his lips to accommodate hers." Then he adds this discerning conclusion, "He wanted his wife to know that the kiss still works."

Isn't that what the incarnation of Jesus Christ is all about? Isn't that what Jesus came to do in accommodating to our condition to save us; to touch us with His love, His mercy, and His grace, so that, in His name, His love, and His power, we can touch others? All of this that Jesus has done for us is to enable us to say to the world, near and far, that the kiss still works.

Oh, and by the way, I hope, unlike Shirley, you are all still awake.

FAITHFUL FOLLOWERS

Luke 9:57-62

In this passage from Luke, Jesus was embarking upon the last phase of His ministry – His final journey to Jerusalem, to the cross, crucifixion, and resurrection. By now people had begun to follow in great numbers – the twelve, seventy others, many of those who had just been served bread and fish on a hillside, and probably many more who were just curious. For them, following this charismatic man was a joyful and thought-provoking experience. For us, who claim to be following Jesus today, this text is also a provocative story. The three men whom Jesus met that day provide a clear evaluation of what it means to be a faithful follower. As we examine their conversation with Jesus, I think I can agree with Socrates when he said, "The unevaluated life is not worth living." As we examine this passage, perhaps we will discover that you and I are not only measuring these three men, but we are also evaluating our own depth of commitment to be followers of Jesus.

The first man said, "I'll follow you, Lord, wherever you go." I don't think this was the first time this man ever saw Jesus. I think he had been following along for a long time; he had watched Jesus, he had seen His eyes, he had heard His voice, he had observed the people around this inspiring teacher, and he wanted to be part of that. He said, "I will follow you, Lord, wherever you go." And then, this strange answer, "Foxes have holes, the birds of the air have nests, but the Son of Man has nowhere to lay his head." Count the costs. That is simply what Jesus was saying, and it costs something to follow Jesus.

The same thing is true for us. We are also impressed. We are impressed by parents, pastors, or teachers, and sometimes even close friends who are exceptionally strong in their faith. We say we would like to be part of that, too. We say that we will follow Jesus to be part of His group. We have heard the Gospel spoken and read to us, and we read it ourselves, and we say, "I'll follow you, Lord." Jesus says, just as clearly to us as He did to that man, "Foxes have holes, the birds of the air have nests, but the Son of Man has nowhere to lay his head." Count the costs!

There are seven contemporary sins, and they are these: policy without principle, wealth without work, pleasure without conscience, knowledge without character, science without morality, industry without humanity, and worship without sacrifice. So often, we want all of those blessings, but we don't want to do any of the things that they require – what it may cost us to get them. Just as surely as Jesus warned this first man to consider the price of discipleship, He also cautions us to be more than realistic. He says, just as probingly to us, "Count the cost!"

How do we discern this cost? How do we avoid these excuses and learn to run our race? Mother Teresa was being interviewed a few years ago by Dan Rather; he said, "Mother Teresa, what do you say when you pray?" She replied, "Sometimes I don't say anything, I just listen." Well, Dan Rather, being a good journalist, had to ask another question, and didn't know how he should follow up, so he asked, "Well, when you listen, what do you hear?" Mother Teresa answered, "If I listen long enough and patiently enough, I begin to hear what God is calling me to do, and what it might cost me to do it."

Jesus does not just want us to be repetitive. He wants us to be resourceful; not just to make promises, but to be productive. I remember a number of years ago when Leighton Ford, Billy Graham's brother-in-law, came to the town in which I ministered to do a crusade. One of the older men of my church, knowing that I was going to be out of town, said, "I'm sorry you are going to be gone when Leighton Ford is here." He added, "I absolutely love crusades; I've gone forward twenty-six times!" The question is, where did he go after he had gone forward, after he had made all those promises? "I'll follow you, Lord, wherever you go!" Why did the man need to go forward so often? Twenty-six times he had done that, but because there was not an overwhelming abundance of positive evidence, I have often wondered where he went after he went forward. James says, "Faith without works is dead." Let me paraphrase that: Promises without evidence are lifeless and useless.

Also, Jesus is not just asking us to be respectable; He wants us to be responsible. Many times, we just feel like it is enough to look good. If we look like a Christian, if we look like what we ought to be, and we act like a Christian, that is enough. A friend of mine, years ago – the late Tommy Bell, who was an official for the National Football League – told a wonderful story about his life as an NFL official. He used to go all around the country to different cities to officiate games. He wanted to go to church on each Sunday morning, but the only churches that were open early enough for him were the Roman Catholic churches. Even though he was a Protestant, he would go. The services in those days were in Latin; therefore, not knowing the language, when someone stood up, he stood up, when they sat down, my friend sat down. One time, he and a friend went to Europe to officiate a football game between two armed forces teams, and they attended a church in Germany. They sat down in front, and there was only one man in front of them. The minister, who spoke in German, began to say something, and the man in front of them stood up. So they stood up. All of a sudden they heard the congregation snickering and looked around, and they were the only ones standing with this man. After the service, the pastor said in English, "Let me apologize for what happened. During the time I was making the announcements, I was announcing the birth of a new child in our church family, and I asked the father to stand up." That is rather silly, but isn't it true that we do that kind of thing even in our lives? We just look like Christians, we dress like Christians, we act like Christians, and we go through regular religious ceremonies, and somehow feel that that is enough. Jesus says to us, "Foxes have holes, the birds of the air have nests, but the Son of Man has nowhere to lay his head." Count the Costs!

To the second man, Jesus speaks first. He says, "Follow me." This man says, "I'll follow you, Lord, but first let me bury my father." We might expect Jesus to say, "Well, let us see, there will probably be the calling hours and the service. By that time, we will be over in Nazareth and from there going down towards Bethany. You can catch up with us there." But, in fact, that is not what he said. He did say, "Leave the dead to bury their dead. As for you, go and proclaim the Kingdom of Heaven." That does not sound like gentle Jesus – meek and mild. Yet, it really fits. A number of years ago, when I was in Israel on an archaeological study tour with Dr. James Kelso from the Pittsburgh Seminary, he told us about an old tradition that was true in Jesus' day, and probably hundreds of years before, that was still true during our time there. The tradition was this: the oldest son does not leave home until the father has died. All of a sudden, that statement of Jesus began to make more sense to us. The chances are, this man's father wasn't dead. He probably wasn't even sick. He wasn't asking for an excuse for two or three days, he was asking for an excuse for years, waiting for his father to live out his time.

Think how often we make excuses. We do it quite easily, sometimes too easily. Before I went to the seminary, I taught school and I kept a couple of the excuses I received as a teacher. One was, "Please excuse Mary for January 31st, 32nd, & 33rd." (I had a sense that Mary's mother had not written that.) Another one was, "Please excuse Tom from gym class because *I don't like it anyway.*" Finally, I'm not sure this was an excuse, but it is one of my favorites. It simply said, "Please excuse Jimmy for being," and then the note added, "it was his father's fault." If you want to make an excuse, don't do it to a schoolteacher or to a parent because they will see right through it. If parents and teachers can see through excuses, how about God, because, you know, He hears our excuses all of the time? We're too young, we're too old, we don't know enough, we don't have enough time, we don't have enough experience; and Jesus says to us, "Leave all those dead excuses to bury themselves. As for you, go and proclaim the Kingdom of Heaven!"

Sometimes, we just need a little encouragement to face up to our excuses. There are times when a friend can point out how selfish and shallow our excuses often are. In the Academy Award-winning film *Chariots of Fire*, there is a scene where Harold Abrahams is sitting in the bleachers with his girlfriend. He is very depressed because he has just lost a race to Eric Liddell, the first loss ever in his life. Harold says to her, "If I can't win, I won't run!" She responds with a penetrating, incisive challenge. "If you don't run, you can't win!" There are times when our excuse is that we can't go on, feeling that everything is futile and hopeless. That is the time when we need to hear her words, as well. "If you don't run, you can't win!"

Another answer for Jesus is for us to do something with what we have already learned, with the gifts and talents we already possess. The answer for these three men is in the very next chapter. Jesus sends seventy people out to do this ministry. "Go and share the Gospel. Go out in pairs of two and tell the message," and they hesitate. They are not sure they want to do that, and I am sure they made lots of excuses. Yet they went, reluctantly, but when they came back, they said, "Even the demons are subject to us in your name." Why? Because they had gone out and used what God had already taught them through this relationship with Jesus Christ. They began to realize that all the excuses they had thought about, or had made, no longer made any sense because God had called them to use what it was they had learned, and when they used those gifts they were effective.

I have a friend who is a police officer in Denver, Colorado. One night, he and a fellow officer went to a PTA meeting at a local school, and the teacher said afterwards, "Would you two stay and talk to me? I want to ask you something." So they waited, and my friend was asked, "What do you do?" He said, "I'm a police officer and I teach self-defense training – karate, all those kinds of things." She said to the other officer, "What do you do?" He said, "I'm in charge of the Canine Corps." Then she said, "Oh, that explains the whole thing. There is a bully in school who was bothering your two boys, and *your* son threw him on the ground, and *your* son bit him." We are asked to do just what God has called us to do and use all the gifts God has given to us. We are to use them spontaneously. Spontaneous does not mean accidental. Spontaneous means something is so much a part of us that we cannot help but do it. Jesus says, "Leave the dead excuses to bury themselves; as for you, spontaneously go and proclaim the Kingdom of Heaven."

The third man is also a person who was impressed by Jesus. He came to Jesus right away, ran up to him and made his promise enthusiastically, but with a small caveat: "Jesus, I'll follow you wherever you go, but first let me say farewell to those at my home." Jesus answered, "No one who puts his hand on the plow and looks back is fit for the Kingdom of Heaven." Didn't this man just want to say goodbye? Just say farewell? The problem was Jesus was going forward and this man was looking homeward. Jesus doesn't want us to go forward one way with Him while looking longingly back the other way, looking back to the old things. We are called to look forward, to that which is new, to that which God is calling us to do.

When I was in junior high school, I had the opportunity to plow some fields behind horses, and I learned by experience what that phrase meant; no one puts his hand to the plow and looks back. You don't walk behind horses and look backwards, you must watch where you step. More seriously, I also learned that, when you are plowing a field, you find a site across the field and you set your eyesight, not on the ground, or not behind you, but straight ahead. You plow toward that site – toward a tree, a fencepost, or something that will keep your furrows straight. "No one who puts his hand on the plow and looks back is fit for the Kingdom of Heaven," because we are tempted to vacillate, to swerve all over the place. Jesus wants us to be focused and to walk face forward.

There is an urgent message that God gives to us in this passage. As Jesus is talking to this man, and He is also talking to us, we may understand what it means to run with perseverance in the race that is set before us. I'm sure that you know the seven last words of the church: "We have always done it that way!" Bruce Larson, in one of his books, *The Emerging Church*, says, "The one word I don't like is renewal," because renewal implies that somehow, back there, somewhere, with old doctor so-and-so, or this pastor, or that person, somewhere back there, it was all perfect – and now we are being asked to *renew* or repeat that. Jesus is calling each one of us to something new – to honor the future without disrespecting the past. In fact, Jesus says, "Behold, I make all things new."

We are to run our race with perseverance – and it is *our* race. It is not just for a few, it is for all of us.

The twelfth chapter of Hebrews begins with this wonderful passage: "Since we are surrounded by so great a cloud of witnesses, let us lay aside every weight and the sin that clings so closely, and let us run with perseverance the race that is set before us, looking to Jesus Christ, the pioneer and perfecter of our faith." Our race!

Forty-five years ago, no one had ever run the mile in less than four minutes. Today, there are several who have done so, but none had then. One cold day in England, Roger Bannister and his friend Chris Chattaway had decided to try to break that record. It was cold and rainy, and Roger Bannister confessed that he didn't think they should try. Chattaway said, "Yes, let's do it. We practiced for this day. This is the day." This is the way they did it. Chris Chattaway had one of those automatic clocks in his head. He knew how to run at a steady speed to allow precisely the right amount of time to leave Bannister enough seconds to attempt to break the record. So Chattaway, for the first three-quarters of a mile, was the pacer – he set the pace at just the right speed. Bannister said afterwards, "Several times I felt like quitting, but I couldn't, because there was my friend, setting the pace. I had to stay with him." After three quarters of a mile, Chattaway moved off to the side and Bannister raced past. Bannister had greater stamina and strength. He was going to race the last 440 yards to try to break the record. He said, "Sometimes I felt like quitting, but now I heard my friend's footsteps behind me with shouts of encouragement." Now those of you who have run a mile, or even the 440, know it's tough enough to run it without calling out encouragement, but that is what happened. Bannister broke the record at 359.4 (by six-tenths of a second). I've seen a film of that race, and Chattaway, at the end, finished just a few yards behind Bannister, running his own best personal record. Usually, when we have heard about Bannister, we have not heard about Chattaway. Let me tell you that any pastor worth his or her salt knows that sometimes he or she needs to have a Chattaway; setting the pace, encouraging, being part of a collegial relationship. Sometimes pastors need to learn that they are not always the record breakers, the Bannisters – sometimes they, also, are the encouraging, pacesetting Chattaways.

Look at the verse I gave you a moment ago. Let us run with perseverance the race that is set before us. Notice the pronoun: it is *us*, not *them*; not the pastors, not the elders, not the deacons, not the trustees. The race is set before *us*; each one of us is to run a race. Some of us are Bannisters. Some of us are Chattaways. However, God calls us all. We are called to run our race, each one of us, looking to Jesus Christ, "the pioneer and perfecter of our faith," which simply means: He has gone before us and He has perfected the pathway, and completed it, so that we can also be a part of that race and run with Him where He has called us to follow.

You and I are called to be followers. Remember again what Socrates said: "The unevaluated life is not worth living." The same is true for us in this day and age. We need to evaluate how we are following Jesus, whoever we are, wherever we are. It is so important that we do. We need to take hold aggressively, intentionally, and decisively to all that God has called us to do. In the *Dead Poets Society,* Robin Williams is talking to his students, urging them to go beyond materialism and a shallow life, reaching for a more positive and productive life. He keeps saying to them, "Carpe diem, carpe diem – seize the day." I can say the same thing to you with two more Latin words, Carpe Diem Pro Christus: *Seize the day – for Christ.* When we make that kind of intentional commitment, you and I will be faithful followers.

Several years ago, I spoke at a Fellowship for Christian Athletes national conference at Lake George, New York, for professional, college, and high school coaches from all over the country. The last day, I was using this text as part of the message for the morning devotions. Sitting back about three chairs on the aisle was the late Dave McClain, who was the football coach at Wisconsin. He died a few years ago of cancer – a very tragic death. I had come to know him well during the four days I was there. As I finished the last devotion, I bowed my head to pray. I paused for a moment to get my thoughts together. Before I could say anything, Dave started to sing a familiar African American Spiritual, "I have decided to follow Jesus, no turning back." As we close today, I would invite you to sing that with me as part of your answer for counting the costs, moving beyond excuses, and running your race.

Let us pray:

I have decided to follow Jesus,
I have decided to follow Jesus,
I have decided to follow Jesus,
No turning back; no turning back. Amen.

(Dr. Jackson and the congregation sang this prayer.)

Send in the Clowns!

Psalm 67
I Corinthians 4:8-16, 20 (Good News Bible)
"For Jesus says, 'Be ye perfect, even as your Heavenly Father is perfect.'"
(Matthew 5:48)

Not long ago, a friend of mine was praying with his kindergarten-age son. By the way, that is a good practice, not just to hear our children's prayers, but to pray with them. God is the One that hears the prayers, and it can be very edifying when we pray with our children, for them and for us. The son was overly impressed with where he lived and who he was, and his prayer began this way: "God, I thank you that we live in the biggest house in the whole block." Then, having just received his allowance, he added, "God, I thank you that we have more money than anybody else." He had been to kindergarten that day and he became a bit chauvinistic as he prayed, "God, I thank you that I am smarter than Janie and Susie." When he finished, his father didn't say a word; he just picked up the prayer and said, "God, please forgive Johnnie for being just a bit too thankful."

The father was giving the son a second opinion. We are used to second opinions, and often we need them. The late Frank Harrington, former pastor of the Peachtree Church in Atlanta, used to tell a story about when he came home one day from presbytery and his wife

255

asked, "Would you please cut the grass?" He said, "Do you realize that I have just been elected moderator of the presbytery?" She replied, "Wear your robe if you want to, but cut the grass!"

Have you heard about the man who went to the doctor, and the doctor examined him and said, "You are crazy." And the man said angrily, "I want a second opinion." Then the doctor said, "You are ugly." Sometimes second opinions are good, and sometimes we are not so sure.

In our Scripture text, Paul gives a very special, important, second opinion to the Corinthians. They had become proud, a bit too arrogant about their faith, feeling exclusive, and looking down on others, excluding them from their fellowship. Paul asked them, "Are you already rich? Have you already become king? I wish you really were kings with us, so that we could be kings together with you. For it seems to me," said Paul, "that God has given us the very last place as apostles; like those who are doomed to die as a spectacle for the whole world and humanity. We are fools for Christ's sake." This second opinion surprised the Corinthians, particularly, because Paul called himself a fool. *"We are fools for Christ's sake."*

Another translation for the word "fool" is the word "clown." We are to be "clowns" for Christ's sake, and there are some compelling characteristics about the clown that speak to us, as Christians. If we are going to be good stewards of God's gifts to us, I think we need to examine these characteristics very carefully.

The first characteristic of the clown is that he or she does the unexpected; the extraordinary, the unusual. So often, the clown in the circus does things that we just don't anticipate. Clowns are frequently unpredictable, spontaneous, and totally surprising. Back in the nineteenth century, there was a man who ran for the state legislature four times and failed; for Congress twice and failed; for the vice presidency once and failed; for the Senate once and failed; started two businesses and failed; he then had a nervous breakdown.

Many people called that a failure. Then, in 1860, he became president. Carl Sandburg once wrote of that man, "I never knew anyone who failed so often and succeeded so ultimately." It was, of course, Abraham Lincoln, whose own secretary of war, Edwin Stanton, who later praised him, once called him the "consummate clown." To both men, Lincoln had been a total surprise.

As Christians, we are called to do many things that are beyond the ordinary, beyond the norm, beyond the average, everyday things. Years ago on the "Tonight Show," Sidney Poitier was a guest. He talked about how he was beginning to write, direct, and produce. He wanted to be more than just an actor. The host, Johnny Carson, flipping his pencil, asked, "Why would you do that? You are so successful as an actor." Sidney Poitier had obviously thought about that question, because his answer was immediate and spontaneous. Listen to his reply: "Success carries with it the temptation to stay with that success, but that is a shortcut to atrophy. I'd rather stretch myself in new directions, to reach for heights that I have not yet attained and goals I have not yet reached, and thereby fulfill myself and be of more worth to others." How true it is that success often carries with it the temptation to stay with that success. We as believers need to stretch ourselves in new directions; to reach for those heights we have not yet attained and goals that we have not yet reached, and thereby fulfill ourselves and be of more worth to others. Jesus looked at a doubting man whose son was about to be healed and said, "All things are possible to one who believes." (Mark 9:23) We have the promise of Jesus Christ that all things can be possible for us. We can reach beyond the ordinary, even if it often seems foolish to the world.

At the base of the Matterhorn in Europe, there is a small cemetery where people who tried to climb that great mountain, and failed, are buried. In that cemetery, there is a tombstone marked with the names of three brothers who were unsuccessful in their attempt. Along with their names are the words their parents selected as an epitaph. These words simply say, "They scorned the lesser peaks." Frequently, we in the church repetitiously climb the same old peaks. We often repeat the same things year after year, just because we know we can accomplish them. We give the same amount of money this year that we gave last year. We repeat the same old goals, not only because we know we can attain them, but also because they are easy. We fool ourselves by thinking that repetition is an accomplishment! What we need to do is scorn the lesser peaks and reach for those things which are higher and better.

In my church in Canton, Ohio, we had a food ministry. During its second year, we began to receive a cashier's check each month for $17.36. That was a surprise; we had no clue where it came from. It was a very odd amount of money. By accident, we discovered who the contributor was. The money came from a woman who was on welfare, and she was tithing her welfare check; exactly ten percent of what she received in welfare. When we talked to her about this, she said, "All of my friends said it was a foolish thing to do. They asked me why I did it. I told them I have never been so richly blessed." Some just called her a fool. I call her a saint, a *fool for Christ's sake*, who was doing the unusual, the extraordinary, the unexpected!

Bruce Larson, in one of his books, asked this very provocative question, "What would you do if you knew you couldn't fail?" Think how many times we keep from doing new and exciting things, because we are afraid to be criticized, we are afraid that it is not going to turn out well for us, or that we are going to be embarrassed. What would you do if you knew you couldn't fail? What kind of evangelist would you be, telling the Good News of Jesus Christ? What kind of a leader or teacher would you be? What kind of a parent would you be? What kind of a student would you be, if you knew you couldn't fail? That question really shocked me as a young man when I first read it. However, his next question was even more provocative, because Larson simply asked, "Why aren't you doing it?"

The fool for Christ's sake does what he or she does in an unexpected, extraordinary, unusual way as a good steward of what God has given to be used for Him. But also, the fool for Christ's sake, the clown, does what he or she does, not for selfish reasons, but for the good of others. Paul said, "Let each of you look, not only to your own interests, but also the interests of others. Have this mind among yourselves that you have in Christ Jesus, . . . who went to the cross for you." (Philippians 2:4-5, 8) The fool for Christ's sake does what he or she does for the good of others.

In Pittsburgh, during World War II, a company had a rule that everyone who worked there had to take Red Cross training. One particular woman took a job in the company a few months before the war was over. Nevertheless, she was required to take the Red Cross training, about which she complained every day. The people with whom she worked became annoyed by her complaints and her constant questions: "Why are we doing this? The war is almost over; we are almost in Berlin; we are almost in Japan! Nobody is going to bomb Pittsburgh. Why do I have to take this Red Cross Training?" But one day, she came into work and exclaimed, "I finally found a reason for my Red Cross training! Last night, a young man was riding a bicycle in front of my house and a car hit him. I ran down and found him broken and bleeding. Right then and there, I found a reason for my Red Cross training." All the people with whom she worked were greatly relieved, until she gave her reason: "I sat down on the curb and put my head between my knees so I wouldn't faint." Think how many times you and I have been well-trained as Christians. We have received effective and empowering gifts from God. Yet so often we use them only for ourselves, "putting our heads between our knees," so we won't faint.

A friend of mine from Egypt once came to visit for six weeks. He went all around the country, visiting churches and shopping malls, as well as many of the regular tourist sights in this country. After he had visited for six weeks, just before he left for home, he returned to our home. He said, "You know, the churches in this country greatly disturb me." I asked, "Why?" He answered, "Because in one sense, they are just like the department stores I visited, except that they put everything on the shelves, close the doors, and sell to each other." What a challenge for us from a person from another country! How it motivates us to think what it means as Christians to look beyond our comfortable walls in order to do what we do for the good of others. We have received unique gifts from God, and what we do with them requires a choice. We need to be willing to make a thoughtful and well-reasoned decision to bring about change and improvement in the lives of others. Change is inevitable; growth is a choice. We need to make the choice to honor God by serving others and thereby grow in wisdom and grace.

The fool for Christ's sake does what he or she does for the good of others. In the old movie *The Fisher King*, there is a scene where a privileged man is standing beside a man in a wheelchair, who has his little cup out begging for money from the commuters as they go to and from work. As they put the coins in the cup, he turns to the man standing beside him and says, "They give to me so they don't have to see me." We need to realize that we are given the challenge to make the conscientious choice to give of ourselves, our talent, our time, our treasure, only because we see the needs of the people who need a loving touch from us.

The fool for Christ's sake does what he or she does for the good of others. But also, the fool for Christ's sake does what he or she does in loving vulnerability. Doing what we do for the good of others is one thing, but doing it in a loving vulnerability is to lay our lives on the line for them. We become willing to pay the cost! We take up our cross for others, and thereby pay the price! That is a little different from just doing things for others. We do it by giving of ourselves.

In Robert Bolt's play *A Man For All Seasons*, the king asks Sir Thomas More, the cleric, to condone his divorce and justify his marriage to Anne Boleyn. He knows that if the cleric agrees, then the people will accept it. Sir Thomas More refuses, and he makes this comment in the play, "I do not have the stuff of which martyrs are made." However, as the play evolves, we discover that he does. He lays himself on the line for that which is good and true, righteous and honest. The stuff of which martyrs are made is the stuff that enables us to lay our lives on the line for others. Good stewards do that willingly and sacrificially.

A number of years ago, a friend of mine was dean of students at Grove City College. One night, the janitor found him and said, "The students over in the men's dorm threw ice cream on the wall, and if they don't clean it up, I am quitting." So, my friend went over to the dorm, along with the janitor, to investigate. Nobody seemed to know who did it. It is amazing how things happen on college campuses and nobody ever knows who did them. The argument went on and on, the janitor blaming the students, the students saying they didn't know who did it. Finally, my friend walked down the hall, opened the closet door, brought out a mop and a bucket, and started to clean up the mess himself. The students said to him, "Take off, Prof." They knew who did it. He could have argued all night and arrived at no decision between the angry janitor and the recalcitrant students. But as soon as he put himself in the middle, vulnerably, the answer came and the problem was solved.

How many times have you heard it said, or you have said it yourself, "If you go halfway with me and I go halfway with you, the world is going to be a much better place?" If the Kosovars and the Serbs go halfway with each other, the world is going to be a better place; the Arabs and Israelis, blacks and whites, husbands and wives, parents and children, brothers and sisters, neighbor and neighbor. "If you just go halfway with me, and I go halfway with you, the world is going to be a better place." I have looked all of my life in Scripture for that verse and I cannot find it; "Thou shalt go halfway." It is not there. What is there is this, "If you would be My follower, take up your cross and follow Me." (Matthew 16:24) And everybody knows when you take up a cross, it is never a halfway thing. Many ministers wear these attractive robes with three stripes on each sleeve. I learned a long time ago that my success as a pastor would not be measured by the stripes on my sleeve, but rather by the stripes on my back – the direct result of giving myself for others. It is still true what Jesus said, "The greatest among you must be the servant of all, and he who would be first among you must be the slave of all." (Matthew 23:11)

Fools for Christ's sake do what they do in extraordinary and unusual ways; they do what they do for the good of others, and they do what they do in loving vulnerability. Finally, the clown, the fool for Christ's sake, does what he or she does celebrating life. Think of the clown in the circus. With a tear, a laugh, or a gesture, they celebrate the joy and vitality of the life that the circus offers. Fools for Christ's sake also celebrate life with whatever skill or opportunity they have. They celebrate the gift of life. That means getting involved. Someone asked Flip Wilson one time what kind of religion he had. He said, "I am a Jehovah's bystander." I don't think that is an authentic denomination, but I'm convinced that still there are too many "Jehovah's bystanders" around.

In the Christian rock opera *Jesus Christ Superstar*, there is a thought-provoking scene where Jesus is making his way from Bethany and Bethphage to Jerusalem. As he is going down a long pathway, there are people sitting on the curb singing, "Hey, Jesus, did you see me wave? We believe in You and God; now tell us that we're saved." But Jesus goes right on by, because they are just sitting on the curb – they are not part of the action, or part of what He is doing or where He is going. We are called upon to be involved. I read the other day

262

about a man who went early to every home game in St. Louis, when Mark McGwire was hitting homeruns, because he wanted to get a seat in the outfield bleachers, hoping to catch one of those baseballs that occasionally came over the fence. He said, "This is really living." Someone should remind him of how much Mark McGwire is paid on the inside of the fence. Life is not about sitting on the outside catching whatever comes over the fence. It is being involved in the game itself. It is being involved in life!

A number of years ago, my family and I and seven college students spent six weeks in Egypt. While we were there, we took a third-class train from Luxor back to Assiut. It was about a ten-hour trip on a third-class train, with windows open, doors flapping, and people constantly boarding. Nobody ever seemed to get off! The train was dirty and people brought animals and farm produce on board. It was, as my wife would say, "a growth experience." As we traveled along, to pass the time, my daughter and one of the college girls took out a Bible and quietly began to read to each other. An older man came by dressed in a well-tailored brown summer suit, wearing an Arab headdress. He stopped and stood beside them. After a few moments, he leaned down to see exactly what they were reading, and then he whispered to the two girls, "I have life." What a great way for one Christian to introduce himself or herself to another. In this country, we don't do it that way. We say, "I belong to First Church and we have so many members. How many do you have? We have a large budget, what is yours?" But we should say, "I have life." What we have to offer, as Christians, is life and we celebrate that life!

The first memory verse most of us ever learned was this word from Jesus, "God so loved the world that He gave His Son . . . that those who believe in Him will not perish but have everlasting life." (John 3:16) The word for "everlasting" does not mean just length. There are other connotations: "everlasting" also means completed, fulfilled, enriched. I probably don't want to live a life forever that is terrifying, or just plain unfulfilled. Jesus does not offer just length. He offers us an everlasting life that is fulfilled and complete, abundant here, and eternal beyond. That is the life that you and I celebrate.

Perhaps you thought I forgot about the text that I quoted early on, another word from Jesus which says, "Be ye perfect, even as your Heavenly Father is perfect." As a preacher's kid growing up, when I talked about God's perfection, I knew what my father had taught me. God was omnipotent, which means He was all-powerful; He was omniscient, He knew everything; He was omnipresent, He was everywhere. Consequently, when I read that verse, "Be ye perfect, even as your Heavenly Father is perfect," I knew I wasn't omnipotent, omniscient, or omnipresent, and so I just ignored that verse for a number of years. It wasn't until I had gone through college, high school teaching, seminary, and to my first church, that while preparing for a Bible Study I came across a new definition. When we read that verse, I discovered that it doesn't mean perfection without any flaw or blemish; it doesn't mean not making any mistakes; it means *completeness*. If we are to translate that verse accurately, we say: "Be *complete* in yourselves, as God is *complete* in God." The verse is not asking me to be God. It is not asking me to be Moses, Elijah, Jeremiah, Peter, Paul, James, or anybody else. It is asking me simply *to be me*; to use all the gifts that God has given me as a good steward, and to use them in unusual ways, for the good of others, in loving vulnerability, celebrating life. When that happens, we can be perfect. In fact, if we are really faithful stewards, we can be *perfect fools*.

I don't know what you see when you look around at the world where you live. It is probably the same thing that I see; the struggles that we hear about: the injustice, the dishonesty, the evil, the homelessness, the hunger, the terrorism, the conflicts, and wars throughout the world. The world says, "Send money." That is a good idea. We need to do that. Send education, technology, armed forces; all of those things are needful in their place and time. But God looks at all of these things that you and I see, and He says there is something else that must be sent. He says, *"Send in the clowns."* You and I must go. You and I are called upon as good stewards in our time to be *fools for Christ's sake.*

A number of years ago, I was doing a weekend retreat at Westminster College in Pennsylvania. Among the several passages of Scripture we were discussing was this one from I Corinthians 4: "We are fools for Christ's sake." We spent a lot of time discussing the texts. I gave a devotional talk at the end of the retreat. I said, "Let us pray," but before I could speak, a talented young woman from the group picked up her guitar and began to strum the tune of that Broadway song, "Send in the Clowns." And then spontaneously, as a result of the conversation and the result of God's Spirit working in her life, she sang this: *"All through the world, all throughout life, people seek answers to sin, freedom from strife. Send in the clowns. We are the clowns. Send in the clowns."* Amen.